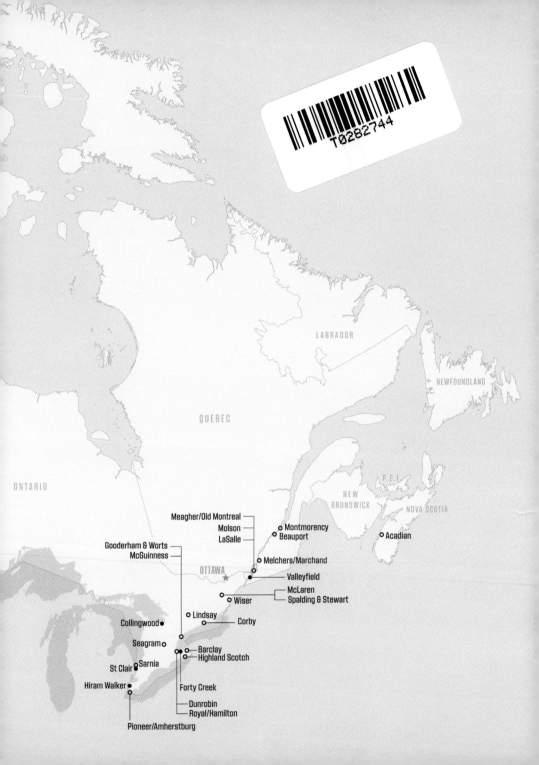

T0282744

LABRADOR

NEWFOUNDLAND

QUEBEC

P.E.I

NEW
BRUNSWICK

NOVA SCOTIA

ONTARIO

Meagher/Old Montreal
Molson
LaSalle
○ Montmorency
Beauport

Gooderham & Worts
McGuinness
○ Melchers/Marchand

OTTAWA ★
○ Valleyfield

○ Wiser
McLaren
Spalding & Stewart

○ Lindsay
○ Corby

Collingwood ●

Seagram ○
Barclay
Highland Scotch

St Clair ○ Sarnia
Hiram Walker ●
Forty Creek

Dunrobin
Royal/Hamilton

Pioneer/Amherstburg

○ Acadian

Praise for *Canadian Whisky, Third Edition*

"Everything I ever wanted to know about Canadian whisky—and a good bit that I never thought I needed to—I learned from Davin de Kergommeaux. Since its first edition, *Canadian Whisky* has offered a wealth of insight and information, presented by a gifted writer and historian. This latest, updated edition illustrates the dynamism and excitement behind Canadian whisky. You could never ask for a better guide."

—**CLAY RISEN**, journalist and author of
American Rye: A Guide to the Nation's Original Spirit

"Davin de Kergommeaux is Canadian whisky's greatest advocate. Single-handedly, he has brought it to the world's attention. In these pages, he charts the saga of the country's own spirit in both senses—the drink and the people. From its earliest days to the hugely exciting contemporary advances, he celebrates Canadian whisky, exploding a few myths along the way, while offering sound advice as to its future. This is not just a story about whisky, it is a story about a country. It is a tale that needed to be told. This is an essential buy for all whisky lovers—and all Canadians."

—**DAVE BROOM**, author of *The World Atlas of Whisky*

CANADIAN
WHISKY

DAVIN DE KERGOMMEAUX

CANADIAN WHISKY

THE

ESSENTIAL PORTABLE EXPERT

Updated and Expanded Third Edition

appetite

Copyright © 2024 Davin de Kergommeaux

All rights reserved. The use of any part of this publication, reproduced,
transmitted in any form or by any means, electronic, mechanical, photocopying,
recording, or otherwise, or stored in a retrieval system, without the prior written consent
of the publisher—or, in case of photocopying or other reprographic copying, license from
the Canadian Copyright Licensing Agency—is an infringement of the copyright law.

Appetite by Random House® and colophon are registered trademarks of
Penguin Random House LLC.

Library and Archives Canada Cataloguing in Publication is available upon request.

ISBN: 978-0-525-61244-5
eBook ISBN: 978-0-525-61245-2

Cover and book design: Andrew Roberts

Printed in China

Published in Canada by Appetite by Random House®,
a division of Penguin Random House Canada Limited.

www.penguinrandomhouse.ca

10 9 8 7 6 5 4 3 2 1

For Janet, with love and appreciation.

_____

To Ronan and Seneca.

CONTENTS

continued

As with *flavour, doughnut, sulphur, cheque,* and many other words, *whisky* has two common spellings. While intended for a global audience, this book is published in Canada, so it uses Canada's preferred spellings, except when referring to specific brands that do otherwise.

A NOTE ON TASTING NOTES

Tasting notes for over 100 Canadian whiskies, included throughout the book, were written specifically for this edition. Canadian whisky makers and brands change frequently, and the whiskies included here are just a sample of those. Tasting notes begin with the name of the whisky. For a few vintage whiskies, the distilling year follows in parentheses. The alc/vol (alcohol by volume) as a percentage comes next, then the producer name in parentheses. And finally, the tasting sketch or impression. Since each drinker's tasting experience is unique, readers are invited to reflect on their own impressions as they review these careful but also personal observations. See pages 334–339 for a complete list of the whiskies.

A NOTE ON MEASUREMENTS

Canada uses the metric system for most measurements, and, except for historical quantities and measures, this book conforms with that practice. Where gallons are used, these are "wine gallons" and can be converted to litres at 1 gallon = 3.78 litres. Similarly, those readers more familiar with imperial measurements can convert litres to gallons at 1 litre = 0.26 gallons. Bushels are units of volume, and their weight varies depending on the grain. For convenience, distillers often equate a bushel to 56 pounds, or 25.4 kilograms, regardless of the grain. One kilogram equals 2.205 pounds. Two thousand pounds equal one ton; 1,000 kilograms equal one tonne. And 1,670.4 furlongs per fortnight equal 1 kilometre per hour.

INTRODUCTION

andles, mickeys, shots, or drams, no matter what its measure, Canadian whisky is a story of Canada. It is a story of a colony becoming a nation, of early settlers finding creative ways to adapt Old World practices to new and often hostile environments, a story of craftsmanship, ingenuity, family feuds, fortunes made, and legacies lost, and of 21st-century artisans reviving a pioneer enterprise that giant conglomerates, abetted by government, had long since absorbed.

The story begins with farmers protecting their crops from pests, and millers turning waste into something they could sell or feed to cattle. It tells of Canadians processing Canadian grain, Canadian water, and that other abundant ingredient, wood from Canada's extensive forests, into something they could sell locally and abroad. Almost from the beginning, Canadian whisky enjoyed global repute, and it is still enjoyed in more than 160 countries. But, until recently, Canadian whisky received little attention as a distinct whisky style. Like Canadians themselves, it tends to fly under the radar. Nevertheless, specialist and consumer media now cover Canadian whisky regularly. Connoisseurs line up to taste it at sampling events, and whisky clubs, once the bastions of Scotch, now celebrate Canadian whisky, too. And though Canada's best whiskies sometimes do not make it out of the country, others are now found only beyond Canada's borders. However, abroad—and, discouragingly, at home—much of the received wisdom about Canadian whisky is still fantasy.

Many of today's misunderstandings began as hypotheses, based on limited information and passed on innocently. Most brands tell their story honestly, or at least try to. Yet even in today's age of authenticity, a few vested interests have usurped the role of historians, massaging, embellishing, or just plain inventing hagiographic stories to reflect well on specific brands or styles of whisky. Sometimes people fill in gaps so that their stories conform with popular cliché. Other times, they leave out inconvenient facts to bolster a desired conclusion and not let the truth get in the way of a good story (or a sale). For instance, the avaricious financiers, indifferent industrialists, and disinterested successors who took control of some brands are made into romantic figures or simply vanish. On their social media feeds, in brand publications and on websites, and on brand-massaged or -created Wikipedia pages, a few cynical marketers tell stories crafted not to inform but to persuade. Some of their nonsense has become gospel by simple repetition.

So while information about Canadian whisky was once difficult to find because the industry rarely allowed prying eyes within its walls, today the truth sometimes gets lost in an oversupply of earnest, but misinformed, and sometimes lavish brand presentations. Just the same, over the past decade or so, fans who recognize non sequiturs, conjecture, and reverse-engineered analyses have begun to tease out more reliable versions. However, the country is still huge, and travel within its borders expensive, so unfamiliar Canadian approaches are sometimes interpreted according to whisky concepts from elsewhere, and misconceptions arise. So to be clear, despite fervent assertions to the contrary, Canada does *not* have the most flexible regulations of major whisky-producing countries; the 9.09% rule was intended to take advantage of US tax incentives, *not* to help blenders improve mundane whisky; and grain neutral spirit is not permitted in Canadian whisky.

Canadian whisky is not Scotch and it is not bourbon. Most Scotch is not single malt whisky, and most American whisky is not bourbon—and even less is straight bourbon. So comparisons of Canadian whisky to Scotch or American whisky based on regulations for single malts or straight bourbon are either disingenuous or naïve. Canadian whisky did not descend directly from Irish or Scotch whisky, nor did it evolve in parallel with whisky in America. Rather, these two now-different North American styles developed along distinct but intertwined paths as part of a single evolution. In North America, making whisky began first in the United States, and over time ideas, recipes, equipment, practices, distillers, and whisky moved freely back and forth across the border. However, two distinct periods in American history led drinkers in the US to associate whisky with their northern neighbour.

The first of these developments was the American Civil War (1861–65), which, in addition to causing violent social and political upheaval, disrupted alcohol production throughout the Union and Confederate states. Thirsty Americans looked north to fill the void. The second disruption came with the Volstead Act. In 1920, Volstead ushered in nearly fourteen years of Prohibition in the United States. In his definitive history of the era, *Last Call*, Daniel Okrent called this period "a sequence of curves and switchbacks that would force the re-writing of the fundamental contract between citizen and government." The act was socially convulsive and created deep rifts among groups who might otherwise get along. Progressives, feminists, libertarians, secularists, and fundamentalists who maybe enjoyed the occasional drink found no comfort in the legislation or the increasingly theatrical antics of its supporters. When Prohibition ended, American distillers had to start over, often with new processes, new recipes, and unfamiliar equipment. Meanwhile, Canada kept America's bottles full.

Despite its stated purpose, Prohibition did not eliminate alcohol from the United States. It simply encouraged the marketplace to find more and more creative ways to bypass or ignore an essentially unenforceable law. In the process, the Volstead Act became founding legislation for organized crime in America. And though Canadian whisky may have made up 10% of the alcoholic beverages consumed during Prohibition, the ensuing folklore has created the false but nearly universal belief that Canadian whisky was the era's drink of choice.

This book tells the story of Canadian whisky by taking the reader inside the bottle, the distillery, and the marketplace. For quick reference, 102 artisanal whisky distilleries, nine traditional distilleries, and 29 historical ones are mapped on its inside front and back covers. The book tells their stories as revealed in early documents and independent reports, and recalled in the memories of people who have lived many decades of Canadian whisky history. It presents insights gleaned through discussions with people at each of Canada's eight legacy whisky distilleries and many microdistilleries. It is not intended to set the "official record" straight; however, it does challenge many dearly held beliefs and corrects some errors that unfortunately wiggled their way into its earlier editions. For example, comments in earlier editions that JP Wiser's successors guarded his recipes carefully, as brand representatives asserted when research for the first edition was underway, are mistaken. The recipes were either lost or discarded. And although historical tenet sometimes changes as new information emerges—as it has, for instance, with the McLaren Distillery—one thing is certain: in the marketplace, the most important ingredient in whisky is not the water, nor is it the grain. No: the most important ingredient is the story. Let's get it right.

1

THE SUBSTANCE OF
CANADIAN WHISKY

$$\left(\begin{array}{c}1\end{array}\right)$$

THE GRAIN

Golden wheat fields stretching to the horizon across barely undulating flatlands define the Canadian prairies. More than 2,000 kilometres east, in southern Ontario, roads from encroaching suburbia crisscross similar expanses of corn. Interspersed with patches of bush, soybean fields, and, more recently, electricity-generating windmills, corn remains a defining presence. If, as Canada's regulations decree, whisky is "a potable alcoholic distillate obtained from a mash of cereal grain," then Canada is rich in the raw materials. Along with wheat and corn, Canada's rural bounty includes rye grain, enough for the global market, and equally plentiful quantities of malting barley. Is it any wonder, then, that from the earliest colonial days, Canadians have made whisky?

Century Reserve 21-Year-Old
40% alc/vol | Highwood

Pure, soft, plush, mouth-filling pleasure. Sweet grain, buttery cob corn, talcum powder, creamy caramel; brisk, gingery spice, wooden decking, farmy. Citrus pith and peel, vague mint. All corn, despite what the label indicates.

Masterson's 10-Year-Old Straight Barley Whiskey
50% alc/vol | Alberta Distillers

Remarkably dusty—almost musty. Clean grain, freshwater plants, wet earth and petrichor, until sourish fruit and basil-esque dried herbs appear. Crème caramel–caressed jalapeños. Gorgeous, lingering, fruity, herbal aftertaste. All barley.

Masterson's 12-Year-Old Straight Wheat Whiskey
50% alc/vol | Alberta Distillers

Aromatic butterscotch, with perfumed hints of vanilla fudge and barley sugar. Medium weight. Glowing spices move slowly deeper. An odd, alluring, sweet-sour finish, almost crisp like soda. All wheat.

North of 7 Single Cask Rye
45% alc/vol | North of 7

Sweet, full, with soft tugs. Searing rye spices. Rich and zesty amid overripe fruit, guava, vanilla, floral tones, dry grain, clean wood, and fleeting dark chocolate. A round, robust beauty. Ninety-five percent rye, 5% malt.

EARLY WHISKY GRAINS

Although Canadian settlers did not invent whisky, they did bring whisky-making skills and tools and, just as important, whisky-making grains with them from their many homelands. Barley came to Canada primarily from England and the Netherlands—not Scotland, as many still assume. Wheat also arrived from England and Europe. Dutch and German immigrants brought rye, the grain that, confusingly, would lend its name to Canadian whisky. But the softest-flavoured, sweetest, and creamiest of whisky grains, corn, originated right here in North America 6,000 years before Jacques Cartier set foot at Stadacona—or the Pilgrims at Plymouth, for that matter.

As Dutch and German communities emerged across Pennsylvania and the northeastern United States, rye grain played a significant role in the development of American whisky. However, Canada was settled about a century after America, and immigration patterns differed. Only one German community of any size developed in Canada: Berlin, now called Waterloo. Thus, except for Hespeler & Randall (Seagram) in Berlin, and later Alberta Distillers in Calgary, when Canadian distillers began making all-rye whisky about a century ago, it was for blending. Most did not bottle all-rye until the 21st century. Nevertheless, in the mid- to late 19th century, some larger distillers began making mixed-mash American-style rye specifically for export to the US.

Canada's first commercial distillers were mainly English flour millers who came to Canada to establish new mills and who turned their milling waste and excess wheat into whisky. Occasionally, some distillers used barley or other grains in their mashes, but the most common whisky grain in pioneer Canada was not rye, or barley, or corn; it was wheat. However, early-19th-century Dutch, German, and American immigrants scattered across Upper Canada found wheat whisky a bit bland. They remembered rye schnapps from home and knew how flavourful distilled rye grain could be, and so encouraged distillers to spice up their all-wheat mashes with a bit of milled rye.

Once the idea of adding rye grain to a mash took hold, there was no looking back. Yet mash bills and grain inventories from the 19th century show that the proportion of rye in a batch of whisky seldom reached one part in five. Indeed, some early mash bills show rye at 1% of the grain mashed, though most are closer to 5% or 10%. To distinguish this new liquor from "common whisky"—that is, whisky made without any rye grain—the rye-flavoured variety quickly acquired the nickname "rye." Although it commanded a slightly higher price, rye soon supplanted common whisky in the marketplace. At the same time, the word *rye* entered the Canadian lexicon and whisky is still the first thing many Canadians think of when they hear it.

Tumbleweed 1888 Triticale
45% alc/vol | Tumbleweed

Clean, clear. Fresh grain, grape juice, then glorious nail polish memories. Wheat explodes into rye, rye into wheat. Dark fruit, chocolate cherries, earthy herbs, rustic. Sizzling chilis, yet lush. All triticale.

Still Waters 12-Year-Old Single Malt
61% alc/vol | Still Waters

Expressive fragrance foretells integrated flavour. Rich, creamy, malty cereal, then bananas, marshmallows, crème brûlée, plum pudding, sweet esters, apple juice. Softest pepper and crispy oak linger into spicy malt. All malt.

TODAY'S WHISKY GRAIN

In the 1850s, Great Lakes shipping and an expanding railway network began to make competitively priced American corn available in Canada. This interested distillers who knew that corn produces more alcohol than other grains. Soon, they were experimenting with part- or all-corn mashes. Essentially, three types of spirit resulted: corn spirit that was matured in new wood to make bourbon; corn or wheat spirit with rye in the mash that matured into "rye"; and corn or wheat spirit, sometimes matured in used wood, to make common whisky.

Distillers still mash a variety of cereal grains to make whisky, but for the most part they use corn. They reserve rye primarily for flavouring, with the notable exception of some all-rye or high-rye whiskies produced by Alberta Distillers, Hiram Walker, Gimli, Valleyfield, and a handful of new artisanal distillers. Wheat, so plentiful, is used less commonly for Canadian whisky now, except by a few microdistilleries and Highwood Distillery, which was engineered explicitly for wheat. Meanwhile, malted barley is gaining popularity with Canada's microdistillers. Triticale, a wheat-rye hybrid, and sorghum, a grain used in the 1970s and 1980s for its lighter flavour, are rarely heard of anymore. In Canada, corn is now number one. Sometimes, Canadian distillers include several different kinds of grain in a mash bill, though more often they mash, ferment, distil, and mature each type of grain separately, then bring them together as mature whiskies.

SOME GRAIN SCIENCE

And now for some whisky-making science. The grains distillers use to make whisky are the seeds of corn, rye, barley, and wheat plants. Each seed contains a tiny embryonic plantlet and a large, starchy endosperm that stores food until the plant sprouts. The seeds also contain starch-degrading enzymes, which become active when the seed germinates. These enzymes change starches in the endosperm into sugars to feed the sprouting seed. Grain that has begun to germinate is called malt.

Specialized firms called maltsters make malt by keeping the grain moist in large drums or on malting floors until it sprouts and its enzymes become active. Then they dry it so it won't germinate fully. Activated enzymes in this "malted grain" will later convert starches in the mash into sugars. Barley makes the best malt, and since the most shrivelled grains are particularly rich in enzymes, maltsters filter it through vibrating screens to separate distillers' malt (for conversion) from brewers' malt (for beer and malt whisky). However, most Canadian whisky is made from unmalted grain.

The non-starchy parts of the grain provide oils, minerals, proteins, and micro-ingredients that nourish the yeast during fermentation and contribute flavour to the final product. The most flavourful part of the grain is the bran— the outer skin. After distillation is complete, distillers recover most of the non-starch grain components to sell as high-protein animal feed. Rye usually makes the most nourishing feed, corn the most palatable.

CORN

It is ironic that the Pilgrims came ashore at Plymouth Rock in 1620 hoping to replenish their dwindling beer supplies, as the original inhabitants of most of North America (including Canada) neither brewed nor distilled alcoholic beverages. It is doubly ironic that the seeds of a plant the Indigenous population had developed for food are exceptionally well suited to making the finest whiskies. The Indigenous people living in what would become known as Canada and the United States cultivated more than 300 different varieties of corn (*Zea mays*) before the first European immigrants arrived, early in the 17th century. Anachronistically, beyond North America, some still refer to it as Indian corn.

Distillers generally use yellow dent corn, a cross between Indigenous flint and flour types. With a higher starch content than most whisky grains, corn yields more alcohol and is easier to process because its mash is less viscous. Unlike other grains, though, corn contains two types of starch, one of which requires higher cooking temperatures than most starches. Thus, it takes more energy to cook corn than other grains. Corn produces a sweet, creamy, fruity distillate. Distillers began importing corn from the US in the mid-19th century, but it was another hundred years before plant breeders developed varieties suitable to Canada's climate.

Mature corn in the field.

RYE

Rye (*Secale cereale*) is cold-hardy and tolerates drought and flood, making it well suited to the harsh climate and poorly prepared soils of pioneer Canada. Rye's long stems also made it easy for early settlers to harvest. As anyone who has eaten rye bread knows, rye has a hearty, somewhat spicy, and slightly bitter taste. In whisky this often translates into intense flavours of hot pepper, clove, ginger, cinnamon, fruit, and a complex floral sweetness, with a refreshing bitterness. Rye spirit begins spicy and fruity and develops scrumptious rich and complex flavours when aged in oak. Depending on how they are fermented and distilled, whiskies made solely from rye grain can be a little overwhelming to the uninitiated palate. Canada's microdistillers have recently uncovered eye-popping new rye flavours, such as lemon custard, by using new processes and yeasts. Still, a little rye can go a long way. Consequently, from the earliest days, rye grain has been added judiciously. When they use an all-rye mash to make base whisky for blending, Canada's distillers may turn to yeasts that generate less spiciness, then strip out much of the remaining rye-grain character in the still.

Rye has its challenges. It contains less starch than other grains, and thus has a higher proportion of nitrogen (protein) and a lower alcohol yield. These high nitrogen levels make it notoriously sticky and messy to work with, and can cause foaming and overflows during fermentation and distillation. Nevertheless, rye's unique flavours are well worth the trouble. The jury is still out on new hybrid ryes developed primarily for the baking industry. They require intensive cultivation, so are expensive and less eco-friendly, while a high ratio of starch to bran means more income-generating alcohol, but proportionally less flavour.

BARLEY

Barley (*Hordeum vulgare*) is often the first grain that comes to mind when people think about whisky. For Canada's legacy distilleries, though, barley is generally a minor component of the mash, if they use any at all. Nevertheless, Canada—particularly the western provinces of Alberta and Saskatchewan—has ideal soil and weather conditions for growing barley. So when large Canadian distilleries use malted grain, they almost always use barley malt because it is so readily available. Malting barley is big business in Canada, but make no mistake: the primary use for malted barley is brewing beer, not distilling whisky. All the same, Canada's growing band of artisanal distillers makes first-rate single malt whisky entirely from malted barley. Unlike Canada's traditional distillers, malt distillers favour plump-grained, starch-laden brewers' malt, and sometimes roasted beer malt.

While some legacy distilleries occasionally use malted barley, until recently, when the price of barley dropped significantly, unmalted barley was pretty much unknown. The Gimli Distillery and Alberta Distillers now mash a little. Seagram mythology tells us that Sam Bronfman always kept a bit of unmalted barley whisky on hand to use for flavouring. More recently, distillers at Gimli have begun experimenting with whisky made from malted and unmalted barley, some of which they bottled as Crown Royal Noble Collection Barley Edition.

WHEAT

Molson's distillery in Montreal was an adjunct to a brewery and used both barley malt and mixed grains, while Wiser's, in Prescott, Ontario, produced feed for JP Wiser's flourishing cattle business, so favoured corn and other grains preferred by livestock. However, most of Canada's earliest commercial distillers began as millers who distilled excess grain on the side. Primarily, that grain was wheat (*Triticum aestivum*). Before Europeans planted grain on the prairies in the 18th and 19th centuries, and long before Canadian Confederation, southern Ontario was known as Canada's breadbasket because great stretches were planted in wheat. Millers ground this wheat into flour, which produced large quantities of milling waste called wheat middlings. They disposed of this waste by distilling it to make animal feed and whisky. No wonder someone suggested they add a bit of rye.

Mashing wheat can be tricky, as wheat contains sticky glucans that can gum up the works. Today, distillers who use wheat take care to prevent the lines (piping) from becoming clogged. At Highwood Distillery, which specializes in distilling from wheat, they do not mill the grain. Instead, they cook it whole until the kernels swell into gelatinous masses and burst like soggy popcorn, releasing their starch-rich contents.

Over the centuries, many varieties of wheat have been developed, including hard and soft wheats, and spring and winter wheats. Experience has shown that soft winter wheat, which is rich in starch, is the most suitable for distilling. Traditionally, wheat yielded less alcohol than corn, but some newer varieties are beginning to catch up. Wheat spirit is usually sweetish, lighter-bodied, and more delicately flavoured than corn, rye, or barley spirit.

Once the grain is ready, the distiller's next step is to add water. Though this water may come from pristine lakes, glacier-fed streams, deep wells, or city mains, it must always be the cleanest, freshest, and purest water the distillery can access. With all the care taken to select the most suitable grain to make whisky, it just wouldn't make sense to process it with anything but top-quality water.

(2)

THE WATER

Distillers mash and ferment grain in water. Partway through distillation, they may add more water to help remove some insoluble by-products of fermentation. After they distil the spirit, they add water again, so the alcohol enters the barrel at an optimum strength for generating flavour. They add water once more when the mature whisky is ready for bottling. In all, distillers use as much as ten litres of water for every litre of whisky produced. This water must be pure and clean and completely odourless. So distillers filter, adjust, and purify it long before it ever touches the first grain. They also purify the water they add to bring the spirit down to barrel strength, and to reduce the final blend for bottling. This ensures that the water does not taint the flavour of the whisky.

Add to this another sixty litres of water used to heat the stills and cool and clean the equipment, and you can quickly see why the first thing people look for when establishing a distillery is a reliable source of pure, clean water. Fortunately, Canada has plenty of it.

Canada has plenty of pure, clean water.

SOME WATER SCIENCE

There's more to water than meets the eye. As it flows over the land, water picks up all kinds of minerals and chemicals that may make it acidic or alkaline, soft or hard. While Scottish distillers extol the virtues of their soft water, American distillers wax lyrical about their hard limestone water. Can both be right? Of course they can. However, as Harold Ferguson, who for more than forty years used limestone-rich Lake Huron water to distil Canadian Mist, put it, "I'd choose to make whisky out of the cleanest water I could get; you can adjust everything else."

It is true, though, that water that has passed through limestone supports enzyme action and the production of particular congeners, the chemicals that give whisky its flavour. Soft Scottish water, however, provides a different advantage: its pH is lower—that is, less alkaline (and therefore more acidic) than limestone water. Yeast requires lower pH during fermentation, so some Canadian distillers add distilling residues, called thin stillage, to make the mash more acidic. This "sour mash process" offsets the alkalinity of limestone water, nourishes the yeast, and impedes bacteria that inhibit fermentation or cause off flavours. For this reason, early Canadian distillers frequently soured their mashes to prevent infection. Today, some distillers have replaced sour mash with improved hygiene and sanitation.

GOING GREEN

Rising energy costs and environmental concerns have led many Canadian distillers to install heat- and energy-recovery systems, enabling them to recycle the energy used to heat the water. Hiram Walker Distillery, for example, reduced energy consumption by almost a third over a five-year period, allowing it to hold energy costs steady despite the steeply rising rates charged by energy providers. As well, filtering and purification practices ensure the water that distilleries return to the environment has been reoxygenated and the impurities removed.

Environmental stewardship is no mere fad. Sixty years ago, the Corby Distillery in Corbyville, Ontario, installed a massive heat-recovery plant along with sedimentation and filtration systems that ensured the water it returned to the Moira River was as clean as when Corby's withdrew it to use for processing. The thriving trout population in the Moira as it flowed past the distillery became a point of pride for Corby's management and distillery staff, who had taken pains to keep the river habitable. In recent years, some distillers have taken steps to reduce water use by as much as 75% to further lower their environmental impact.

Distilling remains an agricultural process, and just as it was sixty years ago in Corbyville, the harmony of nature is never far from the distiller's mind. Distillers also turn to nature to convert starches from the grain into alcohol. To do this, they recruit natural enzymes and living yeast.

Gibson's Finest Rare Aged 12 Years
40% alc/vol | PMA

Crème caramel, maple syrup, vanilla, barrel tones, brisk ginger, baking spices, almond skins, canned mandarins, and hints of cereal. Ends on soft spice and tannins.

Bearface Wilderness Series Matsutake Release
42.5% alc/vol | Mark Anthony

Unusual. Sweetish with hot chilis early in, mouth-filling, damp wood, a rousing earthiness, the meatiness of leaf mould, punky wood, violets, forest rain. Long, earthy, slightly peppery finish.

Canadian Rockies Aged 28 Years
46% alc/vol | Fountana Group

Soft and sweet, with more nibble than bite. Well integrated. Corn syrup, thrilling barrel tones, cedar, kiwi, growing hot spices, burnt fruitwood. Raw lumber with tannins on the finish.

Pendleton Directors Reserve Aged 20 Years
40% alc/vol | Pendleton

Clean oak, lush butterscotch, molasses, almond granola, white pepper, dried orange peel. Herbal tones, worn leather, and dry grain. Creaminess evolves slowly into beautiful oaky tannins. A chest-warming thrill.

2

HOW CANADIAN
WHISKY IS MADE

FROM FIELD TO FLASK

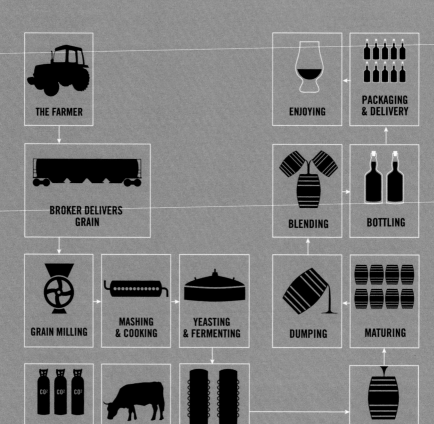

THE FARMER

BROKER DELIVERS GRAIN

GRAIN MILLING

MASHING & COOKING

YEASTING & FERMENTING

CARBON DIOXIDE

CO² CO² CO²

SPENT GRAINS

DISTILLING

DUMPING

MATURING

BARREL FILLING

BLENDING

BOTTLING

PACKAGING & DELIVERY

ENJOYING

(3)

PROCESSING

Each Canadian distillery is unique, and whisky-making practices differ considerably among them. Typically, though, the Canadian whisky we drink is a blend of various "component" whiskies that distillers have crafted individually and blended together to achieve specific flavour profiles. Whatever their methods, skilled workers inspect the grain for quality, clean it, then grind it into meal and cook it. They add enzymes at key points, then yeast to ferment it into a sweet, weakly alcoholic liquid called distillers' beer. This they distil, mature, and blend to make whisky.

Most distillers mash, ferment, and distil each type of grain separately to optimize its performance and create more blending options. Processing each kind of grain independently allows distillers to adapt each step, from grinding to maturing, to suit each specifically. They may tailor milling practices, and cooking temperatures and times, and further increase the number of component whiskies by using various yeasts, distilling regimes, and maturation processes. In addition, some also make one or more mixed-grain mashes. The whisky-making process is almost as complex as the resulting whisky itself. Let's begin with a look at mashing and fermentation.

COOKING AND ENZYMES

Yeast (*Saccharomyces cerevisiae*) feeds on simple sugars, but it cannot consume starch. Since grain stores carbohydrates as starch, distillers convert it into sugar so that the yeast can ferment it into alcohol. This process is called mashing.

Distillery workers begin by milling grain into a coarse flour called grist and adding water. Then they cook it at high temperatures and pressure, and treat it with enzymes. Malted grain, used mainly by small artisanal distillers, contains its own endogenous enzymes, so there is no need to cook it. For malt whisky, conversion takes place in large vessels called mash tuns. Usually, after conversion, distillers filter the converted mash (called wort) and pump it into fermentation vats known as washbacks. They always make malt whisky in batches.

However, Canada's legacy distillers generally stick with unmalted grain and purified microbial enzymes, so they follow different protocols. Depending on the spirit they are making, distillers either cook and mash the grist in batches, or use an automated continuous cooking and mashing process. Cooking the grist makes the starch more accessible to the enzymes and kills any bacteria that might contaminate the mash.

Conversion with microbial enzymes happens in two stages. Sometimes, computer-controlled machines mix the grist with hot water in a large batch cooker to form a slurry. More commonly, though, they pump it steadily through an elongated, tube-shaped, continuous cooker at 100° Celsius. Cooking turns most starch into a viscous, porridge-like gel. To keep it flowing smoothly through the cooker, distillers add amylolytic enzymes to the mash before cooking it.

These enzymes break the starches down into dextrins in a process called lique-faction. The conversion of starch into dextrins continues as the mash passes through the cooker. Once it is cooked, they pump the mash into fermenters and add saccharifying enzymes (and, occasionally, a little malt) to change the dextrins into sugars. Otherwise, the cooked, liquefied starch would return to a more com-plex, less convertible state as it cooled.

At one time, distillers made their microbial enzymes themselves; today, all but one purchase them from specialist enzyme companies. Alberta Distillers is the last Canadian distillery to produce its enzymes on site. To do this, they inoculate a sterilized corn mash with spores from a selected strain of *Aspergillus awamori*

Enzymes are grown in small fermenter-like tubs called reactors.

Royal Canadian Small Batch
40% alc/vol | Sazerac

Grain, creamy caramel, and clean oak with dark fruity accents, hinting at chocolate malt, and cinnamon sticks. Mild dusty rye, barrel tones. Full-bodied and gently oaky.

Signal Hill Founders Reserve
56.3% alc/vol | Signal Hill

Fragrant, sweet, and briskly hot. Oak tannins temper ripe dark fruit and syrupy sweetness. Toasted oak, increasingly fruity, richest butterscotch, hot peppers, clean oak, and pulling pithy tannins.

Stampede Rye
40% alc/vol | Eau Claire

Aromatic butterscotch, hints of spirit, faint dark fruit, dry hay, and weathered wood. Creamy. Sweet with instantly mounting heat. Mouth-filling, round, and robust. Not overly complex.

Wayne Gretzky No. 99 Ice Cask
41.5% alc/vol | Wayne Gretzky

Sweet, syrupy, almost winey, with gentle heat. Icing sugar . . . bath salts? Rising heat turns gentle as spicy herbal tones fade into Indian kewra water and clean oak.

fungus (similar to *Aspergillus oryzae*, which is used when making miso and soy sauce) in small fermenter-like tanks called reactors. Over a period of four to six days, the *Aspergillus* grows, creating a lumpy, buttermilk-like mixture with a characteristic musty aroma. When it reaches maximum enzyme concentration, they add this enzyme-rich preparation to a whisky mash, sometimes supplementing it with commercially produced enzymes.

Because these homegrown enzymes are unrefined, they also induce a broad array of beneficial side reactions during mashing. For example, they break down a number of other carbohydrates and grain components in addition to starch, and they generate various flavour precursors and yeast nutrients. "Using homegrown enzymes is the secret to making 100% rye whisky," says whisky microbiologist Rob Tuer.

YEAST

Yeast is a tiny, single-celled organism—a fungus, really—that consumes sugar and turns it into ethanol and carbon dioxide in a process called fermentation. Yeast excretes these products, in roughly equal amounts, along with many minor but significant by-products that add flavour to the whisky. These include esters, ketones, fatty acids, and an assortment of alcohols and fusel oils. Surprisingly, research shows that yeast generates more whisky congeners than grain contributes. Some of the flavour of whisky thus begins with fermentation.

Once they have mashed the grain and prepared the fermentable sugars, distillers cool the mash to between 26° and 38° Celsius and often dilute it and adjust the acidity with thin stillage. Then they add yeast in a process called pitching. Most distillers ferment their mashes at temperatures low enough to permit yeast to access nourishing nitrogen in the grain. However, some Canadian distillers add diammonium phosphate to the mash, or add protease enzymes at key points so that fermentation will continue until all the sugars are fermented. Often, workers add the yeast well before the enzymes have transformed all the starch into sugar. This kick-starts fermentation so that it proceeds in parallel with conversion. Over a period of about three or four days, as the enzymes create more sugar, the yeast consumes it, so the mash never accumulates enough sugar to encourage bacterial growth. The result is beer with an alcohol content somewhere between 6 and 8% for rye, and about 10 to 16% for corn mashes.

Like most living things, yeast's behaviour depends on its environment. Whisky makers take advantage of this to encourage the yeast to generate specific congeners. For example, raising the temperature of the fermenting mash leads to more fruity, floral esters and fewer fatty acids. Reducing oxygen levels in the mash increases both esters and fatty acids. Other changes, some as simple as stirring the mash, generate different flavour profiles.

While distillers generally use commercially produced yeast for making base whisky, when they make flavouring whisky, they take care to select yeasts that produce specific flavours. For instance, so-called POF (phenolic off-flavour) yeast used by some microdistillers generates flavours that might be considered faults in beer or wine, but are highly prized in rye. Canadian distillers also hire specialist companies to grow yeasts from well-guarded proprietary strains. Among other things, these special yeasts generate unique esters responsible for fruity aromas and flavours. While some of these esters smell distinctly of specific well-known fruits, others bring a more generic sense of fruitiness to the whisky. Some distillers go so far as to check the yeast's DNA sequences before entrusting their fermentations to it.

Yeast companies grow these pure-strain yeasts in a sterile, yeast-propagating mash in vessels called yeast tubs. This mash is similar to regular whisky mash, but is adjusted to maximize the growth and viability of the new yeast. Technicians seed these mashes with yeast from previous batches and collect and store pails of yeast from each new yeast mash to keep the strain pure. There is a school of thought that, because it is added to the mash, yeast is an ingredient in whisky, even though no element of the yeast is incorporated into the final product. However, yeast is more of a processor, much as the stills are, and once its job is done, distillers remove it along with the spent grains.

BACTERIA

Yeast is not the only organism feeding on the sugars in the mash. Bacteria (primarily *Lactobacillus*) also thrive in the fermenters and produce congeners that add to the flavour, though not necessarily in a good way. Small quantities of the esters, fatty acids, and other congeners they generate can add pleasing complexity to some whiskies. So distillers occasionally encourage these bacterial contributions by leaving some fermenters uncovered or allowing some fermentations to go longer than the typical three or four days. However, in all but the smallest quantities, bacterial flavours are generally negative. Distillers usually keep fermentation times as short as possible and ensure that all vessels, pipes, and lines remain meticulously clean so bacteria cannot gain a disruptive foothold anywhere in the process.

Over the centuries, distillers have designed and modified all kinds of machinery, tools, and practices to improve yields and quality. However, conversion and fermentation, two processes central to turning grain into whisky, are biological processes carried out by microorganisms. In the end, distillers must rely on nature to complete the most crucial steps. Nevertheless, the product of fermentation is not whisky; it is distillers' beer. The next step in the process, distillation, transforms this beer into alcoholic spirit with the potential to develop the full range of beguiling Canadian whisky flavours.

Black Velvet makes experimental high wines in a former Gilbey gin still.

(4)

DISTILLING

Water boils at 100° Celsius, ethanol at 78.4°. Long ago, someone figured out that when they heated a mixture of water and alcohol, the alcohol evaporated before the water did, and they could concentrate the alcohol by capturing and cooling the early vapours. This simple observation is the basis of distillation. Ethanol itself is essentially flavourless, but the beer created during fermentation is rich in flavourful congeners. Fortunately, some of these compounds distil along with the ethanol.

The speed of distillation affects the concentration and mix of congeners, and thus the final flavour of the whisky. Slow distillation often produces a more flavourful spirit, so some distillers occasionally dilute their beer or high wines with water to extend the distilling time. The size and shape of the still, and the portion of spirit saved (the "cuts"), also affect which compounds make it into the final spirit. Distillers generally operate several stills to take advantage of the differences among them.

PRODUCTS OF DISTILLATION

77 METRIC TONNE RAILCAR

DISTILLERY

BY WEIGHT

⅓	**⅓**	**⅓**
CO_2 (CAPTURED AND SOLD)	SPENT GRAINS AND YEAST DISTILLERS' DRIED GRAINS (CATTLE FEED) 23–26 METRIC TONNES	WHISKY

HOW MUCH WHISKY IS PRODUCED FROM A CARLOAD OF GRAIN?

- One railcar load of grain weighs 77 metric tonnes
- This produces 7,700 litres of absolute alcohol
- After diluting to barrel strength, this fills 212 barrels
- When mature, this yields 35,400 litres of cask-strength whisky
- When diluted to bottle strength, this gives 62,000 litres of whisky
- At bottle strength this produces 82,685 bottles of whisky
- So one railcar load of grain produces 82,685 bottles of whisky

ALL FIGURES ARE APPROXIMATE

THREE-COLUMN DISTILLATION

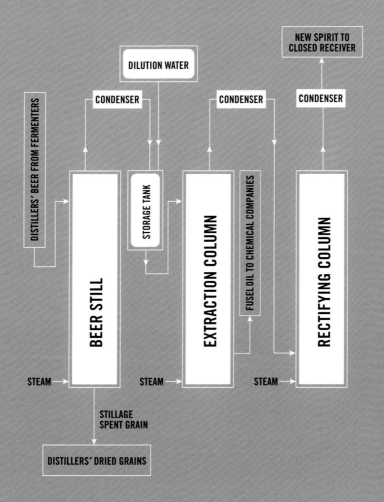

NEW SPIRIT TO CLOSED RECEIVER

DILUTION WATER

CONDENSER

CONDENSER

CONDENSER

DISTILLERS' BEER FROM FERMENTERS

STORAGE TANK

FUSEL OIL TO CHEMICAL COMPANIES

BEER STILL

EXTRACTION COLUMN

RECTIFYING COLUMN

STEAM

STEAM

STEAM

STILLAGE SPENT GRAIN

DISTILLERS' DRIED GRAINS

TYPES OF STILLS

Typically, Canadian distillers use two types of stills: traditional pot stills familiar to the earliest Canadian distillers, and carefully tuned column stills. Both concentrate the ethanol and desirable congeners by removing water and impurities. Distillers began using pot stills many centuries ago. In 1813, however, French inventor Jean-Baptiste Cellier-Blumenthal patented the first practical continuous still. Suddenly, distillers could produce spirit non-stop. Then, on June 10, 1826, the *Register of the Arts and Sciences* (London) carried an illustrated description of an improved continuous still designed and patented by JJ Saintmarc. His still was ingenious because beer entered the top of a distilling column continuously and exited at the bottom after the spirit evaporated. The following year, Robert Stein further improved the column still by heating the beer with steam rather than direct fire. Then, in 1830, Irish exciseman Aeneas Coffey patented yet another version of the column still.

Though modern column stills are often called Coffey stills (which has been confusing to the ear ever since), it was the Saintmarc version that caught the attention of early leading-edge Canadian distillers Thomas Molson and Robert McLaren. In the end, McLaren chose to stick with his forty-gallon copper pot still, while Molson had another idea. He built a square, wooden, steam-heated adaptation of the column still. Later distillers, such as Hiram Walker, purchased tall, round, three-chambered, wooden charging stills with copper doublers attached from Hoffman, Ahlers & Company in Cincinnati.

COLUMN DISTILLATION

Today, Canada's large distillers make their whisky spirits in tall metal cylinders called column stills. Perforated metal plates, or "trays" (usually copper), stacked inside the columns act like a series of interconnected mini-pots. Warmed beer enters near the top of the still and flows back and forth across the trays until it reaches the bottom and is discarded or recycled as stillage. At the same time, pressurized steam injected into the bottom of the still bubbles up through the perforations in the trays. This heats the beer as it flows across the trays, causing some of the alcohol to evaporate. Once the beer has crossed the tray, a short drainpipe called a downcomer carries it to the tray below, where the process begins again.

Meanwhile, the alcohol vapour condenses on the tray above and dissolves in the beer flowing across that tray, where more alcohol then evaporates. As the process repeats, the beer travels down the column, losing more alcohol to the rising steam it encounters on each tray. The vapour that finally exits the top of the still can be up to 94% alcohol. Of course, as the alcohol rises, it leaves some congeners behind in the alcohol-depleted beer. Thus, the spirit produced in a column still is often light in body and flavour.

Column stills must be very tall to be fully effective. So for practical purposes, most are split into two adjacent columns, called an analyzer and a rectifier. The analyzer, more commonly referred to as a beer still, produces a distillate, or "high wine," of about 65% alc/vol (alcohol by volume—also written as ABV). Generally, the spent grain solids are still suspended in the beer as it enters the beer still, and flow out through the bottom of the still with the depleted beer.

Since the high wines produced in the beer still are rich in congeners, distillers sometimes put them directly into barrels to mature into flavouring whisky or redistil them in a pot still. For base spirit, distillers redistil the high wines in a further series of columns. Between the beer still (analyzer) and the rectifier, distillers usually remove unwanted heavy alcohols called fusel oils in an intermediate process known as extractive distillation. Fusels are insoluble in water, so distillers dilute the spirit from the beer still down to about 15% alc/vol and redistil it in a fusel still. They draw the fusel oils off partway up the fusel column and send the remaining diluted spirit to the rectifying column. The rectifier raises the alc/vol to as high as 94% before the spirit is condensed and collected in a receiving vessel. From there, they send it off to be put into barrels for ageing. Trace amounts of fusel oil that survive this process add character to the whisky.

Each distillery uses a custom combination of stills. Highwood, for example, has a pot still with a tall rectifying column mounted directly on top to take advantage of both processes in a single run. Individual distillery chapters describe the specific distillation processes of each, but all derive from this generic process.

DISTILLING, THEN DILUTING

Canadian distillers think long and hard about how they spend money on production, as each dollar they spend increases the price a consumer must pay for a bottle of whisky. Distillers know that oxidation, a critical factor in maturing whisky, requires sufficient water in the spirit. They have found that putting the spirit into barrels at about 70% alc/vol (with a big plus-minus) produces the most desirable flavours during maturation. It seems odd, then, that they would go to the expense of distilling to 94% alc/vol, then turn around and add water back before they put the spirit into barrels. However, to paraphrase the Bard, there really is method to this madness.

Spirit that has been distilled to a lower alc/vol is a soup of congeners. Some of these are more soluble than others, and some react with flavour elements found in the wood. By introducing spirit with a high congener content into some barrels, and spirit with a low congener content into others, Canadian distillers encourage diverse maturation processes to create distinct flavour profiles. Some processes are mutually exclusive, and others are more focused when the chemicals in the wood are not competing with other compounds in the maturing spirit. Chemical reactions tend to favour an overall equilibrium.

When distillers remove congeners derived from the grain and fermentation, that equilibrium shifts in favour of reactions such as oxidation.

POT AND BATCH DISTILLATION

Distillers sometimes redistil spirit from the beer still in a large pot. Most micro-distillers primarily use pot stills, but larger legacy distillers use them mainly when they make flavouring whisky, especially when it contains a high percentage of rye grain. A pot still is simply a copper or stainless steel kettle or boiler with a pipe that leads vapours into a water-cooled vessel called a condenser. Distillers fill the pot with high wines from the beer still, then heat it with steam coils until these high wines boil. The resulting vapours, including most of the alcohol and desirable congeners, and some water, flow into the condenser.

Most malt distillers filter their mash before fermenting it. Since large legacy distillers do not filter their beer, they generally don't distil it directly in a pot, as the grain residues would burn. Pot stills are relatively inefficient, so the final distillate, which comes off the still at about 65% alc/vol, contains many impurities. This is a good thing, as these impurities give the final whisky much of its flavour, especially when blended with lighter whisky from a continuous column still.

In addition to desirable congeners, high wines also contain some unpleasant ones such as highly volatile ketones, often called heads or foreshots, and less volatile heavy alcohols called tails or feints. The foreshots are the first spirits to come from the pot still, while the feints distil off near the end of the run. Foreshots and feints are usually collected separately and recycled into the next batch of beer to recover any remaining ethanol and flavourful congeners. Distillers save the middle portion (cut) of the distillation to make whisky. Meanwhile, the watery leftovers in the pot still, called pot ale or thin stillage, are sometimes added to the next mash in a sour mash process, or dried and sold as cattle feed.

In essence, distillation heats distillers' beer or wort and separates it into components. For flavouring whisky, which draws much of its flavour from the grain and fermentation by-products, distillers retain a large volume of water and congeners in the distillate. For base whisky, they remove most of the water and congeners to make room for other, more subtle flavours to be expressed more fully. As they turn grain into whisky, distillers dry the waste left behind for sale to livestock farmers. And when it comes time to mature their spirits into whisky, they entrust the process to the final whisky ingredient: wood harvested from mature trees in managed oak forests, where a new generation of saplings grows in their place.

Gibson's Finest Venerable Aged 18 Years
40% alc/vol | PMA

Crisp and fresh with clover, vanilla, lemon custard, sawdust, pencil shavings, white pepper. Nutty, dry grain, green hay. Mouth-filling. Dark fruits. Flowers. Nail polish. Oaky, spicy finish. Elegance defined.

Speaker Rota's Canadian Whisky/Rocking R 100% Rye
40% alc/vol | Rig Hand

Brisk, youthful, peppery. Baking spices, caramel, vanilla. Lush and full. Rose petals, soft but grippy barrel tones, sweet and tart fruits. Dusty rye. Finishes on green tea and grapefruit pith.

(5)

MATURING

As clear as water, with a sweet, spicy, and—some would say—harsh flavour. That's Canadian whisky when it first comes off the still. It's drinkable, and that is how most early settlers in Canada drank it. But it does not appeal to the modern palate. And by today's definition, it's not yet whisky. Before it earns that honour, it must spend at least three years maturing in oak barrels. However, three years is simply a legal minimum; there is no single magic moment when the whisky suddenly reaches its peak. Flavour continues to develop as long as the spirit remains in the barrel, and distillers routinely mature portions of the distillate for different lengths of time to create distinct whiskies. Comparing the new distillate to the mature product quickly demonstrates that ageing really does smooth out the rough edges while developing new flavours, dimensions, and complexities.

Most Canadian distillers mature their whisky in barrels made from American white oak harvested in Missouri and Kentucky. Oak is particularly well suited for making barrels as it is sturdy and is porous to air, but not to liquids. It is also pliable, and, when heated, can be bent into the familiar curved barrel staves. Unfortunately, raw new oak contains tree sap, resins, and harsh tannins that can quickly impart astringent and unpleasant flavours to the whisky. Coopers, the craftsmen who make barrels, overcome this "greenness" by weathering the oak staves outside, then charring the inside of newly raised barrels with a gas flame.

AGEING REGULATIONS

For centuries, European wine and brandy makers knew the benefits of oak ageing. It was an easy knowledge transfer to their whisky-making colleagues. Along with knowledge, though, came government regulation. Canada enacted a legal requirement for ageing in 1887, the first such law in any nation. Initially, the minimum ageing period was one year; in 1890, it became two. The stated purpose was to improve the quality of the product. However, many of the larger Canadian distillers already aged at least some of their whisky before sending it to market.

That first ageing law had another purpose altogether: increasing government tax revenue. Small producers who could not afford to wait to sell their whisky were also the ones most likely to evade taxes. Within a couple of years, not a single "nuisance distiller" remained. In 1974, the government increased the ageing requirement to three years and specified that distillers must use "small wood"—oak barrels no larger than 700 litres. In practice, Canadian distillers usually use barrels much smaller than that, with a capacity of about 200 litres.

AGEING PROCESSES

Distillers dilute new spirit to somewhere between 68% and 72% alc/vol before filling it into barrels through a "bunghole" drilled in one end of the barrel. At larger, automated distilleries, the barrels arrive at the filling station in groups of four or six, standing on end on a pallet. Once the barrels are filled, a forklift stacks the pallets in a warehouse, often called a maturing house. Some older maturing houses accommodate barrels on their sides on racks, while workers at the Valleyfield Distillery stack some of their barrels vertically, on top of each other in pyramids.

As the spirit matures, water, alcohol, and traces of some volatile congeners evaporate through pores in the oak. These losses from evaporation are commonly called the angels' share. The warmer the warehouse, the greater the angels' share, although the proportions of water and alcohol differ. In the humid climates of Ontario and Nova Scotia, more alcohol evaporates than water, so the whisky becomes weaker. In drier locations, such as Alberta, the situation is reversed. More water evaporates than alcohol, and the concentration of alcohol in the whisky increases during maturation.

Air moving in and out of the barrel is part of the maturation process, so temperature changes in the maturing house affect how whisky matures. As the weather becomes warmer, the air in the barrel expands, as does the alcohol itself, increasing the pressure. This pushes air out through pores in the oak and forces spirit into and between the barrel staves. Later, as cooler seasons arrive, air and alcohol in the barrel contract, lowering the pressure, which pulls flavour-rich spirit out of the oak and into the whisky. At the same time, more air seeps back into the barrel. Warmer temperatures and greater air exchange increase oxidation, which, in turn, generates more fruity esters. Generally, the warmer the warehouse, the faster the whisky changes. However, not all reactions accelerate at the same pace, so rapid maturation produces a different, often rougher flavour profile than slow maturation. Whisky that matures in one part of the maturing house often tastes different from that in another part due to temperature variations within the building. Canada's harsh winters mean that most maturing houses need to be heated at least enough to ensure the fire sprinklers don't freeze, should they ever be needed.

SOME MATURING SCIENCE

Five different processes that occur in the barrel work independently and synergistically to create an array of whisky flavours, both robust and subtle, and impart colour to the spirit. Understanding these activities enables distillers to emphasize specific flavours in various blending components. For example, distillers maintain the lightness of base whisky by maturing it in previously used barrels. On the other hand, they use flavour-rich new and once-used barrels for robust flavouring whiskies.

As the spirit sits in the barrel, it extracts flavours from the oak. This process happens rapidly at first, before tapering off to almost nothing within about seven months. Like any organic substance, wood is made up of various chemical compounds. In oak, these consist primarily of two large, complex carbohydrates—cellulose and hemicellulose—and an aromatic polymer called lignin.

These substances degrade into simpler compounds during the charring process, then seep into the whisky as it matures, adding significant flavour and colour. For instance, when lignin is heated gently, it breaks down into eugenol, phenols, cresols, guaiacols, vanillins, and various similar compounds that contribute flavours often attributed to rye. Eugenol tastes like rye's signature flavour, cloves. So distillers often mature rye spirit in toasted barrels to accentuate its unique qualities. Toasted oak can also impart rye-like attributes to spirit made with little or no rye grain. Cellulose and hemicellulose, when heated, produce caramels and other similar compounds.

Contrary to what many people believe, a lighter char can deliver more flavour than a heavier one does. Excess charring tends to incinerate the flavour compounds, at least near the inside surface of the barrel. Still, flavours from newly charred wood can be so potent that they overwhelm those derived from the grain. American bourbon makers always use new charred oak barrels, and it does not take long for their robust flavours to become the dominant characteristic of the whisky. This is one reason that younger bourbon can be so flavourful. These primary wood flavourings impart characteristic rich vanilla notes and hints of perfume to bourbon, and Canadian distillers often use new charred oak barrels, too, when they are maturing corn spirit to make flavouring whisky. Another notable effect of heating oak is that more coconut-flavoured oak lactones are available to dissolve into the maturing spirit.

However, for the most part, Canadian distillers mature their whisky in barrels that were used first to make bourbon. At first, it may seem odd to reuse barrels when much of the flavour has already leached out while maturing bourbon, but with the concentration of those primary flavours reduced, more subtle and complex tones can now emerge without the primary flavours masking them. Distillers sometimes refer to these barrels as new bourbon drains or bourbon dumpers. Knowing the source—their "pedigree"—tells Canadian distillers what qualities they can expect from them. Nevertheless, workers often smell, or "nose," the barrels to ensure they are "sweet." Usually, they refill barrels several times and sometimes renew their "activity" by scraping the barrels inside and re-charring them. This removes residual flavours from previous fillings and somewhat extends the cleansing effect of charcoal, but does little to renew wood flavours that have already soaked away in previous uses. Barrels naturally impart fewer wood-derived flavours with each reuse.

CHEMICAL REACTIONS IN THE WOOD

A second process that takes place in reused barrels helps set the Canadian whisky style apart. After the barrel is filled with spirit, new flavouring elements develop slowly through two chemical reactions called hydrolysis and oxidation. Hydrolysis splits large molecules in the wood into shorter, more flavourful ones. Oxidation changes the structures, and thus the flavours, of smaller molecules. Essentially, oxygen dissolved in the spirit, and the ethanol itself, react with certain oak compounds to create a whole array of new flavours. Although the products of hydrolysis and oxidation can be quite delightful, it often takes years to generate enough that you can taste them. This is one reason why long-aged Canadian whisky develops such tempting crisp, woody notes, almost like maple syrup, without the bitterness sometimes expected in whisky that has spent a long time in new barrels. It also explains why wine barrels often need three or more years to confer their most exquisite flavours to the whisky.

CHEMICAL REACTIONS IN THE SPIRIT

The third influence of oak derives from its porous nature. Pores in the oak allow small amounts of water and alcohol to evaporate from the barrel and small amounts of air to come in. Oxygen in the air reacts with ethanol and congeners in the spirit, creating new flavour substances, primarily fruity esters. A fundamental chemical reaction in the spirit, which lends Canadian whisky its highly prized elegance, is the gradual oxidation of ethanol into acetaldehyde and ethyl acetate with estery aromas that some liken almost to sweetish nail polish. Slow oxidation is responsible for many subtle, fruity high notes in blends that contain significant amounts of long-aged base whisky.

CHAR REMOVES OFF NOTES

A fourth influence of charred oak is that charcoal (often simply called char) is a cleansing agent. Char removes many undesirable flavours by adsorbing them onto its surface. For example, corn spirit contains unpleasant sulphur compounds, yet few or no sulphury flaws remain once it has spent time in heavily charred barrels. Before the practice of ageing whisky evolved, many Canadian distillers filtered their raw spirit through charcoal to remove some of the harsher notes and mellow it. Some American distillers still use charcoal filtration. Nowadays, Canadian whisky makers rely on char inside the barrel to take care of this. While excess charring destroys many wood-derived flavour elements, it dramatically increases the effectiveness of the barrel in removing off notes.

GHOSTS OF WHISKIES PAST

Fifth, and finally, the previous contents of used barrels can also affect the flavour of Canadian whisky. Although distillery workers do their best to drain barrels completely, and some go so far as to rinse them afterwards, inevitably, the barrel retains as much as six or seven litres of the former contents soaked into the

A cooper hand chars a single barrel.

staves. This residual bourbon, rye, or wine seeps into the next batch of maturing spirit. Canadian distillers occasionally augment this effect by using an assortment of barrels that previously held cognac, brandy, sherry, rum, or other spirits.

BASE WHISKY

The main ingredient in most Canadian whisky is base whisky, which most distillers make from corn. Alberta Distillers also uses rye and other grains, while Highwood uses wheat. No matter which grain, base whisky must be light in flavour. Thus, distillers remove most of the congeners derived from the grain and yeast in a series of column stills. Then they mature the spirit in barrels they have used several times already. Because the influence of the wood declines with each use, base whisky acquires nearly all its flavour from oxidation and other slow interactions among chemicals in the spirit, rather than from the barrels.

Distillers continue to reuse barrels until they are too leaky to be worth fixing. They often label new barrels with barcodes to track them and record how many times they have been used. This helps them find those containing spirits with specific flavour profiles. Although once they mature these individual spirits are technically whisky, they are more often referred to as "maturates" until they are blended.

Unblended base whisky reveals crisp, delicate whisky flavours. Over time, as the flavours of base whiskies slowly increase, they can become so enchanting that some distillers have been unable to resist the urge to bottle them with just minimal amounts of added flavouring whisky.

FLAVOURING WHISKY

The flavours that distinguish one Canadian whisky from another come chiefly from what is called flavouring whisky. Whether distilled in a beer still, a pot still, or a combination of the two, the spirit destined to become flavouring whisky is already rich in congeners before distillers fill it into barrels. Some of these congeners came from the grain, while the yeast generated others during fermentation. The distiller's objective is to shape and amplify these flavours during maturation. Although rye and corn predominate, distillers sometimes use wheat, barley, or other grains to make flavouring whiskies. Some also use mixed-grain mashes for additional spirit streams.

There is another variable that most distillers use from time to time. The Scottish popularized the practice of maturing whisky in sherry barrels to add rich sherry notes to their whisky. Soon, though, some took a shortcut and put already mature whisky into wine barrels briefly, in a process called finishing. Sometimes this enhanced the whisky with complementary flavours, and other times it simply made mediocre whisky more palatable.

Canadian distillers also mature or finish whisky in sherry barrels sometimes. However, perhaps somewhat cynically, some blenders have taken to "finishing" whiskies simply by adding raw sherry. They claim this is no different from finishing whisky in sherry barrels. But connoisseurs accustomed to whiskies matured or finished in barrels that first spent eighty-odd years filled with sherry in a solera claim they can taste a difference.

MORE THAN A CONTAINER

Whisky makers have learned how their various spirits interact with different barrels and can predict when certain whiskies, stored in specific barrels in particular places in the maturing house, will be ready for blending and bottling. Even so, maturation is not an exact science. As the whisky approaches maturity, blenders taste samples to gauge its progress until, finally, the time is right to disgorge the barrels, a process called dumping. They then mingle the contents of many barrels together, according to carefully guarded recipes, to produce another batch of fine Canadian whisky.

That white oak barrel in which the whisky rests for all those years turns out to be much more than a container. Wood, in fact, is the third ingredient in whisky. Although water and grain contribute most of the volume to the whisky, some distillers estimate that when they mature it in new barrels, as much as 60% of the flavour found in whisky may come from the wood. Regardless, with a variety of base and flavouring maturates at hand, there is only one step left in creating the final product: blending.

Laird of Fintry Tequila Barrel
42% alc/vol | Okanagan

Malty and waxy with gentle nougat, grape juice, vague anise, and some earthiness. The tequila stays subtle, hot, and peppery. Luscious and mouth-filling. Long, spicy finish.

LMD Release 0001 Straight Rye 3 Wood
45% alc/vol | Last Mountain

Ozone fresh and aromatic. Toasted cherrywood and ripe fruit broach Creamsicle and black tea. Vanilla, lovely pith, throat-bound peppery glow. Vaguely sweet with joyful spices, late fruit, and butterscotch.

(6)

BLENDING

"Distilling is a science; blending is an art." So declared Canadian whisky titan Samuel Bronfman. Mr. Sam, as he was known, did not invent blending. British tea merchants adopted an ancient Asian skill and later applied it to whisky. Nevertheless, blenders and whisky lovers owe an enduring debt of gratitude to Mr. Sam and his Seagram Company. Refinements they pioneered in their LaSalle, Quebec, blending lab in the years following Prohibition transformed blending practices globally.

They knew that year-to-year differences in growing seasons affected the flavour of the grain. "Look," he told his blending staff one day, "when a man goes into a store for a bottle of Coca-Cola, he expects it to be the same today as it will be tomorrow. The great products don't change. Well, goddammit, our product's not going to change, either." With that, he challenged his staff to figure out a way to maintain consistent flavour despite annual differences in the grain. Their solution? Include many different component whiskies in each blend and adjust the proportions when some of them change.

They began distilling corn, rye, and several different mixed mashes separately to create distinct spirit streams. Then they matured these in various ways, and for various lengths of time, to emphasize certain characteristics before blending them as mature spirits. Their remarkable success led Seagram's to adopt this practice for its American brands and other brown spirits as well. Other whisky makers took note of this new "Canadian" way to blend whisky, and it became the standard for top-end Canadian whisky. Crown Royal, for example, includes about fifty different whiskies, with the exact number and ratios adjusted each year.

Seagram's chief blender, Art "The Nose" Dawe, and plant manager, Arthur W. Downe, compare blend samples to the standard in the quality control lab at the Waterloo distillery. Seagram's blending practices and insistence on consistency set the pace for the industry.

INCIDENTAL BLENDING

Early Canadian distillers did not consciously blend their whisky. The first deliberate efforts to improve whisky flavours happened early in the 19th century, when they began to add rye grain to their otherwise all-wheat mashes. However, long before Canada's ageing law came into effect, some Canadian distillers were already ageing their whisky. Often, they used barrels made from local oak. When they reused these barrels, they noticed that the whisky, though less robust, developed flavours not found in whisky from new barrels. Innovative distillers such as Joseph E. Seagram and Hiram Walker thus began to mingle whisky from new and used barrels. The result tasted better than either one alone.

BLENDING TODAY

In today's whisky world, Canada is still best known for its blends of gentle base whiskies and robust flavouring whiskies. Distillers develop each blending component individually, using processes that optimize its inherent attributes. This ensures that each component brings specific, predictable qualities to the final whisky. Blenders may further enhance certain flavour elements with minor additions of other mature spirits or wine, either through barrel finishing or directly. They may also adjust the colour with spirit caramel. While these practices might seem at odds with ideas promoted by marketing people from other popular whisky-making nations, in one guise or another, those nations employ them as well. Canadians are simply more open about it. Understanding Canadian whisky requires stepping beyond the paradigm advanced by people more familiar with the product of other countries.

Although single malts, bourbon, and the like dominate the conversations of some aficionados, blended whisky still rules the marketplace. Overwhelmingly, the sheer volume of blended whisky produced in Scotland, Ireland, and the US keeps the whisky industries there viable. Moreover, most single malts are themselves blends of a sort—blends of malt whiskies, all made in the same distillery and, like Canadian whisky, matured using different types of barrels and ageing regimens. Bourbon, too, is usually a blend of corn-based whiskies that have matured in various places in tall warehouses where gradations in temperature generate noticeably different whiskies. It should surprise no one that most Canadian whisky is also blended. What is remarkable, though, is how exceptionally well some Canadian blenders have mastered its complexities.

While Canadian whisky may include many components, blenders draw these from just two whisky streams: base whisky and flavouring whisky. Some distillers begin with a single base spirit and mature it into various base whiskies using a variety of barrels and maturation times. Others distil several different base spirits and further expand their blending options by maturing these in multiple ways. The flavours and aromas of base whisky are less assertive than those of flavouring whisky. Nevertheless, base whisky is the foundation of the blend, providing its texture and its "whiskiness." Because of this, the base for any individual blend is usually itself blended from a selection of base whiskies. Generally, base whisky makes up most of the final blend.

Flavouring whiskies—often all-rye whiskies and bourbon-like corn whiskies—contribute the characteristic flavours of the blend. The use of distilled rye grain for flavouring distinguishes Canadian whisky from that made in other countries. To qualify for the name "Canadian whisky," the liquid you pour into your glass must always exhibit some signature rye notes. Some best-selling blends use rye flavouring whisky alone, but most use several—or many—flavouring whiskies with complementary flavours, including corn, wheat, barley, and sometimes mixed-mash whiskies. Doing so helps balance any flavour peaks and adds complexity.

The measure of a great blend is in its balance. Though it may have many components, the first impression should simply be of whisky. A tiny cohort of whisky fans who mistake boldness for quality will always call for more extreme flavours. To satisfy this demand, you'd almost swear that some blenders mix random base whiskies, slap them in a wine or non-whisky spirit barrel for flavour (or just add wine or spirit), up the abv, and cross their fingers. Powerful, yes, but not very whisky-like. To craft a whisky that sells millions of cases year after year, on the other hand, now that is true blending genius. As legendary Hiram Walker blender Mike Booth, who, among many successes, created Lot No. 40 and Canadian Club Classic 12, opined, "Every blender wants to make the next Crown Royal."

CONSISTENCY

It is the blender's role to ensure that the aromas, flavours, and textures of each new batch match previous ones. The first job of the blender, then, is to monitor the maturing whiskies regularly and gauge how they will fit the recipe. Because each year's growing season influences the flavour of the grain, that recipe is merely a starting point. Fluctuating crop yields and other factors also make some components more costly to produce some years, yet whisky drinkers don't tolerate price increases well. And even the most loyal whisky drinkers tend to complain at the slightest flavour differences. As Joanna Zanin Scandella, a retired blender for Crown Royal, put it, "Close is not good enough." So when specific components become expensive or unavailable, blenders maintain a brand's identity by adjusting the recipe until the new batch matches the standard exactly.

This may sound more like a job for science than art. However, our sense of smell varies from ultra-acute for some congeners to exceptionally dull for others, so we don't smell everything equally. As well, some chemicals smell radically different in the presence of certain others. Instruments can detect known flaws, but no formula, recipe, or scientific analysis can mimic human senses well enough to predict or detect the "X factor"—those tiny nuances and interactions that make each whisky special. So instead, most distillers have a panel of trained tasters assess each batch. They may pour two glasses of the current batch and one of a standard reference blend in a so-called "triangle test." If the panel can determine which is the odd one out, then more work is needed. In the final analysis, the newly blended whisky must pass the human nose test.

NEW BLENDS

Creating a new blend is not the mystical process many imagine. First, the blender identifies their objective. Are they making a high-volume blend with a long life expectancy, or a special release to draw attention to the brand? Are they extending the range of releases of a successful brand? What taste, smell, and feel do they want, and at what price? All of this, of course, is driven by marketing data. With their objectives clear, they determine whether they can make the necessary components cost-effectively and as needed.

The blender then prepares test blends in small batches in the blending lab. Trained tasters review these, and the blender tweaks them to reflect any comments. After several iterations, they choose one for scaling up. If blenders are working from within existing whisky stocks, the new whisky may go into production quickly. In other cases, production must wait until all components are ready in sufficient quantities.

Then workers withdraw barrels of each component from the maturing houses. In the past, and occasionally today, they would dump the requisite number of barrels of each component directly into the dumping trough, creating the blend as they went along. More commonly, they pump the various components into separate holding tanks until they reach appropriate volumes, then the blender noses samples to ensure they match the expected profiles. Once everything is sampled and approved, they mingle the various maturates. Sometimes they all enter the blending tank together, but more often, blenders mix certain components and leave them to marry before adding others. For high-volume whiskies like Canadian Club or Crown Royal, they might start a new batch nearly every day.

Workers then reduce the whisky to bottle strength with demineralized or deionized water. Usually, they add a tiny amount of spirit caramel to adjust the colour. Although the amount of caramel is below any taste threshold, adding spirit caramel is said to have the extra benefit of improving the marriage among the various maturates. The caramel-like flavours often tasted in Canadian whisky are natural oak caramels from the barrel and not the few drops of spirit caramel added by blending staff.

After blending and dilution, workers check the final whisky for colour, strength, pH, and flavour. If it passes all these tests, it goes on to the bottling department, where filters remove any residue of charcoal or debris and make sure it is crystal clear. Often, they chill the whisky to about 10° Celsius before filtering it, so less soluble components will remain on the filter pads. Some tasters feel that whisky that has not been chill-filtered feels a little richer in the mouth.

ASSEMBLING THE COMPONENTS

Canadian whisky is a blend of many components, each made to contribute specific characteristics to the final whisky. Usually, though not always, a single distiller makes all the component whiskies for an individual blend, although they may, on occasion, buy base whisky to fill an immediate need. Blenders mingle the components together to create a final product, which, in Canada, is simply called, bilingually, "Canadian Whisky Canadien."

American whisky regulations require that, in the United States, most Canadian whiskies be labelled as blends. Unfortunately, this confuses some consumers because blending in America is different than it is in Canada. Although some brands' sales staff claim otherwise, American blenders have many options available to them that are not permitted in Canada. For instance, Canadian blending regulations do not allow the American practice of mixing neutral spirits into mature whisky. Let us dispel the "GNS myth" right now: Canadian whisky is never made with grain neutral spirits. Tiny amounts of young rye or base whisky may occasionally be used skilfully as top dressing to brighten or enhance certain flavours, but neutral spirits? Never. But, according to chapters 4 and 7 of the *Beverage Alcohol Manual* published by the US Department of the Treasury's Alcohol and Tobacco Tax and Trade Bureau, blenders in the US may routinely add up to 80% unaged neutral spirits to blends labelled as American whisky. So, too, can they augment the flavour of some bourbon, blended whisky, and some other whiskies with up to 2.5% of anything that is not harmful, including 0.1% of ultra-potent flavourings synthesized in flavour laboratories, with no need to mention these on the label. Again, this is not allowed in Canada. Canadian blending is closer in concept to the practices used to blend Scotch, except that in Scotland they bring together whiskies from many different distilleries.

DIFFERENT FORMULAS FOR DIFFERENT MARKETS

In the decades following American Prohibition, producers could barely keep up with demand for Canadian whisky. But when a trend towards white spirits put all categories of whisky into decline, dozens of distilleries closed. Canadian distillers sought ways to cut costs and improve profitability. So some were pleased when the US government offered tax incentives for Canadian distillers to add small amounts of American spirits or wine to their blends. There were various reasons for these subsidies, such as the failure of the Florida orange crop in the 1980s. American producers made a spirit they called orange wine by fermenting and distilling otherwise unsaleable oranges. Since taxes are the most significant expense in making whisky, including small amounts of American spirits would provide substantial savings for brands that sold millions of cases in the United States.

Retired Seagram's chief blender Art "The Nose" Dawe remembers those days. Although Seagram's management—and Dawe himself—did not like the idea, he sometimes adjusted formulas to include American wines or spirits as a cost-saving measure. However, this tax break applied only to whisky exported to the United States, and most distillers continued making whisky for Canada and the rest of the world according to their long-established recipes. Wine or other spirits added for the US market did affect the flavour, so Dawe compensated by making other adjustments to the blend. The debate became academic, according to Dawe, because Seagram used the Canadian version as the standard and adjusted the US version until quality panels could not tell the difference.

But how could blenders add American spirit and still call it Canadian whisky? The answer to this question dates to the mid-20th century. The expense of ageing whisky contributes significantly to its final cost, yet Canadian regulations insist that all components of Canadian whisky be fully matured. Thus, Canadian economy brands faced stiff price competition in the United States from American blends made with up to 80% unaged neutral spirits. To help address this disparity, the Canadian government implemented regulations permitting distillers to add small amounts of wine or other spirits to whisky. These regulations did not subsidize distillers or reduce taxes in Canada, but they did allow them to take advantage of US tax breaks and add unaged wine or spirits as young as two years to comprise up to 9.09% of the final volume. (The regulation is exacting: it says distillers can add another 10% to the existing volume of whisky. For example, they can add 10 litres of young spirit or wine to 100 litres of whisky, so 10 litres in a total volume of 110 litres is one-eleventh, or 9.09%.)

There was no advantage for high-end whiskies, which are less price-sensitive, or for low-volume whiskies. However, for very high-volume, low-margin whiskies, known as "value brands," the new regulations effectively reduced US taxes. This, in turn, lowered overall costs, allowing Canadian distillers to price their high-volume "mixing" brands more competitively in the vast US market. For the most part, distillers were slow to apply this practice to deluxe and premium brands. Initially, not all distillers took advantage of the new regulations for their value brands, either.

Eventually, though, the law of unintended consequences kicked in. For example, some blenders who knew that immature rye spirit could be exceptionally vibrant began blending in small amounts of it to recapture those untamed rye notes. Others, noting the benefits the Scottish achieved with "rejuvenated" wine or sherry casks (barrels they deliberately impregnated with litres of sherry or wine), began adding small amounts of plush wine, mature cognac, or rum directly to their blends. Sometimes, they did this to stretch out the more expensive aged spirit; other times, simply to develop new flavour profiles. As long as blending does not veer into mixology, such innovation has been said to keep Canadian whisky exciting. Still, while technically this practice is legal, some whisky lovers find it a bit unsettling, and long-experienced blenders often reject it. Blending whisky, after all, is about authentic whisky flavours, not about gaming the system.

Canadian Hunter
40% alc/vol | Sazerac

Butterscotch, vanilla, crème caramel, hot chilis, cloves, cinnamon, allspice. Simple, spirity, and luscious with a slippery mouthfeel and hints of oak that fade into heat and sweet.

Howitzer
40% alc/vol | Howitzer

Rolls from soft toffee to tangy pepper, recalling distant barrel tones. Orange peels, fragrant on the nose, tug gently at the cheeks. At ease, soldier. Simple, solid, traditional.

Hunter Rye
45% alc/vol | Sazerac

Sweet, woody, dark maple syrup, vanilla, and prickly spirit with grapefruit juice and pulling oak tannins. Simple, hot, spicy, and surprisingly long.

Rich & Rare Reserve
40% alc/vol | Sazerac

Crisp oak, raisin pie, soaring white pepper. Suggestions of sherry. Lemons and orange blossoms. Grain, more oak, spicy rye, earthy, whispering herbal tones, and maple syrup.

3

THE JOYS OF
CANADIAN WHISKY

MATURING WHISKY

GRAIN AND FERMENTATION FLAVOURS
WOOD FLAVOURS

IMMATURE
GRAINY + SPIRITY

MATURE
BALANCED + COMPLEX

OVERAGED
WOODY + BITTER

(7)

FLAVOUR: TASTE, AROMA, AND TEXTURE

"Taste" can refer to style and connoisseurship. More often, though, the taste that interests whisky enthusiasts is their experience when they take a sip. As with tasting anything else, tasting whisky is not some mysterious process reserved for experts—almost anyone who drinks whisky can relate their impressions of its flavours and aromas. Enjoying whisky is all about flavour, and knowing how whisky is made, where these flavours come from, and how we detect them make tasting it all the more interesting. It also advances us from tasting whisky to appreciating it, setting us on our way to connoisseurship.

Scientists can tell us what pigments the painter Picasso used to create his masterpieces, and the chemicals that give those pigments their colour. As fascinating as this may be, though, to an art lover this information is entirely beside the point. Keep this in mind as you read on, because science also tells us that whisky is a solution of ethanol and water containing minute quantities of flavourful chemicals called congeners. Flavour scientists have worked diligently to identify the aromas and flavours of specific chemicals, and to some extent they have succeeded. For instance, they tell us that isoamyl acetate smells like bananas. Unfortunately, the reverse is not true. Bananas smell like a lot more than just isoamyl acetate—unless you agree that those little yellow candy bananas really do taste like bananas. They may be reminiscent, for sure, but in truth, most flavours are not the product of a single chemical, but of complex patterns of scents, tastes, and textures that together evoke bananas, oranges, cigars, cognac, or whatever.

Just as blue and yellow mixed together become green, some congeners also lose their individual identities when combined with others. To complicate matters further, some congeners are so potent that we taste them clearly in concentrations as low as parts per billion (ppb) or parts per trillion. Even when well beyond the capability of practical lab instruments to detect them, tiny amounts of these may mask larger volumes of other, less potent congeners. According to Maria Palafox, whisky chemist and quality manager at Alberta Distillers, "There are some things that the nose and taste can pick up that the instruments can't—for example, some sweetness or barrel notes. The GC [gas chromatograph] only tests the chemical compounds, and you set what chemicals to look for. It has a 7 ppb detection limit." As well, the way the whisky feels is an important part of the tasting experience. So do not be overly enchanted by whisky sellers' chemical hocus-pocus. Science can describe some of it, but only human sensory perception can judge whether whisky is great or merely good enough.

Strictly speaking, taste refers to the five flavour elements detected by our taste buds: sweet, sour, salty, bitter, and savoury. Although we tend to detect certain tastes mainly on specific parts of our tongues, these regions are not as distinct as some people believe. Taste buds at the tip of the tongue focus on sweetness—caramel, toffee. On the sides, just behind the sweet area, and also way at the back of the tongue, they tend to work hardest at detecting saltiness. However, there is no salt in Canadian whisky, so these regions focus more on their secondary interests: sweetness and sourness. Behind these receptors, though still on the edges of the tongue, concentrations of taste buds sense the sourness of acidic or citrus notes in the whisky. And way at the back, the tongue's bitterness sensors respond to pithy rye notes and tannic elements of the wood. To talk of bitterness, though, is to oversimplify, as several different kinds of bitter stimulate other receptors in other ways. Some of these bitter flavours are more enjoyable than others, particularly to a mature palate.

Receptors for a fifth taste, called umami or savoury, are distributed across the front two-thirds of our tongues. Umami sometimes imbues the oldest whiskies with a meaty, savoury richness. However, unless you drink forty-five- or fifty-year-old Canadian Club, you'll likely not come across it in Canadian whisky. Recent research on the molecular basis of taste has led some observers to talk about a sixth type of taste: astringency. In proper balance, astringency adds "structure," creating pleasant "pulling" sensations in the mouth, just as grape tannins do in red wine. Softly astringent oak tannins lend a sense of elegance to long-aged Canadian whisky.

Of the five primary tastes, only sweet, sour, and bitter are commonly found in whisky, yet whisky has so many extraordinarily subtle nuances. This is because our noses differentiate thousands of aromas, even without our intentionally smelling them. Modern research on the molecular basis of smell suggests that estimates of 10,000 distinguishable aromas are conservative.

When we take a sip, vapours from the whisky enter the back of our nose in a phenomenon called retro-olfaction. Various parts of our brain integrate these aromas with textures our mouth feels and tastes that stimulate our taste buds. Together, taste, texture, and aroma make up the flavour of the whisky, what some

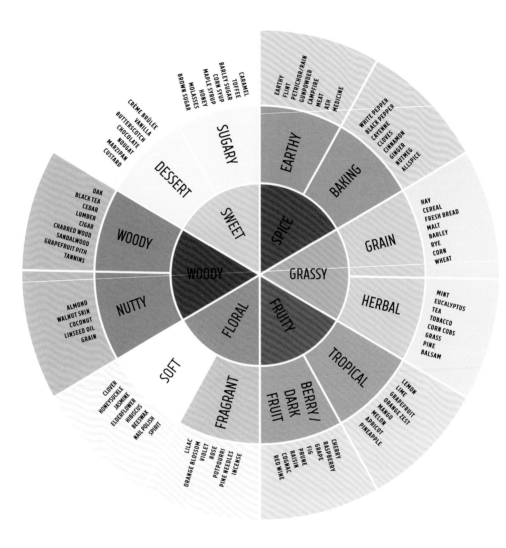

Whisky Tasting Wheel, adapted by Reece Sims.

tasters call the "palate." The "nose" of the whisky—that is, the aromas we smell before we taste it—often predicts the flavour.

TASTES LIKE GRAIN

Each grain brings its own essence to the whisky. Corn provides that smooth, creamy, voluptuous mouthfeel, and sometimes, in long-aged whisky, a trace of boiled corncobs. Wheat has a creaminess, with freshly baked bread replacing the oiliness of corn. Barley shares its cereal nuttiness, while rye delivers pepper, flinty mineral notes, lilac-like florals, faint echoes of sweet, ripe fruit, and spices. These spicy notes revolve around cloves, along with allspice, nutmeg, ginger, cinnamon, and more. Together, they are sometimes called baking spices or rye spices.

Grain yields these flavours because of compounds in the outer layer of each kernel, which, incidentally, is chemically and structurally like wood. Both consist of long carbohydrates called cellulose and hemicellulose, bound together by lignin. While cellulose and hemicellulose lend generic caramel flavours to the whisky, lignin breaks down into its chemical building blocks during cooking, fermentation, and distillation. These building blocks and their flavours differ for each grain. It is this lignin that provides the grain-derived flavours we taste in whisky.

OR IS THAT YEAST?

If only it stopped there. According to one distiller, yeast contributes twenty-five times more congeners than wood or grain. Most people would agree that, although chickens eat grain, roast chicken has its own distinct flavour. If you compare the flavours of organic free-range to factory-farmed roast chicken, you quickly discover that it makes a difference what chickens eat and how they are cared for. Nevertheless, roast chicken tastes like chicken, not chicken feed. If chickens were whisky yeast, they would feed on mashed grain. Thus, while grain affects the whisky flavours produced during fermentation, it is yeast that generates most of the flavour molecules. So is it really yeast we taste? Not at all, but distillers can make those fruity, floral notes that we so often equate with rye almost disappear by changing yeast.

STILL MAGIC

The still also influences flavour. It can concentrate flavourful congeners in the spirit, or it can strip them out. For example, Alberta Distillers makes two contrasting whiskies from the same mash of 100% rye grain. For Reifel Rye, distillers use the still to concentrate the products of fermentation, producing a robust whisky that many would call typical rye. For Alberta Premium, the distiller deliberately distils out some fermentation flavours usually associated with rye, creating a lighter whisky with less robust rye character.

As well, distillation itself creates some flavour components. For example, some almond, caramel, and fruity flavours result from chemical reactions initiated by heat in the still. Additionally, when two of the amino acids from the grain (cysteine and especially methionine) degrade in the hot still, they become important sources of sulphur, which contributes both positive and negative flavours to the whisky. On the other hand, copper in the still removes some unpleasant sulphur compounds from the spirit.

WOOD, AT LAST

The role of wood is often oversimplified to the point of being misunderstood. Believing that the wood makes the whisky, inexperienced distillers sometimes use small barrels or even bags of oak chips to speed up the extraction process. In small quantities, wood flavours such as oak caramels, coconut, lumber, and tannins contribute pleasing flavours and, just as important, structure. Eugenol and other congeners associated with rye are also present in toasted oak, so whisky made with absolutely no rye grain can still taste like rye. But overexposing whisky to wood ignores a critical contributor to flavour development: time. It is not wood, but air seeping slowly into the barrel and reacting with ethanol that produces those notes that bespeak well-aged whisky. Most importantly, the key to great whisky is balance, and whisky that is overexposed to wood becomes—it's not hard to guess—woody.

PAINFUL PLEASURES

There are two other key elements of flavour in Canadian whisky. The first is the ubiquitous pepper. Pepper extends from flavourful black pepper through hot, spicy white pepper to volcanic cayenne. Alcohol in the whisky enhances the peppery heat by stimulating pain sensors on the tongue. While this sensation can become painful, many people enjoy the tingle that moderate amounts of alcohol cause. Think of hot mint or spicy food. Gingery flavours tend to accentuate the intensity of pepper, while creamy sensations smooth it over.

HOW DOES IT FEEL?

The other aspect of flavour is mouthfeel. This takes two forms, the first being a creaminess or buttery sensation often associated with corn whisky. Mouth-coating whisky that feels syrupy is said to have "weight." Quite the opposite of creaminess is the pleasantly bitter sensation that sometimes emerges when other flavours have subsided. Because distillers age most Canadian whisky in reused barrels, it accumulates significant woody tones without becoming overly bitter. In addition, some rye congeners feel almost like grapefruit pith. This pithiness enhances the mouthfeel as it refreshes the palate.

Given that each production step affects the flavour of the whisky, it is pointless to wonder, for example, how much rye a particular whisky has in it. How the distiller fermented the mash and distilled and matured the spirit are far more important. Nevertheless, understanding the various ways whisky's flavours might arise enhances your enjoyment, whether you are a casual but curious whisky drinker or a budding connoisseur. If you are the latter, though, you may want to take the next step and learn some techniques to discern, differentiate, and describe all the subtleties you find in your glass.

Rich & Rare
40% alc/vol | Sazerac

Butterscotch, vanilla, sultanas, pepper, and smatterings of oak with a creamy smooth mouthfeel, yet searing heat. Fresh cedar sawdust, ripe fruits, hints of sherry, and pulling oak.

Signal Hill
40% alc/vol | Signal Hill

Crème caramel, strawberry tart, vanilla, molasses, brown sugar, ginger, cloves, pepper. Soft oak goes solid. Candied citrus peel, a bit fruity and almost nutty. Hot spicy, oaky finish.

(8)

TACKLING TASTING
TECHNIQUES

I f you know what apple juice tastes like, or recognize the smell of freshly baked bread, you already realize it does not take specialized training to identify and enjoy flavour. That said, Canadian whisky has so much more to offer those who make even the slightest effort to understand it. This means starting with the basics: tasting it neat, and with a few drops of water, while focusing on its nuances and subtleties.

Making notes forces you to name the aromas, flavours, and textures you encounter, and records your thoughts for later. For the best results, make separate notes for the nose and palate, and categorize the aromas, flavours, and textures the same way each time. For example, do you detect woody tones? Describe them. Any sourness? What about fruit? Spices, flowers, cereal?

Creaminess or pulling tannins? When you focus on these one at a time, the subtleties and character of the whisky become more obvious.

After you nose the whisky and taste it, note its "finish," those flavours that remain long after your final swallow. Generally, a long finish is considered preferable to a short one. Length, of course, is personal, given that flavours linger on some people's palates longer than on others'. Now leave the empty glasses out overnight and note any residual aromas next morning. You'll be surprised how different they are sometimes. As your catalogue of tastings grows, you can sort them into your preferred styles, another excellent way to train your palate. Of course, if you write tasting notes to share, you may want to add a bit of flourish later. Research with wine tasters, though, has shown that most people cannot detect more than about four flavours or aromas reliably at a single sitting. So when they are not just entirely whimsical, published tasting notes are often composites of several tasting sessions.

Whisky writers commonly describe whiskies by listing other things they remind them of, be they oranges, coffee, cloves, pipe tobacco, black pepper, barbecue-blackened pineapple, the beach, and so on. Novice whisky drinkers may feel inadequate when they cannot detect these flavours, but everyone's olfactory experiences are unique, and tasting whisky is also a personal experience. Where one person smells mango, another might sense melon and pine needles. As well, aromas may evoke deeply personal memories, leading people to describe them in different ways.

By all means, develop your own vocabulary. You can look for ideas in the tasting notes or flavour wheel on page 64, but these impressions should be no more than a guide. Base your own assessment on your personal experiences and not what a whisky marketing department or writer tells you. Once you record your own ideas, see how they compare to others' and take delight in any differences. The fun comes in sussing out the nuances you detect, and the more you taste, the better you become at doing so.

The pleasures of good whisky are pretty much self-evident, but there are tasting techniques that help amplify them. Yes, you can simply throw the whisky back, shooter-like, wipe your mouth on your forearm, wince, and gasp, and everyone will know you're a real tough cowboy—or cowgirl. A little bit of flavour might linger on your tongue, but your mouth will be anaesthetized, your eyes watering, and you will have missed 95% of what you could be enjoying. Better to take a more structured approach, based on smelling, tasting, and savouring. It's called "sippin' whisky" for a reason.

There are many theories on the proper way to taste whisky—so many that you can quickly surmise that none of them can be entirely correct. Indeed, people who conduct whisky tastings love to inject a bit of showmanship and a bit of ego into the event. Some will have you take a mouthful of whisky, then lean forward and chew it with your front teeth—the so-called Kentucky chew. Others have you tilt your head back and gasp for air like a carp in a summer pond. Some say you should warm the glass in your hands, even though this makes the most volatile aromas evaporate. Others insist that you taste at room temperature, as the typical consumer would. It's probably best to experiment a bit before you settle on an approach for analytical tastings. For social occasions, just go with the flow.

ADDING WATER

About the only factor most experts agree on is that adding water helps reveal hidden aromas and flavours. According to blender Maria Palafox of Alberta Distillers, diluting whisky to 20% alc/vol makes aromas easier to recognize. Retired distiller Rick Murphy, also of Alberta Distillers, adds that diluting the whisky makes any flaws easier to detect. Many explanations are given for this, some fanciful, others more sound. Whisky scientists tell us that whisky is not a homogeneous solution of alcohol and water. Rather, "clumps" of pure ethanol, called micelles, form within the whisky, and congeners that are not soluble in water dissolve in these microscopic pockets of pure alcohol. They tell us that these micelles shrink as you add water, and as they do, they expel the "hydrophobic" congeners, making them more obvious. No doubt adding water to high-alcohol whiskies can enhance the flavour, if only because it reduces the anaesthetic effect of the alcohol on the nose and tongue.

Most whisky judges nose and taste whisky first at bottle strength, then again with a splash of water. This is probably the best approach for the casual whisky aficionado and the budding connoisseur, too. Start by adding just a few drops of water and see for yourself what happens. It won't be the same with every whisky. To amplify the effect, you may want to cover the glass for a few minutes, so the hydrophobic vapours collect before you smell them. Some people prefer to taste a whisky first to see if it needs water at all, fearing it may cause some very old whiskies to lose their delicacy and fragility.

One thing that's for sure is that mixing water and alcohol creates what is known as an exothermic reaction: it produces heat. This warms the whisky, making some of the more volatile elements evaporate. Try this experiment: Take a small amount of water into your mouth and hold just a drop of it on your tongue. Then draw a small amount of whisky—cask strength, if possible—into your mouth and let it mix with the water. See how warm it gets?

Professionals usually taste at room temperature, but if your boozehound father-in-law is on his way over and you fear for your most precious bottles, put your worst bottle of Scotch in the refrigerator. The cold will disguise most of the harshness (along with the flavour, of course), and you can make points with dad-in-law by pouring him giant drams, all the while disposing of that bottle that you knew at first taste was a terrible waste of money. Add a few ice cubes as insurance, to keep it cold to the very last sip.

OUTSIDE INFLUENCES

Glassware also influences your tasting experience. A glass that narrows at the top, as an ISO tasting glass does, concentrates or focuses the aromas. For rich sipping whiskies, the Glencairn glass favoured by single malt drinkers enhances the pleasure. Canadian whisky can be comparatively sweet, so some people prefer to introduce the whisky a little deeper into the mouth, where its sweetness does not swamp the nuances and complexities. A glass with an out-turned lip helps, but if you don't have one, take a sip anyway. Just wait, and everything will reveal itself. For cocktails or mixing whiskies with spirity overtones, a wide-mouthed glass helps dissipate the alcohol. However, spirit is an integral part of the drinking experience, so don't wait too long for that first whiff, or it will pass you by.

Analytical assessments work best in flights of four or five whiskies tasted one after another in identical glasses. People often taste what they expect to find in a whisky. This is why analytical assessments are best done blind, so you won't taste what you think you should instead of what is in the glass. If you calibrate your palate first by starting with a whisky you know well, then you can compare the others to it. The order in which you nose and taste them affects the flavours, too, so it helps to taste each whisky several times, changing the order or even the lineup of whiskies.

Analyzing more than five or six whiskies at a sitting can be difficult because of a phenomenon called sensory-specific satiety. When you smell the same aroma many times in a short period, you come to enjoy it less. This is like eating a large meal until you are unable to take another bite, yet still having room for dessert and coffee. As well, smelling the same aroma repeatedly can make you less aware of its presence—a factor called olfactory fatigue. This can throw off the balance in a flight of whiskies that have both common and differing aromas. However, olfactory fatigue also has benefits, as it tends to help us ignore any background odours. Refresh your nose every now and then by smelling something else. Some people keep a glass of water handy to smell between whiskies; others simply smell their arms.

Some people like to comment on the whisky's colour, believing it suggests what flavours to expect. However, distillers often adjust the colour so that minor differences among batches will not put off those customers who demand consistency. Other people comment first on the "legs" or "tears" that run down the inside of the glass. Larger and slower-moving legs are said to indicate a weightier body. But not all raw glass is equally "sticky," so these legs vary depending on the materials used in manufacturing the glass. As indicators, legs are much more useful for lower alc/vol drinks such as wine.

STRUCTURED TASTING

The whisky tasting begins with smelling the whisky's bouquet—its nose. Swirl the glass gently, then, leaving your mouth partly open, take a whiff. Very simple. Think about the different aromas you smell and the order in which you smell them. Our noses are very good at detecting even the tiniest differences between aromas. Use this ability to enhance your analysis by smelling a second whisky, then going back and forth between the two to compare. Deep breaths are not necessary.

It can take several minutes to uncover a whisky's complexities, but eventually you will want to taste it. As with nosing, begin with a small sip. Some people like to aspirate a little air with the whisky to help spray it in tiny droplets around their mouth. Because much of the flavour comes from aromas drifting up from the tongue, it also helps to savour the whisky with your mouth slightly open to increase airflow. Right away, you should recognize the special

Wayne Gretzky No. 99 Red Cask
40% alc/vol | Wayne Gretzky

Molasses, burnt sugar, and leather, then a creamy, nutty, grainy body warmed by mild peppers. Sweet dark fruits. Classic Canadian with a vaguely minty black tea finish.

Gibson's Finest Bold Aged 8 Years
46% alc/vol | PMA

Big, rich, rum and Coke with strong oak-cereal backbone and creamy texture. Orange blossom water and dark fruit. Rye spices and blazing heat. Cleansing grapefruit pith finish.

Pendleton Rye 1910 Aged 12 Years
40% alc/vol | Pendleton

Sweet molasses, gingery white pepper, maple cream, vanilla. Green fruit, raisins, limes. Grassy meadows, wildflowers, mint. Fresh-milled lumber, crisp charred oak, steely rye. Rich, weighty, balanced.

Pendleton Original
40% alc/vol | Pendleton

Luscious, rich, creamy caramel with ripe fruit, prickly pepper, and candied ginger. Clean lumber, pine bark, Nutella, light rye bread, kiwi, lovely pithiness, and comforting warmth.

spiciness of fermented rye grain, and detect notes from the barrel—vanillas, caramels, tannins. For people used to single malts or bourbon, Canadian whisky can be a bit difficult at first, but after a little practice, you'll be surprised how quickly you learn to detect a broad range of flavours. Remember, it's finesse, subtlety, nuance, balance, complexity you're looking for, not a firewater kick in the face.

But there's more to tasting than focusing only on the flavours. Let the whisky roll around in your mouth and feel it. Is it rich, creamy, and weighty, or is it watery, perhaps even a bit thin? A luxuriant mouthfeel is one of the characteristics that help set the great Canadian whiskies apart. And if it ends with a cleansing feeling of grapefruit pith, not only have you experienced one of the unique pleasures of Canadian whisky, but you are also ready to taste it again. This time, add a dash of water and note any new aromas.

Whether you choose to focus hard on your tastings or simply have fun with them, you will, with practice, learn to differentiate among whiskies and identify which ones you prefer. You may even develop your own approach, which, in turn, will give you confidence in your opinions. After all, you have only one person to please: yourself.

4

A CONCISE HISTORY OF CANADIAN WHISKY

(9)

CANADA'S FIRST
DISTILLERS

The name of Canada's first whisky maker, and where or when they toiled, can never be known. Canada's original inhabitants did not distil alcohol, but when European settlers began arriving en masse, whisky and whisky stills arrived with them. While there have been reports that James Grant operated a rum distillery in Quebec City with a 70,000-gallon-a-year capacity as early as 1767, this remains uncertain. What we do know is that when Grant died in 1789, his distillery had a 240-gallon pot still (or *chaudière*), and another of 1,500 gallons. He had also installed four copper pots of 65, 75, 350, and 2,000 gallons in a second, larger distillery adjacent to the first. Five thousand tonnes of wheat and 300 barrels on hand suggest that, by then, he was making whisky.

A brewery built by New France intendant Jean Talon in Quebec City in 1768 may have housed a still during the five years it operated. However, the earliest records pointing unequivocally to distilling date to 1769, when British immigrant Colin Drummond began buying land for his St. Roc rum distillery, also in Quebec. It was 1783 before English entrepreneur John Young arrived in Quebec and became business partners with Simon Fraser (not the explorer you may be thinking of). In 1791, Young joined James Grant's son Thomas to purchase the St. Roc Distillery and convert it into a brewery. The following year, they, along with Fraser and his son, built a large-scale malt distillery in nearby Beauport. Clearly, Canada was now making whisky. By 1810, when the sheriff sold off the assets and physical plant of the debt-ridden Beauport Distillery, others had begun distilling whisky in both Lower and Upper Canada. Almost certainly, though, dozens, if not hundreds of small home distillers had preceded all of these. Throughout the 18th century, stills arrived across Lower Canada (later the province of Quebec), in Rupert's Land (Manitoba), and eventually in Upper Canada (Ontario) with the earliest European settlers and United Empire Loyalists fleeing the American Revolution (1775–83).

In 1794, when Métis fur trader Nicolas Montour bought the derelict Montreal Distillery Company from Isaac Todd, Canada was still seventy-odd years from nationhood, but already some distilling businesses had flourished and failed along the way. At the same time, 480 kilometres west, in York (later Toronto), Upper Canada's lieutenant-governor, John Graves Simcoe, reported that residents were distilling their excess grain into spirits. And he encouraged this effort. By 1801, fifty-one licensed stills served a population of fewer than 15,000 residents in Upper Canada. The tiny size of these "distilleries" well into the 1850s is illustrated in Port Hope, where eight of them served a population of 2,500. That's one distillery for every 300 residents—children included. However, no trace of these distilleries remains. Although we assume that many other Upper Canadian stills operated unofficially, several hundred people did the Canadian thing and bought distilling licences. Some of these stills were adjuncts to small gristmills, while others were simply household appliances.

ROBERT MCLAREN, PERTH

Some settlers certainly did try their hand at commercial distilling, but for most, success was short-lived, as the record for Bathurst District and its commercial centre, Perth, illustrates. Robert McLaren founded his distillery, with its forty-gallon copper pot still, in the late 1830s. His illegitimate son John later purchased it and operated it more profitably. In 1879, one Robert Stewart left McLaren's employ to join James Spalding in a competing distillery. They occupied the former premises of William Locke's malt distillery, established in 1841. McLaren's and Spalding & Stewart had significant early success with wood-smoked Scottish-style malt whisky. However, as distillery taxes rose, moonshining and bootlegging increased steadily and chipped away at their profitability, just as expanding rail networks brought competition from factory distillers such as Molson's, with their efficient column stills. Licensed stills in Bathurst District dropped from twenty-two in 1827 to seven in 1841, and just two in 1845.

McLaren's profited from a lucrative export trade, but in 1916 the government of Ontario introduced its Temperance Act, and both distilleries soon folded. McLaren's last gasp came in March 1919, with a $125,000 shipment of 3,700 cases sent to Quebec, Montreal, and New York in four carloads. Across the province, most other small distillers had preceded McLaren's and Spalding & Stewart into bankruptcy. From 153 licensed distilleries in Ontario in 1850, just nineteen remained in 1871. Meteoric increases in distillery taxes and accompanying enforcement beginning in 1862, along with an 1883 bottling-in-bond law and an 1890 ageing law, drove any remaining small distillers out of business or underground.

From the late 1830s until 1916, McLaren's made
Pure Malt Whiskey in Perth, Ontario.

Contrary to popular supposition, it was largely English and continental
European immigrants who successfully introduced commercial whisky making to Canada. They used Canadian-made column stills adapted from European
and American designs. In effect, Scottish, Irish, and American settlers were
sidebars to the larger story, their tiny gristmill distilleries pushed out of sight
or out of business. It was Molson, Gooderham, Worts, Corby, and Seagram—all
of them English—who laid the foundations for Canadian whisky. Wiser and
Hespeler were of German descent, while Randall and Walker came from New
England. The Scots and Irish who first settled the Atlantic provinces had ready
access to Caribbean molasses, and so they distilled rum, as did settlers along

the St. Lawrence River as far inland as Montreal. No doubt, early Canadian distillers learned sour mash techniques from their American counterparts. American distillers were themselves influenced in their selection of grains by those Dutch and German settlers who, since the 15th century, had been distilling rye to make alcohol in their homelands.

Revolution in the mid-18th century convulsed the territory that was to become the United States. People loyal to the British crown trekked north. Some of their descendants credit these United Empire Loyalists with introducing whisky making to Canada, and no doubt some of them brought stills. However, beyond this mythology, no record yet confirms anything close to production at a commercial level. By 1890, the Loyalists' tiny mill- and farm-based operations had disappeared entirely. If the United Empire Loyalists had any influence at all, it was perhaps from the Dutch and Germans among them, who encouraged Canadian distillers to add a few shovelfuls of rye to their mashes, marking a turning point for Canadian whisky.

Although the governor and committee of the Hudson's Bay Company authorized the establishment of a distillery at the Red River Settlement (Manitoba) as early as 1837, records of distilling there are scant beyond mention that the Hudson's Bay Company (based in London, England) brought in stills to make cordials. Work on a grain distillery begun in 1843 at Lower Fort Garry seems to have come to nothing, in part due to poor barley crops. Nevertheless, alcohol flowed west in torrents with fur traders from the Montreal-based North West Company and with plundering traders from the US. It was 1878 before Radiger & Erb offered pure spirits, alcohol, old rye, malt whisky, and distillery slop for sale in Winnipeg.

There had been at least two small short-lived distilleries in BC in the mid-1860s, but the first large commercial distillery west of Ontario did not break ground until 1904, when William Braid opened his $300,000 British Columbia Distillery in Sapperton (New Westminster). A Who's Who of Canadian whisky history passed through BC Distillery in its seventy-one years, beginning with its first distiller, AT Morrow, and manager GA Laing from the Hamilton Distillery Company (better known as Royal Distillery). George C. Reifel bought the distillery in 1923, the early days of American Prohibition, and then his successors sold it to Seagram's in 1941. His son George H. Reifel later built and operated Alberta Distillers in Calgary. Stan Brown Jr. left BC Distillery to assist Reifel in Calgary, then moved on to Langley, BC, for the heyday of Potter's.

But the threads are beginning to tangle. To better understand the evolution of Canadian whisky, first we need to explore the roles of some key early players. We begin with Thomas Molson, the second son in the first Canadian-born generation of Molsons.

Twenty-two men and boys from Seagram's early-20th-century cooperage.

(10)

THOMAS MOLSON AND MOLSON DISTILLERY

O n June 10, 1791, King George III of England gave royal assent to the Constitutional Act, splitting the province of Quebec into Upper and Lower Canada. Three months later, on September 1, in Montreal, with neither royal fanfare nor public notice, an English immigrant named John Molson and his housekeeper, Sarah Vaughan, celebrated the birth of their second child, whom they named Thomas. John had sold the Lincolnshire estate he inherited from his father to invest in a new life abroad as a brewer, an enter- prise he began well before reaching the legal age of twenty-one in December 1784. In time, young Thomas would turn the brewery in the east Montreal suburb of St. Mary's into a booming distillery.

Although Molson's generally cites 1786 as the brewery's founding year, John Molson was likely familiar with brewery operations even before arriving in Canada in 1782. His family, or their tenants in Lincolnshire, ran a brewery on the property. In 1783, he joined Thomas Loid, another Lincolnshire native, who had begun brewing beer in Montreal a year earlier. By 1785 Molson owned the brewery outright, and in 1786, he brought the latest steam-operated brewery equipment in from England and built a maltings to supply the brewery.

A FALTERING START

While visiting rum distillers McBeath & Sheppard at L'Assomption in 1801, Molson bought their old copper pot still. He could not have known the auspicious provenance of that still. Whisky historian Charles MacLean credits another McBeath, an Irishman (who spelled his name "MacBeath"), with bringing the first whisky still to Scotland some four centuries earlier. However, except for a £334 sale in 1803, Molson remained a trifler, distilling only occasionally during those early years.

Montreal-based North West Company agents likely used the little whisky Molson produced to fuel the dying days of their notoriously exploitative trade in furs with Canada's Indigenous peoples. Their plan to wrest control of the fur trade from the Hudson's Bay Company ended ignominiously in 1821, when the English firm absorbed them. Nevertheless, their introduction of alcohol to the trade left a long and appalling legacy. Molson, of course, was far from their only source.

By 1811, John Jr. and Thomas were partners with their father in the brewery. They shared in the profits, but John Sr. retained ownership of the brewery and received an annual rent. The arrangement continued when their younger brother, William, joined them. The brothers soon had a new copper pot still shipped from England, but it was a decade before they used it.

Thomas Molson.

As a youth, Thomas Molson enjoyed demonstrating his physical prowess and agility, had an insatiable curiosity, and, unlike other family members, was fascinated with distilling. He was forever experimenting with processes and recipes, never missing an opportunity to discuss his trade with other distillers or travel to learn more about brewing and distilling. While visiting England and Scotland in 1816, Thomas toured as many breweries and distilleries as he could, jotting down notes, making sketches, and recording their dimensions carefully.

In January 1820, he wrote: "A still and heads of copper with pewter worm containing a charge of 180 gallons to 200 gallons. First charged with stale beer, run off 12 gallons low wines and sometimes 20 gallons but the spirit will not be so good but generally run off altogether 64 gallons from one still. There is a small piece of soap put in wash every still full."

Thomas Molson clearly had the whisky bug, but it was two more years—October 19, 1821—before he tried his hand at distilling. He charged the 200-gallon direct-fired copper pot six times over two days, using eight hogsheads and half-hogsheads of stale mild ale, adding feints from earlier distillations to the charges. An inch-and-a-half cube of soap Molson put in each charge reduced surface tension to keep the still from boiling over. He sealed his still with a paste made from rye flour, then heated it directly with a wood fire.

On November 17, 1821, Molson exported his first two puncheons of high wines, also called spirits of whisky, to London merchants Grayhurst & Hewatt. The following year, he shipped them another 1,385 gallons of rectified spirits (whisky), but a year after that, the London agents had difficulty selling Molson's whisky. Despite this setback, Thomas was keen to continue, but without a reliable export market, the rest of the family wanted out of the distilling business.

Molson's was not the only distilling operation in Montreal in 1821. Among others, William Wilson also distilled whisky there, relying on Molson's to grind his malt and provide his yeast. That they were neighbours is not surprising.

Transportation was a challenge in early Canada, so businesses tended to serve their local markets or cluster around transportation hubs. Thus, Molson and later Handyside and Harwood located their distilleries at St. Mary's Current, the highest navigable point on the St. Lawrence River.

A FAMILY DIVIDED

There were further complications for Thomas—who, it seems, could be quite difficult. On a trip to England, he had impetuously married his cousin Martha Molson, and either without thinking or because he was unaware of Quebec's succession laws, neglected to have her sign a prenuptial agreement. This meant that, should he predecease her, his wife would inherit at least half of his share of the brewing business and could then leave it to whomever she pleased. This greatly worried John Molson Sr., who wanted the business bequeathed to his Canadian family, not Thomas's in-laws back in England. As a result, John Molson prepared a will leaving his entire estate to his eldest son, John Jr., and so Thomas, the only Molson with a passion for distilling, was effectively—and, it turns out, unnecessarily—disinherited. Thomas outlived his cousin-wife.

With his brothers' loss of interest in distilling and his long-term future in the family business seemingly bleak, Thomas Molson left Montreal late in 1823 to seek new prospects. At first, he considered opportunities in England, but then returned to Upper Canada to settle in Kingston, some 275 kilometres west of Montreal, where he built a new brewery and distillery. He bought waterfront property in Kingston early in 1824, and by September was advertising to purchase barley. Meanwhile, the Montreal whisky operation went silent even as Thomas Molson was becoming Canada's largest whisky distiller. In 1832, he licensed a single steam-heated still with 910 gallons capacity, just under 20% of the total licensed still capacity of 5,138 gallons for all of Upper Canada. His was, without a doubt, the largest still in the province.

In 1834, with fourteen years' experience behind him and new distilleries flourishing right on the Molson doorstep, William Molson decided that the Montreal firm should fire up its still once again. But William was a brewer; it was his disinherited brother, Thomas, who knew how to make whisky. Their father, encouraged by William, took the first step, inviting Thomas to make what would, surprisingly, turn out to be a joyful return to the family business in Montreal. Amidst this new-found family harmony, the firm also realized a respectable profit on the £802 worth of whisky that Thomas produced in the old copper pot that first year.

To further secure these lucrative family bonds, John Sr. devised a plan that allowed Thomas and his descendants to share in the future of the business. By willing his assets not to Thomas, but to Thomas's son "named John," the elder Molson avoided the unpleasant prospect of his life's work falling into the hands of Thomas's in-laws. Thomas liked the idea so much that he named a second son, born shortly thereafter, John as well. When he returned to Montreal, Thomas, always the entrepreneur, leased his Kingston distillery to James Morton, who also enjoyed considerable success.

Increasing profits emboldened Molson. By 1835, the firm's whisky sales had jumped to £4,460, so it invested £1,000 in new equipment, including a 700-gallon steam coil–heated wooden still. Molson used the large wooden still to make low wines, then brought them up to strength by redistilling them in the copper pot. The new still enabled him to increase production, and before long, whisky sales surpassed the income from the brewery. In those days, distilling, like brewing, was a seasonal business that shut down during the hot Montreal summers. Nevertheless, Molson's production for just the first half of 1836 reached nearly 31,000 gallons.

SOME THOMAS MOLSON WHISKY SCIENCE

Thomas, who had an accountant's eye for precision, puzzled over a seeming loss in volume when he added fourteen gallons of water to 376 gallons of overproof spirits and got only 386 gallons of whisky, rather than the 390 he was expecting. We know now that water and ethanol molecules insert themselves among each other in solution, so the volume of a mixture of alcohol and water is always a little less than the sum of the two volumes separately. Unaware of this, Molson repeated this experiment over and over for years, each time attributing the loss to "concentration"—presumably of the solution, although he might have been referring to his own.

EUROPE'S WAR: CANADA'S BOON

The early success of Molson's distillery had as much to do with international politics as with the quality of its whisky. Between 1792 and 1814, Britain's Napoleonic Wars with France brought frequent brandy and wine shortages to England. These hostilities helped awaken the British palate to the pleasures of grain spirits and kick-started Canadian whisky making as an industry. At the time, Scottish Highland distilleries were largely craft operations, restricted by law to using a single small still and mashing no more than twenty-five tons of grain annually. This left them woefully unable to supply the growing English demand for whisky. An interim option was the product of Lowland distilleries, but these were operating under outrageous taxation pressures. All they could offer was a rapidly made product so unpalatable that many went out of business. Consequently, Britain turned to its North American colony to meet demand.

To get some sense of the scale of this activity, let's look at some numbers. Thomas Molson distilled his first whisky in 1821, and within a year he was able to export 1,385 gallons of whisky to England. By 1827 there were some thirty-one known distilleries in Lower Canada. Four years later, that had more than doubled to seventy, and Molson's continued to dwarf all the others. Indeed, Molson's has the double distinction of being the first industrial-scale distiller in both Upper and Lower Canada in the decades prior to Confederation. Having just been weaned off French brandy, British tastes weren't forced to undergo yet another complete transformation. This early Canadian whisky was almost certainly blended with Scotch malt whisky and British spirits once it reached England.

FLAVOUR AND STRENGTH

Canadian whisky of those days, like Scottish or English whisky of the time, would not be recognized by today's connoisseur. At best, it was little more than "rectified" raw spirit, which meant someone had filtered it through charcoal to reduce any off flavours. By adding flavourings, distillers could then sell it as any of several beverages, including gin, rum, brandy, cognac, or whisky. However, other than Hiram Walker, in Canada, most distillers skipped this step, too.

In addition to flavour, there was also the issue of strength, and whisky was often much weaker then than today's potation. While some distillers sold what we would now call high wines or new distillate as whisky, others commonly sold what is known as low wines, the product of a single distillation, with a strength of about 20% alc/vol or less, about half the strength of today's whisky. Barkeeps and retailers often further diluted these low wines before serving them, perhaps explaining why our ancestors could drink so prodigiously and still do an honest day's work.

Molson usually double-distilled his spirits to produce high wines, concentrating the whisky he exported to England to 34 degrees over proof. He made his export whisky from barley malt and rectified it using fine-rolled pine charcoal. For the

Canadian market, Molson mashed a mixture of grains, often with some rye, in a sour mash recipe, and again, double-distilled it. Whether they sold it in England or Canada, 19th-century distillers generally did not age their whisky. After as little as a month in wood, whisky was considered old and commanded a premium price. By 1840, though, the quality and consistency of Canadian whisky was improving, and a standard strength of 12 degrees over proof became common.

DEVELOPMENTS IN UPPER CANADA

Molson's first serious competitor, Gooderham & Worts, entered the market in 1837, a turbulent year in Canadian politics, with insurrection in Upper Canada and outright rebellion in Lower Canada. Molson's also faced competition from lesser Canadian distillers: Harwood & Sons, Handyside Brothers, and William Dow in Montreal; John A. McLaren in Perth; and James Morton in Kingston. In 1838, Molson's rebuilt much of its distillery after a devastating fire, and in 1839, produced about 150,000 gallons of whisky (proof spirits), while Gooderham & Worts managed to turn out a mere 28,863 gallons.

By 1845, Molson's production had climbed to 250,000 gallons, but the following year, the British export market collapsed. Scottish production capacity had grown as a railway boom brought commercial distilling to formerly inaccessible places. It took Molson's nearly a decade to recover lost trade by developing new markets in the Maritime provinces, the eastern United States, and Canada West. Other distillers weren't so lucky, and by 1853, only William Dow's and Molson's distilleries remained in Montreal. Upper Canada's distillers, with more robust local markets, were less affected, but their numbers, too, were declining. Canadian whisky making was becoming organized as an industry, with the larger distillers trading supplies and firmly adhering to mutually agreed prices, making it difficult for small producers to compete.

BACK TO THEIR ROOTS

As directed in his grandfather's will, when he came of age in 1847, Thomas's son John Henry Robinson, or JHR for short, inherited the brewery, and the following year became a partner in running it and the distillery. JHR did not share his father's enthusiasm for distilling. Moreover, with improved transportation links, a growing population in Upper Canada to support economies of scale, and the loss of the export trade, Molson's whisky sales plateaued, while several larger distilleries gained momentum. Despite producing nearly 350,000 proof gallons in 1863, with the death of Thomas Molson that year the demise of his distillery was inevitable. Although JHR had inherited the brewery from his grandfather, Thomas had left the distillery to his other son named John—John Thomas—who, probably influenced by growing temperance sentiments, had no appetite for the liquor business, either. He sold the distillery to JHR, who, in 1865, consolidated it with the brewery business and began re-equipping it as a sugar refinery.

In 1867, almost exactly seventy-six years after King George III assented to the Constitutional Act, Queen Victoria gave royal assent to the British North America Act, creating the Dominion of Canada. But 1867 also marked Molson's withdrawal from the whisky business. Until 1848, taxes on alcoholic beverages were the largest single source of revenue for the developing nation. Despite record distilling profits, in 1867, when the government increased taxes on whisky to sixty cents a gallon, JHR Molson finally closed the distillery altogether. Faced with stiffening competition, a growing temperance movement coupled with the family's strong Protestant faith, increasing taxes, and declining market share, the Molsons returned to the business that eighteen-year-old John Molson Sr. had begun eighty-four years earlier when he first arrived in Montreal. It had been a great run, and Molson's brewing legacy is still going strong five generations later. However, few remember that, for one generation, Molson's was also the largest distiller in the Commonwealth.

(11)

GOODERHAM & WORTS

n May of 1831, James Worts and his fourteen-year-old son, James Gooderham Worts, arrived by boat at "muddy York." Worts, a Yorkshireman, had been the proprietor of Kirtley Mill in Bungay, Suffolk, England, and planned to establish a gristmill in Canada. His brother-in-law William Gooderham underwrote Worts's expenses. British colonists had founded the town of York on the northern shores of Lake Ontario less than forty years earlier, and by 1831, four thousand people had settled there. Worts's mill would be an important stepping stone in the town's transition to a flourishing industrial centre soon to be called Toronto.

Why he would leave his mill in England and rely on Gooderham to re-establish him in business in Canada is a matter of speculation. Still, that Worts—a sometimes troubled man, known to carry on loud conversations with himself—died by his own hand at forty-two, leaving five children as orphans, may provide some insight. Fortunately, James, his eldest, did not inherit Worts's troubles, and in time, he became the prime mover in what would one day be the largest distillery in Canada—and, for a brief period, reputedly the world.

All this aside, Worts was nothing if not effective. By November of 1831, he had built a twenty-two-metre-tall red-brick millhouse on the Lake Ontario waterfront near the mouth of the Don River. His plan to install a windmill for power, as millers in Suffolk did, had to wait until spring, though, when the ice broke up and lake schooners could deliver the main mast, millstones, and mechanisms.

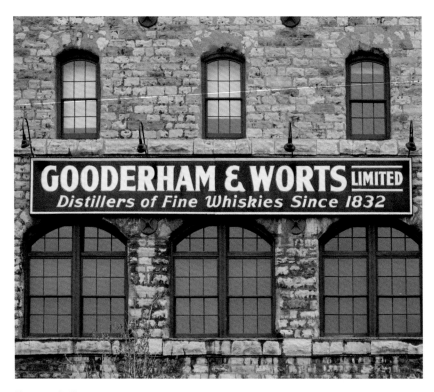

The stone distillery.

FAMILY AND MISFORTUNE

On July 25, 1832, William Gooderham arrived with his and Worts's families, several servants, and eleven orphans he encountered along the way—fifty-four people all told. Gooderham, it seems, was happy to share his own good fortune with others. Two days after setting foot in York, he invested another £1,823 in Worts's mill and formalized their partnership. A few days later, they bought their first wheat, and by early October, Worts and Gooderham's mill was in full operation. Wheat was the primary cereal crop in Upper Canada back then, and by year's end they had milled 2,991 bushels of it into flour.

In Suffolk, the wind was steady and reliable, but as anyone who has landed at Toronto's Billy Bishop Airport can attest, sometimes it blows off Lake Ontario in blasts, and other times not at all. The partners soon realized they needed supplementary power, so in 1833, they installed a steam engine. When a storm blew the windmill's sails away not long after, they abandoned wind power altogether.

In 1834, with their families settled nearby and the future of the flour mill secure, Worts looked forward to the birth of his sixth child. But the birth was difficult and his wife, Elizabeth, died, and the child soon after. Two weeks later, the despondent Worts was found, drowned, in the company well. In the space of a fortnight, his two boys and three girls had lost both their parents. True to form, William Gooderham and his wife raised their orphaned kin together with their own six children. With Worts's death, Gooderham renamed the mill the William Gooderham Company.

MILLING AND DISTILLING

As wheat farming expanded in Upper Canada, Gooderham's business prospered. By 1837, he had built a distillery to dispose of wheat middlings, a mixture of flour, bran, and wheat germ that collected when milling white flour. Gooderham distilled his mashes just once to make low wines of about 22% alc/vol. He gave no hint of the great distilling success to come. That would wait until Worts's son joined the firm some years later and turned distilling from a waste disposal necessity into a business activity on its own.

Yet from the start, Gooderham found a ready market for his whisky, selling the first day's production of 128 gallons to Joseph Lee, a grocer on nearby King Street. Until a month later, when other grocers began stocking Gooderham's whisky, Lee bought everything Gooderham distilled. For his first batch, Gooderham mashed twenty-seven bushels of malt that he purchased from the Cull brothers, with thirty-six bushels of wheat and 304 bushels of middlings. In 1838, to make the distillery more self-sufficient, he built a small maltings. However, he continued buying yeast from nearby breweries. In 1842, Gooderham added a rectifying column filled with charcoal to remove some fusel oils and other impurities. He renewed the charcoal regularly and began adding small amounts of caramel to the final product to give it the colour of more prestigious wood-aged brandy.

In the 1820s and 1830s, engineers in New York developed new distilling technologies that allowed distillers to add beer to the still continuously. The ingenuity early American inventors applied to distilling technology is largely lost in the stories of Scotch whisky, in part because the evidence of their work often fell victim to Prohibition. They understood the concept of using rising steam to drive alcohol vapour up the still, but early mechanisms for doing so were fairly crude. Gooderham's still consisted of a large, square wooden box packed with stones. Alcohol and water exchanging heat on the surfaces of these stones caused rising steam injected at the bottom to strip alcohol from beer descending from above. It was primitive, but it worked.

If making whisky was a profitable way to recycle the waste from flour milling, feeding that waste to cattle took it one step further. Turning middlings into whisky depleted them of their starch and left a nutritious, protein-rich residue known as spent grains. Cattle fed on spent grains gained weight rapidly. At first, Gooderham sold this waste to William Lumbers, a local feed broker, but in 1843 he established a feedlot next to the distillery. When the neighbours complained of the smell, he moved the feedlot across the Don River, where it generated a strong revenue stream.

William Gooderham seems to have been a man of incredibly generous spirit. He helped his nephew James Gooderham Worts set up a new gristmill; then, in 1845, after it failed, he brought James back as a partner in the firm he then called Toronto City Steam Mills and Distillery. Thus, he reunited Gooderham & Worts, millers and distillers, on the site of James Worts Sr.'s original mill. Time would prove this to be a most profitable reunion.

Gooderham's experience as a merchant and miller in England helped make the mill a resounding success. He added a company wharf and lakeside elevator to receive wheat, which now arrived not just from Upper Canada, but from the American Midwest as well. Whether it was the energy of youth or simple gratitude for his uncle's confidence in him, James threw himself into making the distillery a going concern. This was exactly the sort of complementary leadership the firm needed. Though he does not seem the type to have kept score, Gooderham must have been pleased to see his generosity so amply rewarded.

It was Worts's nature to deliberate carefully before making decisions, then spare no effort to implement them. He soon installed two copper pot stills in the old windmill to distil low wines into full-strength whisky. At the same time, he began adding small amounts of rye to the mash, as Gooderham had sometimes done, to improve the flavour of the whisky. It would be some time before the distillery hit its stride, but these were two giant steps in that direction.

Worts also involved himself in several other ventures, including banking and railways. It seems inevitable that early Canadian distillers would dabble in politics, and in 1867, the year of Canada's Confederation, Worts considered running for Parliament to represent Toronto East. Vociferous opposition at his nomination meeting revealed simmering resentment towards the powerful influence wielded by Gooderham and Worts and convinced him to withdraw. Worts was never particularly sociable, and the Toronto *Globe* had already given him little chance of winning. Perhaps this negative reception to his candidacy was a helpful wake-up call. Thereafter, he and his firm contributed generously to city charities, including a major donation to expand the Toronto General Hospital.

THE STONE DISTILLERY

In 1856, William Gooderham's son George, the real visionary behind the distillery, joined the blossoming business as a partner and, like Worts, seized on the potential in making whisky. He lobbied his partners actively, and by 1859 the firm had embarked on a major undertaking: to build a $200,000, five-storey distillery that would be at the leading edge of industrial technology. There, grain would pass from railcar to whisky barrel with barely any intervention by human hands.

The citizens of Toronto had never seen such an undertaking, and with the Canadian economy in depression, it was a godsend. Four schooners ferried limestone in from Kingston, and 500 men laboured on the construction. The new stone distillery, complete with thirty-metre chimney and a twelve-metre wooden still, was quite an accomplishment. As well as the lakeside elevator, the partners added a fourteen-car siding to the Grand Trunk Railway. A modern bucket elevator carried grain to the top floor, and a 100-horsepower steam engine powered eight sets of grindstones. They installed two 1,500-gallon pot stills in Worts's original millhouse, and forty-two tall wooden rectifying columns, each filled with charcoal, received the new spirit, which slowly percolated through to be sold or filled into barrels to mature.

With annual capacity boosted to 2.5 million gallons, Gooderham & Worts now dwarfed Molson's distillery in Montreal, making it the key player in Canadian distilling. Despite its advanced automation, in 1861, the distillery employed 150 people and paid excise duties exceeding $100 a day. It was soon the largest source of tax revenues for both the government of Canada and the city of Toronto. The company fed 400 contented milk cows and fattened 1,000 beef cattle each year.

Flour milling continued, but distilling had become the firm's principal business. And though the distillery produced fully half of the whisky distilled in Canada West, time would demonstrate that Gooderham & Worts, and its successors, were not whisky men, they were distillers. As long as the stills were running, they were just as happy to make industrial alcohol, acetone, antifreeze, or rum. For the time being, however, common whisky and rye whisky were their only distilled products. As export markets in the United States, Europe, and South America expanded, the Montreal *Gazette* asserted that Gooderham & Worts had become the largest distillery in the world.

Once distilling became the focus of the business, they brought numerous supporting activities on site. They built a new maltings and a cooperage, where forty coopers made barrels from oak harvested locally and farther inland. As if to seal the transition from incidental distillers to distilling magnates, in 1864, the partners demolished Worts's old windmill. It had been a city landmark since 1832.

The walls of the new limestone distillery were more than a metre thick at the base, with interior beams set onto protruding stone mounts rather than embedded in the walls. So while a fire in October 1869 gutted the interior, the walls remained standing, as they still do today. The partners took the fire in stride, perhaps finding some solace in the fact that large quantities of grain stored in the top of the distillery fell through the burning floors and smothered the fire before it could destroy the equipment. Within two days, the firm called for tenders to rebuild, and four months later, at a cost of $100,000, the distillery was back in production.

On August 21, 1881, nearly fifty years after he arrived in Canada, ninety-year-old William Gooderham died. His nephew, James Gooderham Worts, followed him, less than a year later, on June 20, 1882, at age sixty-four. This left William's son George to run the distillery alone. Although he maintained the Gooderham & Worts name, George Gooderham bought Worts's interests and became the sole owner of the distillery he had been instrumental in building.

The business continued to thrive, and when new government regulations required that, by 1890, whisky must be aged a minimum of two years, he added twelve additional warehouses. The ageing law further bolstered an already strong reputation for quality enjoyed by Canadian whisky around the world, and particularly in the United States. Canadian distillers had long been barrel ageing their best spirits anyway; now the government of the Dominion of Canada was prepared to certify it.

In 1902, directly across the street from the five-hectare distillery site, George Gooderham established the General Distilling Company to make industrial alcohol, in a joint venture with Hiram Walker & Sons. It would not be long before non-beverage distillates would be the firm's primary products.

GOODERHAM'S WELL-TEMPERED ENTHUSIASM

When William Gooderham brought his son George into the business, his focus was still on milling flour. His nephew James had seen the potential in distilling, but it was George who really propelled the firm to become an industry leader, and his enthusiasm never waned. However, when he died in 1905, at age seventy-five, and the distillery passed to his three sons and six daughters, the temperance movement had exactly its desired effect: it tempered the family's interest in whisky. Production continued, but the younger generation behaved more like caretakers.

The First World War offered a reprieve from the disapproving gossip of the temperance fold, as the distillery switched production to making corn-based acetone for the war effort. British Acetones took over management of the plant, and Gooderham & Worts became a major supplier to the Allied effort. As well as acetone, the firm launched a successful business distilling and canning anti-freeze. The viability of making products other than whisky was clear.

Gooderham's Rich & Rare
40% alc/vol | Gooderham & Worts (defunct)

Closed nose, then prune juice, mash, and dusty grain. Soft, creamy, sweet, then suddenly ablaze. Dark fruits, fleeting cedar, more fruit, cinnamon hearts. Finishing glow fades quickly to black tea.

Gooderham's Canadian Centennial 15 Years Old (1956)
alc/vol not stated | Gooderham & Worts (defunct)

Big dark fruit, brown sugar, celery salt, and oily hints of spirit. Toasted oak, vague cedar, black pepper, almost malty. Shortish, with pithy herbs. Such sophistication from unassertive barrels.

THE SEEDS OF RIVALRY

The war ended in 1918; American Prohibition commenced in 1920. Folklore notwithstanding, most Canadian distilleries, Gooderham & Worts included, suffered badly during Prohibition. The Corby Distillery in Corbyville, however, did not. Its owner, tobacco magnate Mortimer Davis, had hired Harry C. Hatch, a top sales agent with good connections in the United States, and he generated tremendous sales volumes. Davis trusted Hatch and asked him to negotiate a buyout of the floundering Gooderham & Worts. Hatch claimed he had tried and been unable to make a deal. However, in 1923, he resigned from Corby and, with his brother Herb and friend Larry McGuinness as partners, bought Gooderham & Worts for himself. Davis, who was in France at the time, felt betrayed. Meanwhile, Hatch set himself to building a Prohibition empire. The network he had established to sell Corby whisky switched to selling Gooderham & Worts almost without skipping a beat, leaving Davis to scramble.

Without Hatch's American connections, Gooderham & Worts likely would not have survived Prohibition. Low Canadian sales volumes, coupled with the Gooderham family's disinterest, could not have sustained operations. However, the rejuvenated distillery made so much money for Hatch and his partners that, within three years, they bought Hiram Walker's distillery as well and hired Corby's general manager, WJ Hume, to run it. An enraged Davis was spitting nails as he declared Corby better off without the turncoats. While the two firms continued to operate separately, in 1927, Hatch merged them on paper to form Hiram Walker-Gooderham & Worts.

Although a few individuals profited immensely from Prohibition, sales of Canadian whisky to smugglers could not match lost sales to legitimate distributors. When the US repealed Prohibition in 1933, Hiram Walker-Gooderham & Worts expanded its manufacturing capacity rapidly in Canada, America, and abroad to feed those legal channels of distribution. At the same time, American whisky makers restarted production, but with updated equipment and new production methods, they were slow to recapture the bourbons and ryes of the pre-Prohibition era. American producers found stiff competition in established Canadian producers and their well-loved product.

In recent decades, developers have conducted extensive research on the architecture of the Gooderham & Worts complex with an eye towards maintaining its historical integrity. However, details of its whisky-making operations remain vague. Perhaps this absence of documents confirms stories that, following Prohibition, Hatch sought to distance himself from that lawless era and ordered all records of pre-1933 dealings be destroyed.

In 1957, the last grain alcohol flowed from the stills at Gooderham & Worts. The new owners had consolidated beverage distilling in an expanded Hiram Walker plant in Walkerville, making the Toronto distillery redundant. To keep their distillery licence—and thus their bonded warehouses—active, the firm distilled rum one day a year at the Toronto site. However, most production switched to antifreeze and other industrial products. The end finally came in 1986, when a British firm, Allied-Lyons, bought Hiram Walker-Gooderham & Worts from Hatch's heirs. Within four years, all production ceased at Gooderham & Worts.

The Gooderham & Worts Distillery, with its extensive and unique Victorian architecture, has been identified as a national historic site. This ensures that the stone distillery and many of the other buildings will survive. It truly is a beautiful location. In 2005, real estate developers purchased the Gooderham & Worts site and converted it to retail and residential use. However, the Distillery District, as it is now called, has not become the tourist magnet its developers must have hoped for, and in truth, other than some beautifully preserved facades, little remains of the old distillery but simulacra. Mill Street Brewery brought whisky making back to the site in 2012, when it opened Toronto's first microdistillery in its restaurant on Tank House Lane. There, they make gin and a respectable single malt whisky. More recently, the Spirit of York has begun distilling spirits on site. Nevertheless, the last of Canada's original distilleries remains at least superficially intact as the only place in Canada where an imaginative whisky lover can sit, eyes closed, and breathe in a legacy that, for the most part, has been forgotten.

Gooderham & Worts and Consolidated Alcohols barrel stencils.

(12)

JP WISER AND WISER'S DISTILLERY

On October 4, 1825, in the small Upstate New York town of Trenton, Isaac Wiser and his wife, Mary Egert, had a son. They named him John Philip. From adolescence, JP, as people called him, was hard-working and ambitious, with a good nose for business. While still a youth, he began buying cattle to sell to butchers between Trenton and Albany, 160 kilometres to the east. Wiser never lost his love of the cattle trade.

Two of Mary's relatives, Amos S. and Charles P. Egert, were established merchants in Gouverneur, New York, about 150 kilometres north of Trenton. When, together with Ogdensburg distiller James G. Averell, they began a new enterprise, fattening cattle on distillery waste, they hired JP—initially to work in their dry goods store in Gouverneur. Before long, he was travelling around northern New York, buying and selling cattle for them. JP's dedication and keen interest in the cattle business earned him a partnership in the Ogdensburg venture.

Just across the St. Lawrence River from Ogdensburg, in Prescott, Ontario, four distilleries produced about 200,000 gallons of whisky a year. In 1857, Averell purchased Charles A. Payne's distillery, the second-largest of these, and JP moved to Prescott to manage it. Payne sold 69,680 gallons of high wines, proof, and common whisky in 1858. JP increased that to 84,836 gallons the following year. Early grain bills show that Wiser mashed wheat, rye, and corn in eight pine mash tubs. The corn came by boat from the United States and the rye by train from within the province. He also planted rye, a crop the local newspaper claimed was two metres tall. At one point, Wiser was removing the unfermentable bran from his corn before mashing it. He also added hops to his mashes, as brewers still do, almost certainly to prevent contamination by bacteria. From the start, Wiser aged his whisky in new charred and re-charred barrels, each one made on site from oak wood harvested as settlers cleared land for farms.

Staff at Wiser's distillery in Prescott, Ontario, November 1890.

Prescott was a bustling community of 2,500 souls when Wiser arrived in 1857, and its location on the St. Lawrence River made it an eastern Ontario transportation hub. Rail lines from Ottawa, Montreal, and Toronto passed through the busy border town. Some trains boarded a steam ferry in Prescott for the short trip across the St. Lawrence to Ogdensburg and the American northeast. Prescott was also an active river port, serving steamships and schooners. The comings and goings on the river were clearly visible from the distillery, which was right on the waterfront at the western end of town.

Averell had been a good tutor, and the energetic JP learned the distilling business quickly. Four years later, when Charles Payne left, JP had the good sense to hire a competent distiller. Many of the area's top artisans and skilled trades already reported to distillery foreman George Lane, and Wiser paid them generously by the standards of the time. For five ten-hour workdays, and another half day on Saturday, he paid $10 to $15, plus generous bonuses at Christmas. Cash went home with the men; some liquid bonuses did not make it off the premises.

As well as a flourishing business, Wiser—and his wife, Emily Goddard of Richville, New York—had a growing family. Their son, Harlow Goddard Wiser, arrived in 1859, followed by two sisters and three brothers over the next few years. The mid-19th century was difficult for small-town distillers, as expanding transportation systems favoured larger operations. However, JP realized that the distillery was a valuable feed source for his primary business—cattle. Within five years, he bought out Averell and Egert to become the sole proprietor of the company.

The year 1864 started badly, though, when fire destroyed most of the distillery. Undaunted, JP seized the opportunity to expand and incorporate up-to-date equipment, including a shiny new copper column still and storehouses that could hold up to 10,000 bushels of grain. Ninety metres west of the distillery, he built barns to house 2,000 head of cattle. Emily's family may have helped underwrite JP's purchase of the distillery, allowing him to take over and expand so rapidly. However he financed it, on the strength of his thriving cattle business, JP Wiser was soon the only distiller of any size left in Prescott. Nevertheless, his barnyard did have a certain impact in the community. The west end of Prescott had been a good neighbourhood until the cattle arrived. So to minimize complaints, JP built his home adjacent to the barns.

POLITICAL INFLUENCE

JP Wiser was a commanding figure. He walked with a gold-tipped cane, could be gruff and driven, and had an innate ability to find people's strengths. And though he owned the business, much of Wiser's success was the work of company treasurer Albert Whitney. Cranky and slightly stooped, but shrewd in business, Whitney was not a people person. Nonetheless, he dedicated fifty years to the firm, and until 1906, he, and not JP, held the licence to distil.

Whitney, who was known for his sarcasm, was a solid man with a short, sandy-coloured beard. The brother of Ontario premier James Whitney, he was prominent in local politics, often accused of ensuring that every political decision would benefit the distillery. Accusations of conflict of interest came to a head in the election of 1896, when opponents dubbed Whitney and a group of like-minded councilmen the "Distillery Ring." They fought back on the hustings, and when the votes were counted, Whitney and his ring were re-elected and the matter was settled.

As dedicated as Whitney was to the distillery, he was also committed to maintaining his routine. Workdays were long, and he practically ignored his family, often choosing to spend his Saturday afternoons and Sundays playing poker at JP's home. And though Whitney was married and had at least one daughter, he also kept a mistress, whom he visited weekly, in full view of the town. When his wife died, Whitney did the socially acceptable thing and married his lover, the long-widowed Anna McDonnagh.

The American Civil War brought increasing sales in the US, making Wiser a principal supplier of beef cattle and whisky to the border states. Despite stiff postwar tariffs introduced by the Americans, Wiser's reputation helped him keep some of this market. Comfort Whitney, his distiller and blender (and no relation to Albert), shared Wiser's mantra: "Quality is something you just can't rush. Horses should hurry, but whisky must take its time."

A decade after he purchased the distillery, Wiser employed sixty workers who supported forty-six families. Each day, excise duty on his production put $2,000 into the Canadian treasury. In ten short years, its more than $1 million annual operating costs had made JP Wiser's distillery the largest contributor to Prescott's prosperity, and JP himself had become one of the leading city fathers. Employees and townspeople alike regarded him as a benevolent guardian. He took Canadian citizenship, served on town council for eleven years, and in 1878 was elected a Liberal member of Parliament. Oddly, he supported Canadian prohibition, an act that, had it been passed, would have had dire consequences for the town. Wiser was not much of a drinker, but neither was he teetotal. Likely, he realized that prohibition was not on the near horizon and felt safe endorsing it for votes.

Nevertheless, JP found politics a distraction. He preferred the political back-rooms, often financing his favoured candidates. During his term in Parliament, however, he did exercise some influence. Debating Conservative Prime Minister Sir John A. Macdonald in the House of Commons, he convinced Macdonald to alter his party's plans for development in the west. Wiser toured western Canada to learn more about the issues, then reported his conclusions to the House. In the next election, a grateful Liberal leader, Sir Wilfrid Laurier, spent a few days visiting JP in Prescott. When the campaign was over, Laurier had replaced Macdonald as prime minister.

A CATTLEMAN AND A RANCHER

In the late 1860s, Wiser purchased a twenty-five-hectare farm just west of Prescott. Each day, draught horses made the short trek there from the distillery, with barrels of spent mash. Although distillery waste was the main fodder for 1,000 head of cattle, the farm was more than a waste disposal plant. It soon became one of Canada's foremost breeding centres for cattle and racehorses, and JP spent extravagantly to obtain and improve the best bloodlines. He named his farm Rysdyk after a particularly outstanding $10,000 stallion he had purchased in Connecticut. He also established a brickworks on the farm that, at its peak, employed forty men.

In 1875, a boat loaded with several hundred distillery-fattened cattle left the dock at Wiser's distillery for Britain. Before long, he had steady markets in several British ports. A man interested in the details, Wiser accompanied a load of cattle across the Atlantic in 1879, so he could learn how best to care for them on their journey and better understand his market. His beef business launched a new Canadian export trade, one many others soon replicated.

Wiser's love of the cattle business also led him to establish a vast ranch called the Dominion Cattle Company in Texas. Early in the 1880s, his son Harlow spent three years there managing the 4,000-hectare property and learning the cattle trade. JP then expanded his 12,000-head US cattle operation to include another 60,000 hectares in Kansas. He owned some of the land, but most was free range or leased. The ranches sent 2,000 cattle a year to be fattened in Prescott and shipped to markets in Glasgow, London, and Liverpool. Many more found their way to stockyards throughout the United States.

The gregarious and popular Harlow Wiser returned to Canada to work at the distillery in 1887. The promise of a Wiser legacy seemed assured until, one day in 1895, Harlow suffered a heart attack. By the next day, the thirty-six-year-old was dead. Although the Wisers were Canadians, the family buried Harlow across the border, in Ogdensburg. JP sent another son, Frank, to Kansas to manage the ranch, but he returned a year later, complaining that the cowboy business did not agree with his constitution. Harlow's brothers Ike and Frank (a third brother, John, had died in childhood) did not share JP's enthusiasm for the business.

Wiser carved in a barrel head.

DISTILLERY Nº I.   PORT Nº 41-E.

PEBBLE-BROOK

Kentucky Type
BOURBON

BOTTLED UNDER SUPERVISION OF
THE FEDERAL GOVERNMENT
IN DISTILLERY BONDED WAREHOUSE
CONTENTS 32 FLUID OUNCES

WISER'S DISTILLERY LIMITED
PRESCOTT. ONT — CANADA.

Wiser's Pebble-Brook Bourbon was distilled in 1924, after owner Canadian Industrial Alcohol had rebuilt Wiser's distillery and switched production to non-potable alcohol. The whisky more likely originated at their Corbyville distillery.

From the time he took it over, JP constantly improved the distillery, and in 1885, that meant installing eight copper tanks in a new brick building. Fabricated on site from huge sheets of copper, they weighed two tons each and held 11,000 gallons. More enhancements followed in 1887, after fire struck the distillery again. Determined not to be distracted by these challenges, Wiser rebuilt, and within sixty days a new and improved distillery was back in production.

Before 1893, JP sold his whisky in kegs, barrels, and bulk containers. Then, at the Chicago World's Fair, he introduced his first bottled whisky. Although Hiram Walker's Canadian Club whisky was already widely known in the US, most likely Wiser's was the first to be specifically designated "Canadian whisky." In addition to Canada and the US, by the early 1900s Wiser was also exporting whisky to China and the Philippines. At a time when quality was equated with purity, JP's whisky was considered among the purest. In 1977, Edward McNally, a veteran excise officer who worked at Corby Distillery in Corbyville, which by then owned the Wiser's name, remembered Wiser's Red Letter Rye as "a little too dark in colour but smooth and well matured." Red Letter, of course, was a Corby creation, and despite what the label claims, it had nothing to do with JP Wiser.

On April 30, 1911, John Philip Wiser's long and distinguished career ended with his death at age eighty-five. Following funeral services in Prescott, his cortège crossed the St. Lawrence River by boat to New York state, where he had been born. There, his remains were interred in the family plot in a shady nook on the banks of the gentle Oswegatchie River.

About a year after Wiser's death, hay in a new cattle shed caught fire, again devastating the distillery. JP Wiser had built a thriving business in Prescott and earned a stellar reputation, but sometimes stories involving families take surprising turns. Wiser's distillery, for all its innovations and skilled workforce, languished after his death. His sons lacked the skills—or perhaps the interest—to run it. In October 1920, they sold the remnants to Mortimer Davis's Canadian

Industrial Alcohol Company, which merged it with Corby's into Consolidated Distilleries and, after shipping its 40,000 gallons of mature whisky to Montreal, rebuilt Wiser's distillery as an industrial alcohol plant. Nevertheless, during Prohibition, Consolidated Distilleries put Wiser's brand on Pebble-Brook Kentucky Type Bourbon, Old Hickory American Rye Whiskey, Old Dominion Canadian Rye Whisky, and Robert Hope's Regent London Dry Gin. No mention of Wiser's Old Rye, or any other Wiser's brands, though.

In 1932, the year before Prohibition ended, Consolidated closed Wiser's distillery for good. Corby owned the brand and exercised its right to put Wiser's name on whisky it produced in Corbyville, but the original recipes were no more. Then, when management consolidated Corby's distillery with Hiram Walker's in 1991, operations moved yet again, this time to Walkerville. Today, not even a trace of Wiser's distillery, nor his equally successful cattle and horse farm, remains. Radiant stained glass windows made by the renowned Prescott glass artist Harry Horwood for JP Wiser's home are now in storage at Upper Canada Village in Morrisburg, Ontario. And though they bear his name, today's "Wiser's" whiskies are more recent creations.

Based on comparisons with mature "Wiser's" whisky distilled during the 1940s in Corbyville, Corby Spirit & Wine (which now owns the Wiser's name and operates the Walkerville Distillery) has done an admirable job of emulating the 1940s flavour profile, the Corbyville version leaning a bit more into dark fruits, tobacco, and barrel tones. But, of course, this is the work not of Wiser, or his distiller, Comfort Whitney, but of someone unknown in the now-demolished Corby Distillery, which by then was controlled by one Harry C. Hatch.

(13)

HENRY CORBY AND CORBY DISTILLERY

I n 1832, at age twenty-six, Henry Corby left nineteen brothers and sisters behind in Hanwell, England, and, with his wife, Alma, sailed for Belleville, Ontario. Belleville, on Lake Ontario's Bay of Quinte, was a growing lumber town of 2,000 residents at the time. Although Corby was described as "a thorough Englishman," his family descended from French Huguenots named Corbil. The oft-told story that Corby arrived in Belleville with a single sovereign in his pocket seems doubtful, as he soon opened a small grocery shop and bakery.

On December 24, 1835, with thoughts of a warm and joyous Christmas celebration with friends, Corby, his wife, their three young children, his wife's sister Matilda, and a friend set off by sleigh across the frozen surface of the Bay of Quinte. Just off Massassauga Point, the sleigh plunged through thin ice. Alma and the three young children drowned.

ALMA MILLS

The grieving Corby became consumed by business and soon had enough money to buy a steamboat and move into the grain trade, which, in turn, led him to purchase a gristmill. Corby married Matilda and they started a new family, but Alma's grim demise never faded from their memory. Corby named his gristmill Alma Mills, and three decades later his son (with Matilda) successfully promoted an iron bridge across the Bay of Quinte to avoid future tragedies.

It's hard to imagine a lovelier site for a distillery than this spot on the Moira River, but Henry Corby had really wanted to build six kilometres downstream, in Belleville. However, he was a Liberal, and the Conservative city fathers opposed his damming the river to power a mill. So in 1855, Corby bought Silas Reed's 1812-vintage flour mill on 1.6 hectares at Hayden's Corners in Thurlow Township. It took him two years to get the mill working, and another two before he was ready to start distilling. And it was whisky that Corby distilled, whisky that soon made him wealthy.

While he commuted daily from Belleville by horse and buggy, a settlement that eventually became Corbyville grew up around the distillery. Although this was Corby's first venture into distilling, as a baker he had been partners with Silas Reed's brother, a distiller, in supplying the Hastings Rifle Company as it fought against William Lyon Mackenzie's Upper Canada Rebellion. The rebellion quashed and politics being what it is, Corby later went on to become mayor of Belleville, then a Conservative member of the provincial legislative assembly. His confidence, large stature, and booming voice made him a natural leader.

HARRY CORBY TAKES THE REINS

By August 1881, Corby was seventy-five and frail, and ready to sell the mill and distillery. For the sum of $10,000, his twenty-one-year-old son, Henry Corby Jr., better known as Harry, became its new owner. Within three months, the old man died and Harry closed the flour and feed mill to focus on whisky. Harry had big plans for the distillery and expanded it to include an ageing warehouse and a modern bottling line in Belleville. This allowed him to sell whisky in bottles, as well as the pails, jugs, barrels, half-barrels, and kegs that his father had favoured. He also had track laid for a rail spur from Belleville to the distillery. Harry not only expanded production at the distillery, but also modernized its methods. Harry Corby had a theory about the popularity of his whiskies in the United States: "The fact [is] that the extremely cold weather of Canadian winters adds a peculiar quality to Canadian cereals in the form of certain esters and aromatic compounds which Canadian distillers have learned to preserve. It is these esters which make the 'bouquet' of Canadian rye and bourbon whisky so distinctly pleasant."

Like his father, Harry was interested in politics. In 1888, he was elected to represent Belleville as a Conservative member of Parliament, and in 1912 was appointed to the Senate of Canada in recognition of his civic-mindedness and political career. The town was proud of Harry Corby, and thereafter people referred to him exclusively as Senator Corby. Nevertheless, it is Henry Corby Sr. who is best remembered for his distillery. The legacy of his son Harry is his contribution to his community.

PROHIBITION TO THE RESCUE

By 1905, it was Harry Corby's turn to think about the future of the business. With three daughters and no sons to take it over, he sold the distillery to Montreal businessman Mortimer Davis for $1.5 million—quite a tidy profit. Davis did well with his new acquisition, and further expanded exports to key markets in the United States. When fire destroyed the original distillery in 1907, Davis not only rebuilt but enlarged it on the same site. Then, after a promising start under Davis's management, whisky making came to a sudden halt in 1916, by government order. For the balance of the First World War, the firm's output was restricted to industrial alcohol. When the war ended in 1918, whisky sales had declined to a measly 500 gallons a month, and Davis,

Fermenter bases in derelict Corby distillery.

enraptured by the industrial alcohol trade anyway, renamed the firm the Canadian Industrial Alcohol Company, and declared it would devote its entire attention to making cologne spirits, fusel oil, denatured alcohol, antifreeze, and other non-potable spirits, most of it for export. Why waste time ageing something you could sell minutes after it was distilled? However, the opportunity presented by Prohibition promptly intervened to drag Davis squarely back into the whisky business. Soon, the firm also had nine million gallons of whisky maturing in fifteen rack warehouses under the watchful eye of ten government excise officers.

Davis purchased the late JP Wiser's distillery in Prescott in 1920, merged its management with that of the Corbyville plant, and incorporated the two firms as one, called Consolidated Distilleries, a division of his Canadian Industrial Alcohol Company. The names were predictive of further consolidations to come, and Davis's plans to convert both distilleries to industrial alcohol. By 1921, the old Wiser and Corby distilleries were producing 600,000 gallons a month of non-potable alcohol, most of it made from molasses, leading Davis to claim they were the world's largest suppliers of industrial alcohol. He had also begun to experiment with making fuel alcohol. When lightning struck the Corbyville plant in 1923, the $1 million loss included 6,000 barrels of denatured spirits.

ST. HYACINTHE DISTILLERY

About this time, Davis also acquired the short-lived St. Hyacinthe Distillery, just east of Montreal, and began bottling liquor there. Local veterinarian JA Tellier had founded the distillery in 1902, to make vinegar. Two years later, he sold the plant to Joseph-Ovide Brouillard, who expanded it to fourteen buildings to distil and age spirits. Served by a rail line and with a cooperage on site, the St. Hyacinthe Distillery Company turned local grain into more than

150,000 gallons of spirits annually, and paid over $300,000 in taxes. A 1,200-square-metre barn built in 1906 housed 200 head of cattle until a storm tore its roof off in 1919 and the firm quit the cattle business. Its National Canadian Whisky brand was popular in Canada. Meanwhile, it exported Greenbrier American Bourbon Whiskey and Chesapeake American Rye Whiskey to the United States. In the mid-twenties, as temperance sentiments set in, the distillery began to falter, and management sold it to Davis's Consolidated Distilleries, which used it first as a bottling plant, then for storage. In March 1935, Consolidated sold it to be demolished for salvage.

DAVIS VS. HATCH

It was 1921 when Davis hired Harry Hatch to handle whisky sales. Hatch had begun his liquor industry career as a bartender at the Oriental Hotel in Deseronto, and then the Shannonville Hotel on the Tyendinaga Mohawk Territory near Belleville. In partnership with his brother Herb, he soon moved on to operate package liquor stores in various places, including Whitby and Toronto. However, Canada has its own history of prohibition. The Ontario Temperance Act of 1916 made it illegal to sell liquor in the province, but not to make it or import it for personal use. Hatch immediately seized this opportunity and opened a mail order liquor business based in Montreal. A persuasive salesman, Hatch was soon bringing Ontario-made whisky into Montreal, then "exporting" it by the case to Ontario residents—and, with the arrival of American Prohibition in 1920, by the truckload to bootleggers in the United States. Harry, Herb, and a partner, Larry McGuinness, had built an extensive underground sales network there.

American Prohibition was not an instant bonanza for Canadian distilleries. Sales at Davis's Corbyville distillery were lagging badly, and the interprovincial mail order trade had just been shut down when Davis persuaded Hatch to join

Consolidated Distilleries as sales manager with the prospect of partnership. Or did he? The terms of this "arrangement" would later be hotly disputed.

The Volstead Act of 1920 made the sale of whisky for other than medicinal, sacramental, or baking purposes illegal throughout the United States. In Canada, however, it was not illegal to export whisky, provided the proper Canadian duties were paid. Canadian authorities were not responsible for what happened to the whisky after it left Canada. Corbyville was in a perfect location to dispatch whisky by boat across Lake Ontario to small ports such as Oswego, New York. Hatch and his partners established "Hatch's Navy"—a loosely organized but highly effective flotilla of wharf rats and fishermen. Some used their own craft; others used one of Hatch's fleet of forty-two boats to carry whisky across the lake to a country willing to pay almost any price to quench its thirst.

Sales grew to 50,000 gallons a month, making the distillery one of the world's largest. With their American connections and surging demand created by Prohibition, Hatch and his partners had saved Davis's distillery from whisky oblivion. In 1923, Harry Hatch moved to exercise his option to join Mortimer Davis as a partner in this now thriving whisky business. Davis, however, denied having made such an offer and claimed he had simply agreed to pay Hatch and his partners a dollar for every case of Corby's whisky they sold south of the border. Hatch left Corby's later that year to buy Gooderham & Worts's then-silent distillery in Toronto, putting a serious dent in Davis's sales.

If Prohibition had closed Gooderham & Worts, Hatch was about to revive it. Meanwhile, Davis moved west, opening a distribution centre for whisky on Granville Island in Vancouver in 1923, and in 1924 announcing a new fuel alcohol plant in St. Boniface, Manitoba, with capacity to distil a million gallons a year from grain. In 1925, in response to a reputed trademark infringement, Consolidated Distilleries announced, "The distillery from whence Embassy comes [Corby's] has been in operation for sixty-six years by this firm, and is neither affiliated with, nor connected with any other company or firm in the trade." Hmm . . . but what about Wiser's? St. Hyacinthe?

Mortimer Davis became Sir Mortimer in 1916 when King George V knighted him, and doing business with bootleggers was somewhat beneath his dignity. Though his office in Montreal accepted their telephone orders—and, of course, their cash—Davis never deigned to deal directly with smugglers, delegating that task to Harry Hatch. When much of Hatch's Navy followed him to Gooderham & Worts, Davis had to seek out other means to move his whisky. Demand was great, though, and even with the serious blow of losing Hatch, sales of Corby brand whisky doubled between 1923 and 1926. Soon, trains carried Corby whisky west to Vancouver and east to Halifax for forwarding, with much of it transiting the French islands of St. Pierre and Miquelon. From there, it was dispatched by ocean-going ships to America's Atlantic "Rum Row," stretching south from Boston to New York. Ahh, the pillars of today's American society who rose from scoundrels by bootlegging Corby whisky on the Eastern Seaboard! But Sir Mortimer was clean. Despite enormous distilling profits, his real wealth came from another product with huge sales returns and tax revenues for governments: tobacco. He was the president of the Imperial Tobacco Company of Canada, and as early as 1906 had toyed with the idea of bringing Corby into the tobacco business, too.

While Davis and Hatch appear to be studies in contrast (Davis was suave and urbane, with corporate directorships and a Montreal mansion; Hatch, a foul-mouthed wheeler-dealer with vulgar tastes and ambitions, was a salesman through and through), they were not that dissimilar. Both owned horses: Davis, a stable of jumpers in Cannes, France; Hatch, racehorses in Toronto. Both died suddenly in middle age: Davis at sixty-one at Les Glaïeuls, his private villa in Cannes, in 1928; Hatch eighteen years later, at sixty-two, in a public Toronto hospital. And neither had a clue nor cared about whisky, while both coveted the lucre it could bring them.

CORBY'S WHISKIES

National styles were neither well established nor protected in the early 20th century. By 1935, along with two million gallons of Canadian whisky, seven million gallons of Canadian-made bourbon and rye sat in the Corbyville warehouses, waiting to be bottled. Labels on William Penn American Rye Whiskey, Twenty Grand Bourbon, Twenty Grand Straight Rye Whiskey, Old Crow Bourbon Whiskey, Stewart Old American Rye, and Wiser's Old Rye Whisky, as well as Corby's own brands, clearly stated that they had been made under Canadian government supervision. Throughout the 1930s, Consolidated Distillers owned all these brands. Walkerville (Windsor)-based Hiram Walker-Gooderham & Worts had finally purchased Mortimer Davis's shares in Canadian Industrial Alcohol—a controlling interest—in 1937, and, with similar disregard for national or distillery origins, by 1941 production of Corby's Special Reserve Canadian Whisky had shifted to Walker's new American distillery in Peoria, Illinois. The American plant did not always follow the original Canadian recipe, though, substituting raw alcohol for aged Canadian base whiskies.

The Second World War (1939–45) again forced operations at Corbyville to switch entirely to industrial alcohol. When the hostilities ended, the 400 staff at the eighty-building, 9.3-hectare complex returned to producing whisky and gin from grain, but molasses-based industrial alcohol remained the distillery's leading product. The firm installed a new dedicated column still with four million gallons annual capacity to make it. Nonetheless, in June 1950, by letters patent, it changed the name back from Canadian Industrial Alcohol to H. Corby Distillers. Then, in 1978, in partnership with Dutch distillers De Kuyper, Corby's purchased the Meagher's Distillery in Montreal, but shut down its stills and reduced it to a bottling plant. At about the same time, Corby's extended and modernized spirits production at Corbyville, adding a new up-to-date distribution centre there.

1980S CONSOLIDATIONS

Alas, the boom was temporary, and in 1987 the Corbyville plant closed and the company moved its maturing processes and new production to Walkerville. A glimmer of hope appeared when Corby's bought the McGuinness Distillery in 1988 and moved its bottling and blending operations to Corbyville, installing a modernized bottling line in March 1989. However, in May 1991, the company announced that all operations would cease within five months.

For decades, people driving between Toronto and Ottawa would pass a sign for Corbyville and a tin-hat water tower painted with the words "Corby's London Dry Gin" that stood just north of Highway 401 near Belleville. Erected in 1923, when the distillery was rebuilt and expanded after a million-dollar fire, it held 100,000 gallons of water and stood 166 feet tall. Just off the highway, on River Road, the last bonded warehouse of the abandoned distillery now houses Signal Brewing, a microbrewery with a restaurant and large riverside patio. The old brick buildings across the road are gone, and metal-sided warehouses and a distribution centre built in the 1970s have been sold. All that is left today of Henry Corby's once-thriving distillery are a brick-built stable, a hall that was once the lab, and an old fading sign down the road, inviting redevelopment.

French multinational Pernod Ricard now owns Corby's brands and administers them from corporate offices in Toronto. Wiser's distillery has disappeared without a trace, as has McGuinness's. Only the regal stone house in Corbyville, formerly the home of Corby's president, maintains its original purpose, as a residence. Although each originated in its own distillery before being consolidated in Corbyville, Corby's, Wiser's, and McGuinness's whiskies are all now made at the Hiram Walker & Sons Distillery. Based in Walkerville, the distillery was built expressly to make Canadian Club, but now, somewhat misleadingly, flies massive Wiser's banners.

Since it took over from Canadian Club in 2005, Corby's successor, a firm that maintains its founder's name as Corby Spirit & Wine, runs the illustrious Walker Distillery. As departing Corbyville distillery worker Bill Nicol opined presciently in 1991:

> *Now we're here: now we're gone,*
> *But Corby's Spirit will live on.*

Wiser's De Luxe 10 Years Old (1974)
40% alc/vol | H. Corby (defunct)

Lush, round caramel, burgeoning peppery rye spiciness. Oaky echoes evolve into pleasing barrel tones, then grapefruit pith. Classic sweet, chest-warming, then pithy palate. Lingering heat. Had it only survived.

Wiser's Oldest 18 Years Old (1949)
40% alc/vol | H. Corby (defunct)

Rich and brimming with prune juice, raisins, pleasing woody tones, pipe tobacco, clean grain, barley sugar, and white pepper. Creamy and mouth-filling. Long, fruity, pithy tannic finish.

Hiram Walker.

(14)

HIRAM WALKER AND CANADIAN CLUB

As much as we enjoy drinking whisky, making it is a business, and businesses must earn profits for their owners and shareholders. Even so, the great whiskies, the ones connoisseurs extol, are created by people who take pride in a high-quality product and balance profits with reputation. For Hiram Walker, who understood the intangibles of brand equity, profits and longevity came as one with whisky that put flavour first. It was Walker, after all, who brought us the icon that is Canadian Club.

A WHISKY ICON

If ever there was a Canadian icon recognized almost as widely as the beaver, the moose, or maple syrup, it would be Canadian Club. Since its official introduction in 1882, Canadian Club has embraced good times (as the television series *Boardwalk Empire* reminded viewers for five blockbuster seasons) and bad, to become the last Canadian whisky to survive (somewhat) intact from its 19th-century origins, and the sole heritage whisky still made in its original (albeit modernized) distillery. Prior to Prohibition, Canadian Club Rye, as many called it then, was the largest-selling imported whisky in America. Now available in 155 countries, Canadian Club is still Canada's third top-selling whisky. And how did Walker's Canadian Club achieve such elite status? Let's begin at the beginning.

The Canadian Club sign atop the Hiram Walker distillery was removed after Corby's took over management in 2005.

ROOTED IN AMERICA

Before building Canada's longest-surviving whisky distillery near Windsor, Ontario, Hiram Walker was a Detroit-based grocer, tanner, grain merchant, rectifier, whisky compounder, and vinegar maker. Born in Douglas, Massachusetts, on the Fourth of July in 1816, Walker was a sixth-generation American. His father's death from smallpox nine years later left Hiram in the care of his mother and eldest brother, thirteen-year-old Chandler. Hiram later credited his success to good friends in Douglas who sent him to school and taught him the value of a penny and the importance of work.

When Chandler married in 1836, Hiram made the seventy-kilometre trek east to Boston, a thriving metropolis of 60,000, where he worked in a dry goods store. Then, at twenty-two, he caught "Michigania fever" and joined the throngs heading west to Detroit. The Detroit that welcomed Walker in 1838 was a booming, 9,000-person frontier town where he found work as a grocery clerk. Not long after, Walker joined 190 others to stand watch over Detroit during the Battle of Windsor. Had he only known how profoundly Windsor would later change his fortunes—and he, Windsor's.

At age thirty, Hiram Walker married Mary Williams from the nearby Saginaw Valley. Three years and several false starts later, he opened his own grocery store, where he stocked 500 barrels of wheat whisky. In the mid-19th century, groceries often included whisky, and some Detroit grocer's shops were little more than saloons. North America's governments have a complex relationship with whisky makers. They love the tax revenues from whisky, but must not appear to condone the sin that certain Protestant denominations say it incites. This has led to some puzzling, contradictory, and outright incomprehensible laws. Thus, while Walker was operating his grocery business in Detroit, and until the US Internal Revenue Act was passed in 1868, American distillers were not allowed to make or sell rectified whisky, and no one else could rectify it within roughly 180 metres of a distillery. So numerous grocers, Hiram Walker among them, purchased new distillate from local distillers, carted it away, then leached it slowly through tall columns of charcoal. After adding a dash of burnt sugar for colour and prune juice for flavour, a practice known as compounding, they had what was then called whisky ready for market. Walker was the only one of Canada's founding distillers who had such experience.

CANADA BECKONS

The year 1856 was pivotal for Walker. Growing prohibition sentiments and conflicting alcohol legislation in the US had led him out of whisky and into the grain business. It irritated him that he would be able to distil, rectify, and compound whisky undisturbed just across the Detroit River in Canada. He had already cut out the middleman and made the vinegar he sold in his grocery store. It was natural that he would also think about distilling spirits. Moreover, Canada offered untapped opportunity to buy, sell, and mill grain. And so Walker bought 190 riverfront hectares on the outskirts of Windsor and built a flour mill and distillery.

Although he is rightfully one of Canada's best-known distillers, Hiram Walker lived all but the four-year period of his life beginning in 1859 in the United States. He commuted to Canada daily from his home in Hamtramck, Michigan, to build and operate his steam-powered Windsor Flouring Mill and Distillery. Two modest distilleries in nearby Windsor offered little competition, and there were no other flour mills in the region. As the name suggests, distilling was more than an offshoot of the mill. From the beginning, Walker clearly had his eye on the more accommodating Canadian legal climate for whisky. His distillery in the four-storey wooden mill began operations in June 1858, within months of Walker grinding his first flour. With two of its four sets of millstones dedicated to making grist for the distillery, twenty 15,000-litre fermenters (some were slightly larger), and five days fermentation, Walker produced up to 60,000 litres of fermented mash each day.

Friends had helped Walker raise $40,000 to build the facility, and the Bank of Montreal loaned him another $60,000. However, he found servicing that debt difficult at first, and the bank continually pressed him for payment. Thirty years later, his enterprise was so successful that the bank opened a branch in Walkerville specifically for his workers. By 1859, John McBride, one of his key employees from Detroit, was travelling the length and breadth of the United States by train, drumming up business for Walker's two products: whisky and flour. Soon, he added a third: hogs fattened on distillery waste. The distillery could barely keep up with McBride's sales.

From the start, Walker mashed corn, rye, and barley malt, and used wheat strictly to make flour. In 1860, corn imported from the US made up about 80% of the mash bill, rye 14%, malt 3%, and oats 2%. His flavouring was 94% rye and 6% malt. He distilled the fermented mash in a 10-metre tall, 2.5-metre diameter, three-chambered wooden continuous still, and then passed it several times through a single-chambered copper doubler and a 7.5-metre water-cooled copper worm condenser to bring it up to high-wines strength. It was 1871 before Walker installed a Hoffman, Ahlers–style continuous copper column still in his distillery.

Although some other Upper Canadian distillers had begun to age their whisky in oak barrels, this was not yet a legal requirement. Walker had learned the art of rectification well during his days as a grocer in Detroit, and established a positive cash flow at the distillery quickly by selling rectified high wines. His Old Magnolia whisky, a name curiously reminiscent of the popular Monongahela whisky from Pennsylvania, quickly found a steady market locally and in the US.

Walker's sales mushroomed with the demand for Canadian whisky created by the American Civil War. The war also brought Walker another opportunity.

As it dragged on, the value of the American dollar plummeted, and Walker scraped together every Canadian penny he could to buy American dollars. When the war ended, the US dollar raced back up. At the same time, smugglers intent on avoiding tariffs the US introduced after the war bought volumes of whisky equal to those of the Prohibition era. Although popular myth credits Prohibition with creating the American taste for Canadian whisky, Prohibition-era smuggling was merely a reprise of events that had occurred sixty years earlier. Returns from his flourishing whisky sales and the profits of his currency speculation made Walker, for the first time, a truly wealthy man.

PARTNERSHIPS AND EXPANSIONS

Hiram Walker was the driving force behind the distillery, but as the business grew, he needed help managing it, and in 1863, he recognized John McBride's outstanding service by making him a partner in the firm. Walker was delighted with the arrangement, but just four years later, McBride left to revive a small, failing distillery called Rolf & Melchers, about a mile east up the river. Walker thought highly of McBride and gave him a generous settlement of $12,500. Nevertheless, McBride and his two partners could not make a go of their distillery and ended up selling it at a loss to Walker, who closed it. In 1871, Walker tried partnership again, inviting his son Edward Chandler Walker, known affectionately as Mr. Ed, to join the firm. Two years later, he brought in his middle son, Franklin Hiram Walker, followed by his third son, James Harrington Walker.

The year 1867 saw the birth of Canada with Confederation. It also brought a new tariff structure that made the mill less profitable and favoured the distillery by lowering the price of corn. At about this time, Walker began a campaign to move beyond the US and Canadian markets. He established beachheads in

England and Ireland, where steadily growing sales led to reliable markets around the world.

Global recession in 1873 drove thousands out of business, but Walker responded with an aggressive—some called it reckless—expansion in the face of this adversity. He extended his lumber business and purchased two ships, one of which he had built to carry logs and lumber. It was a tough few years, and Walker's fortunes wavered between ruin (some weeks he was unable to meet his payroll) and halting success. Nevertheless, he pressed on, emerging from the recession stronger, if not wealthier. Distilling profits now so overshadowed milling that Walker closed the mill in 1878.

Walker was an American citizen, so he could not vote in Canada. That did not stop him from taking an active role in backroom politics, though. His close personal friendships with some of Canada's Fathers of Confederation, including prime ministers Sir John A. Macdonald and Sir Charles Tupper, gave him considerable influence. In 1878, he endorsed Sir John A.'s protectionist National Policy of tariffs and made large donations to Macdonald's campaign. Similar policies in the United States had reduced Canada's trade there, and he reasoned that Macdonald's tariffs would benefit Canadian manufacturers in the home market. When Sir John A. was swept back into power in that year's election, Walker had not yet introduced his Canadian Club whisky, but there is little doubt that both the triumphant prime minister and Walker's local member of Parliament celebrated their victory with Walker's whisky.

Walker anticipated that tariffs would increase his business in Canada, and so he began a coast-to-coast advertising campaign. However, he did not abandon the idea of rebuilding strength in his primary market, the United States. If US tariffs meant he could no longer compete there based on price, he would appeal to people's palates instead. Walker studied the American market carefully, and in 1882, with the advent of affordable bottles, introduced his first true brand,

Canadian Club. Until then, whisky had been sold in barrels, each one slightly different from the others, with a name indicating its "style." The Canadian Club brand was a mature and consistent product, blended from corn and rye spirits distilled separately and then aged together. Today, Canadian Club managers refer to this process as pre-barrel blending. The whisky was expensive and slow at first to gain acceptance. However, Walker persisted, and gradually his Club brand developed a devoted following.

The area where Walker built his distillery had been a mix of rough farmland and untamed bush when he arrived. Naturally, his mill, distillery, and cluster of outbuildings attracted curious locals, and they began calling the area Walker's Town. As his business grew, Walker built accommodations nearby to house and service his workers. There was already a Walkerton in Ontario, so when the government opened a post office in Walker's Town, in 1869, they renamed it Walkerville. Among other things, Walker's distillery and other enterprises provided Walkerville residents with subsidized rents, free electricity and water, paved roads, streetlights, and fire and police services. Eventually, they also underwrote schools and a hospital. There were great benefits in working for Walker.

NEW REGULATIONS

In 1883, the government of Canada introduced the practice of bottling in bond so that distillers could defer paying taxes on whisky until they sold it. Distillers, however, were quick to see a marketing opportunity and began affixing government seals to their bottled whisky to certify its age. In 1885, the government responded with new measures that would take effect over the next five years, requiring that all whisky be aged before it was sold. Until the United States passed a similar law in 1897, Canadian whisky enjoyed an unparalleled official seal of approval.

Major distillers benefited greatly from having the government certify the age (i.e., quality) of Canadian whisky. Meanwhile, small distillers who could not afford to wait to sell their whisky went out of business. Walker had begun ageing some of his whisky as early as 1869 and had instituted ageing as a practice in 1880, so he did not bat an eye. Instead, he launched a major expansion project in 1886, and by 1890 the thriving distillery included five warehouses, enough to hold nineteen million litres of whisky. Since then, several further expansions have brought an initial output of 2,700 litres a day to annual production in the neighbourhood of thirty-six million litres.

THE MYSTERIOUS WILLIAM ROBINS

In the spring of 1888, Walker hired a mysterious figure named William Robins to help manage the distillery's finances. With an eye on the firm's increasing debt load, in 1890 Robins recommended incorporating the business, with Hiram Walker and his three sons as equal partners. He was also instrumental in convincing the Bank of Commerce to assume an $800,000 loan that the Bank of Montreal had called in. Details are scarce, and though Robins saved the day, this severely strained his friendship with Hiram Walker, and it was only on the urging of Walker's sons that Robins remained with the firm. Finally, following disagreements with Edward C. Walker, he left in 1912. Then Edward died in 1915, and Robins returned in a failed bid to challenge Hiram Walker's will. The family's disenchantment with him over this is almost certainly why his past contributions to the firm go unrecognized.

Walker's Canadian successes extended beyond whisky to include lumbering, farming, oil and gas, a hotel, steamships, and railways. To shorten his commute, he also built and ran a ferry between Walkerville and Detroit that soon emerged as yet another profitable business. Not content with his success in Canada, in

1864, when he moved back to Detroit, Walker opened another short-lived vinegar factory, then turned to the newspaper business. However, through it all, making whisky remained his primary interest.

CANADIAN CLUB

Hiram Walker is best remembered for his distillery, and particularly its Canadian Club whisky. He is credited as the first Canadian distiller to blend powerful flavouring whiskies from a pot still with lighter corn whiskies from a continuous still. As Molson's distillery, Gooderham & Worts, and others had done before him, Walker installed pot stills and wooden continuous stills heated with steam. But whether that was Walker's idea remains uncertain. Although he was an experienced rectifier, Walker never distilled whisky in Detroit and may not have had the skills to do so. In 1863, distillation in Walkerville was the responsibility of William McManus. Those original wooden stills are long gone. Walker's successors rebuilt much of the distillery in the 1950s and 1960s, and early in the 21st century, Kentucky's Vendome Copper & Brass Works recreated a large copper pot still from the 1930s that had finally worn out.

Walker's Club whisky first came on the market in 1882, and, as the legend goes, was made famous in the United States when distillers there attempted to tarnish its name by petitioning their government to force Walker to label his product as Canadian. However, the whisky was so distinctive, the plan backfired, and American customers just bought more Canadian whisky, boosting sales for Walker—and for other Canadian distillers, too. This, they say, was a true testament to Walker's marketing acumen. However, the lore of whisky is built on an oral tradition that sometimes lacks hard evidence. So it is in this case. Despite considerable research, no documentary evidence of an actual petition or the resulting regulations has ever been found. Furthermore, in 1886, Walker managed to sell just 616 cases of his Club whisky in the US. In 1889, this quadrupled to 3,156 cases for Canadian Club. Impressive, but still minuscule compared with what American distillers were selling—or, for that matter, Walker's other whiskies. In 1890, sales of Canadian Club grew slightly, to 4,817 cases. Even the most paranoid US distiller could not have felt threatened. Walker did add the word *Canadian* to his Club whisky in 1888, but not to his better-selling brands. Some American distillers adopted it, though, hoping to polish the image of their own products. In truth, there was no law requiring Canadian distillers to include the word *Canadian* on their labels until the 1950s, and even then, it had no impact on sales. Canadian Club remains a coveted favourite to this day.

Without question, Walker was an innovator and fiercely protective of his reputation. He was the first Canadian distiller to sell whisky in bottles, a practice he instituted as early as 1882 to ensure that his customers always knew what they were buying. However, canny counterfeiters in the US were soon selling copies of the popular Canadian Club, complete with fake Canadian government tax strips. The diminutive but feisty Walker was not prepared to sit back and watch inferior whisky damage his reputation. In 1892, at the urging of William Robins, he identified counterfeiters by name in print ads and posters and dared them to challenge him in court. None ever did. US whisky makers learned not to copy Walker's label, but the perceived superiority of Canadian whisky did inspire some to display "Canadian process" prominently on their labels. Walker was quick to point out that there was no such thing as a Canadian process, and at the time he was correct. Early distilling practices moved freely, north and south, across the border. And so it was that, thirty-five years later, the tables turned and Walker's successors obtained a court order against Lindsay Distilleries of Lindsay, Ontario, that they refrain from using the words *American Club* or *Club* for their whisky. Lindsay, incidentally, made its "whisky" from molasses.

HARRY HATCH

Hiram Walker died in January 1899, having achieved what no other Canadian distiller had done before, and only one other, Seagram, has since. He created a whisky that became a distinguished symbol of Canada and a global top seller. After Walker's death, his three sons, in turn, managed the distillery: Edward, until he died in 1915, then briefly Franklin, and in 1916, James. When James died in 1919, Hiram Walker's grandson Harrington E. Walker took charge. The third generation of Walkers, raised in luxury, lacked the founder's passion for the business. Although the firm had sold whisky to smugglers legally during the American Civil War, they felt somewhat queasy about resuming the practice during Prohibition.

While making and selling whisky was legal in Canada, in 1926 lingering temperance sentiments among polite society prompted Hiram Walker's grand-sons to sell the family business to Harry Hatch. The official story claims that they feared for their American citizenship if they sold whisky to rum-runners. However, Harrington was born in Walkerville, so he was a Canadian citizen, and both brothers had long since established themselves there, having built lavish homes in the company town. They had been in protracted negotiations to sell the distillery to Hatch's former employer and now archrival, Mortimer Davis, who owned Consolidated Distilleries (Corby), when Hatch's salesman-ship prevailed, and on December 22, 1926, he persuaded them instead to turn all the company's assets over to a consortium led by him. It was a sweet deal for Hatch. For the sum of $14 million, he and his partners acquired whisky worth more than $14 million; the distillery complex itself, worth at least that much again; plus the trademark for Canadian Club, then valued at $9 million. Under Hatch, servicing rum-runners became corporate policy, and by 1929 profits reached $4 million. However, improved law enforcement on both sides of the

Harry Hatch bought the Hiram Walker distillery during Prohibition.

border, and the devastation of the Great Depression, trimmed profits to a mere $255,000 by 1930. Legend claims that, from 1929 to 1932, more whisky evaporated from the warehouses than was sold.

Unlike Hiram Walker, Hatch kept his business affairs to himself, but he was passionate about selling whisky. Once firmly in control, Hatch moved to consolidate his distilling interests by having Hiram Walker Ltd. acquire all outstanding shares of Gooderham & Worts. In 1927, shareholders agreed to merge the two firms into a new one named Hiram Walker-Gooderham & Worts, although the two distilleries continued to operate separately. Business was booming, and in 1928 the new firm built a rack warehouse at Walkerville, adding a million and a half gallons capacity to the nine million already there and the four million in Toronto. They planned another warehouse in Walkerville, to hold 2.86 million gallons, for 1930.

In 1929, the acquisitive Harry Hatch proposed another merger, this time with Corby's, now known as Canadian Industrial Alcohol. Mortimer Davis had died recently, and Hatch had his eye on the large stocks of bourbon and American rye whiskies held by Industrial Alcohol's subsidiary, Consolidated Distilleries. The merger failed when the Davis family objected, in part over hard feelings from tactics Hatch had used to purchase Gooderham & Worts and Hiram Walker.

In 1933, Hiram Walker acquired a six-hectare site at Peoria, Illinois, and built a distillery five times the size of Walkerville, with capacity to make 2,000 barrels of 100-proof whisky a day, most of it bourbon and rye. Peoria would also bottle large volumes of mature whisky shipped in bulk from Toronto and Walkerville, at times circumventing Canadian ageing regulations. To head off any nationalist opposition in the US, WJ Hume, the president of Hiram Walker Distillery, reminded the media that Hiram Walker had been an American citizen, and more than half the parent company's stockholders lived in the United States. However, when production commenced in 1934, Peoria was selling more gin than expected, and less whisky, and the firm began looking for ways to make younger (and thus less expensive) whisky more palatable.

Late in April 1937, Hiram Walker-Gooderham & Worts finally purchased the Davis family's shares, and Hatch took control of his old rival's Canadian Industrial Alcohol Company. Hiram Walker already owned several Scottish blending houses, and that same year, it purchased the Glenburgie and Miltonduff Scotch malt distilleries and began work on a massive grain whisky plant at Dumbarton, near Glasgow. By that time, Canadian Industrial Alcohol specialized

Hiram Walker's Winfield Distillery.

in pure and denatured alcohol and magnesia insulating materials, and, through Consolidated Distilleries, bottled about 500 cases of liquor a day. It also owned Scottish blender Robert McNish & Company. Hatch was expanding rapidly beyond Canada. Before long, the firm would expand beyond distilling as well, beginning with Jordan Winery and Bright's Wines in Niagara, and Hofer Brewing in LaSalle. Soon after, oil and gas would become its primary products.

Harry Hatch had very different ideas of corporate citizenship than Hiram Walker. In 1943, he disputed about a million dollars in municipal taxes. The City of Windsor sued, Hatch and company fought back vigorously, and in 1949, the city that Hiram Walker so generously helped to build lost its case at appeal in the Supreme Court.

Harry Hatch died unexpectedly in 1946 while still in his early sixties, and the board appointed his son Clifford as a director. However, others held the reins until 1964, when Clifford was elected president. Unable to keep up with the demand for Canadian Club, Hatch's successors announced in 1960 that they had neared completion of a new bottling plant and would install new equipment in Walkerville to increase output by 20%. Altogether, they spent over $35 million on upgrades and expansions. The Hiram Walker Distillery that exists today dates primarily to modernizations undertaken in the 1950s and 1960s, and a major expansion in 2002.

Unprecedented demand for Canadian whisky led the firm to build a new distillery near Kelowna, British Columbia, in 1971. Known as the Winfield Distillery, it was intended to serve the western market for Canadian Club and other whiskies. Within a year, Winfield had secured a ten-year contract to make malt whisky for Suntory of Japan. Walker's installed two wash stills and two spirit stills, in typical Scottish fashion, and named the new add-on malt distillery Kel-Whisky. Renowned Scottish blender Robert Hicks dubbed this Canadian single malt "Glen Ogopogo," and for a couple of decades, collectors searched in vain for a bottle. It had been sold exclusively in bulk to Suntory for blending, and none was ever bottled.

Consumer preferences had begun shifting to spirits with lighter colour, taste, and strength in the mid-1960s. By 1982, Canadian whisky faced serious competition from low-margin, light American whiskies and white spirits, making the Winfield plant surplus. When Suntory did not renew its contract that year, Hiram Walker closed the plant and sold it to a fuel ethanol company. Hiram Walker had already closed its Peoria distillery in 1981, and had bought a 12% interest in white rum distiller Bacardi in 1978, along with a 20% share of Bacardi's Brampton-based FBM Distillery.

THE CONGLOMERATES

Early in 1980, Seagram made overtures to purchase Hiram Walker-Gooderham & Worts, but Walker's management was unwilling to disclose competitive information to establish a price. Then, on April 8, 1980, Hiram Walker-Gooderham & Worts sold out to Consumers Gas-Home Oil. Suddenly, the firm became Hiram Walker Resources, a subsidiary of a major energy sector player. It lasted just seven years, but if there were any whisky people left on the board, the merger changed their tone. Hiram Walker Resources still made whisky, but its focus had turned to oil and natural gas, and the firm soon boasted it was exploring for oil on "the largest land spread" of any company in western Canada. In 1983, Clifford Hatch retired, and the board appointed his son, H. Clifford Hatch Jr., a Harvard MBA, as president. In 1986, Gulf Oil tried to take over Hiram Walker Resources. High finance, it seems, was more intoxicating than whisky ever had been, and it could also lead to greater foolishness. Panicked by rumours that Gulf just wanted the oil and gas side of the business and planned to sell the distillery to Walker's arch-enemy, Seagram's, Hiram Walker's apoplectic board hived off the distillery business itself and sold it to Allied-Lyons, a food and beverage company based in Britain. The Allied board rewarded Hatch with the role of finance director for Allied-Lyons, and he moved to London, England. About four years later, the personable industrialist resigned in disgrace, having cost Allied over $300 million in miscalculated currency exchange. He was eminently well educated, but he was no Hiram Walker.

In 1994, Allied-Lyons purchased the spirits firm Pedro Domecq to become known as Allied Domecq. The new firm scored a major coup for Hiram Walker in 2002, when it acquired Malibu Rum and embarked on the largest expansion the distillery had seen in years. Malibu remains a major brand in the Corby portfolio, far outselling its whiskies, and Hiram Walker & Sons Distillery blends and bottles every drop of Malibu sold in North America.

However, even bigger changes were on the horizon, beginning in 2005, when Pernod Ricard launched a takeover bid for Allied Domecq. When the dust settled, Pernod Ricard owned the distillery that built its reputation on Canadian Club, but, to comply with competition legislation, it had not purchased the brand itself. No, when the deal was finalized, the American conglomerate Fortune Brands (now called Beam Suntory) owned that iconic brand, creating the bizarre situation where Canadian Club must now buy its whisky from a competitor, Pernod Ricard. Nothing changed except the paperwork, although the brand owners shifted quality control, bond selection for batches, research, and product development to their blending lab at Alberta Distillers. Today, Corby Spirit & Wine, a subsidiary of Pernod Ricard, manages the distillery and owns the brands that Harry Hatch brought into the company. Yet despite managerial turmoil and neglect, and efforts by current distillery staff to scrub its name from their history, Canadian Club remains one of Canada's bestselling whiskies of all time.

LEGENDARY CANADIAN CLUB

That Canadian Club has remained a strong favourite over the years has led brand managers to introduce several new versions (also called line extensions). These include twelve-year-old Small Batch Classic, 100-proof Black Label, and a twenty-year-old. An eight-year-old Canadian Club exclusive to Japan emphasizes the woody notes of the original, a six-year-old called Canadian Club 1858. About a decade ago, managers at Canadian Club stepped beyond Hiram Walker's to create a robust Canadian Club 100% Rye with whisky from Alberta Distillers.

In 2017, brand managers began releasing whisky from two dusty old bonds (batches) in their Pike Creek warehouses. The first, a forty-year-old Canadian Club, was the longest-aged Canadian whisky sold in North America. Connoisseurs went wild, particularly given that brand managers priced it so much lower than other comparably aged whiskies. Then, for the next five years, they released new versions: forty-one, forty-two, forty-three, forty-four, and finally forty-five years old, in a series they named Chronicles. If this sounds exciting, it is. However, even without these gems, Canadian Club held the record for the oldest Canadian whisky ever bottled, with a vatting of whiskies it distilled in the 1950s and bottled in 2014 for Australia. At the same time, they also released 1960s and 1970s versions of the venerable old-timer. College hangovers be damned! If you don't yet know some of Canadian Club's longer-aged versions, a wonderful tasting experience awaits—which, beginning in 2027, should include a fifty-year-old Canadian Club.

Canadian Club is still the major whisky product of the distillery Hiram Walker founded in 19th-century Windsor. However, it feels a little strange to drive past that distillery now that the doors to the gorgeous Florentine palace from which the founder conducted business in his later years are locked. Profits from Canadian Club built the distillery and the brick houses in the town that grew up around it. Canadian Club is the first Canadian whisky ever to make a

Canadian Club Chronicles Issue No. 5 Aged 45 Years
50% alc/vol | Hiram Walker

Sweet nail polish, complex barrel tones, sizzling spice, jute rope, dry hay, cooked fruit. Oak—ever-present but not overbearing. Dark fruit, ice cream. Ends on fruit, citrus pith, and oak.

Canadian Club 1950s
40% alc/vol | Hiram Walker

Oatmeal porridge with brown sugar. Vanilla, mild spices, bold wood, and bitterish tannins. Herbal tones, fruit, old books, sandalwood, and blistering spices. Sweet nail polish. Seemingly endless.

Canadian Club 1858 Original
40% alc/vol | Hiram Walker

Caramels, white pepper, and CC signature dark fruit. Prune juice, apricots, sweet marmalade, and vague tobacco notes, crispy barrel tones, soft tannins. Fades into sweet, spicy oak.

Canadian Club 1960s
40% alc/vol | Hiram Walker

Clover honey, vanilla, and pulling barrel tones. Plum pudding, nutmeg, cloves, and brisker spices. Sweet nail polish, kiwi, strawberries, poached pear, white cedar, tobacco, leather. Elegance defined.

name in the American market, opening doors for others to follow. So there is a certain melancholy that Canadian Club, the brand born and bred here more than a century and a half ago, has been relegated to the status of "customer." As if to emphasize the end of an era, the giant silo-top Canadian Club sign that had become as much an icon of Windsor as the CN Tower is of Toronto was taken down. Instead, Wiser's signs on an overhead walkway across Riverside Drive refer to the defunct and long-demolished Wiser's distillery that once made whisky more than 700 kilometres away, on the other side of the province. Yes, others may own Hiram Walker's distillery, but its heritage is the history of Canadian Club.

The strands of ownership can quickly intertwine, so let's recap: Corby Spirit & Wine, the successors to Henry Corby, now operate Walker's distillery on behalf of Pernod Ricard, which currently owns the distillery. Corby's major whisky brand is Wiser's, bought after the death of JP Wiser, and now distilled in the Walkerville plant. Walker's distillery, under Corby's, also makes the highly esteemed Gibson's line of whiskies. Canadian Club has expanded from a single bottling to nearly a dozen versions, yet the lone acknowledgement of the brand that started it all is a discreet plastic sign and closed pair of gates on the entrance to the former office of the great whisky master, Hiram Walker. Should Corby ever acquire Canadian Club, as some allude, it could reopen these gates and end the brand's term in sourced-whisky limbo, though it might also mean adapting Canadian Club's quality-first traditions to Corby's economies.

DISTILLER.   MILLER.

Joseph E. Seagram.

Waterloo, Ontario, Canada.

Seagram's Waterloo distillery.

(15)

SAM BRONFMAN
AND SEAGRAM'S

The temperance crusaders, who finally drowned out common sense in 1920s America, launched an insatiable demand for booze—any booze—that put unscrupulous wheeler-dealers on an equal footing with principled craftspeople. Money-hungry opportunists reaped enormous profits, as did whisky makers who were determined to maintain some sense of integrity. Schenley's Lewis Rosenstiel and Seagram's Samuel Bronfman both entered Prohibition selling questionable, rapidly made products, but Bronfman's thinking soon changed. While he remained silent when Rosenstiel remarked crassly, "I'm out to make money, not cultivate the public taste," when Rosenstiel later suggested Sam's preoccupation with quality was not the way to make money, Sam fired back, "It's not a question of making money. It's a question of meeting changing tastes, of setting high standards, of maintaining quality, of protecting the integrity of our brands." The two had been friends, and briefly partners, but Rosenstiel's focus on volume and Bronfman's growing preoccupation with substance ended that.

Seagram's whiskies are now synonymous with two things: unwavering quality and Samuel Bronfman. But it was twenty-five years before Bronfman's birth when Joseph E. Seagram joined the milling and distilling firm that would one day bear his name. Nineteen years old and newly married, Joseph's father, Octavius Augustus Seagram, had arrived in Galt from Wiltshire, England, in 1837. A mostly English-speaking pocket in a largely German area of Upper Canada, Galt was about 100 kilometres west of Toronto.

Octavius had left England with an ample endowment from his father and visions of owning an estate in Canada, and he quickly bought property in nearby Fisher Mills. There, on April 15, 1841, he and his wife, Amelia, had their first son, Joseph Emm, followed seventeen months later by Edward Frowde. The Seagram brothers joined other privileged boys from across Canada and the United States in attending Dr. Tassie's Galt Grammar School. Tragically, when Joseph was just seven, Octavius died, followed four years later by Amelia. Their orphaned sons were left in the care of the Anglican church. When he graduated from Dr. Tassie's School at the age of eighteen, Joseph travelled to Buffalo, New York, to study commercial law. A year later, he returned to Galt to seek employment as a bookkeeper, and before long, he was working at a local mill.

GRANITE MILLS

In 1857, while Joseph Seagram was still at Dr. Tassie's School in Galt, right next door, in the 500-person-strong German settlement of Waterloo, an Alsatian-German merchant named William Hespeler and an American-born contractor for the Grand Trunk Railway named George Randall built a steam-powered flour mill and distillery. Although they called their business Granite Mills, at first most of their income came from selling liquor and dry goods from the mill's shop.

In 1861, their four sets of millstones produced 12,000 barrels of flour and enough grist to make 2,700 barrels of whisky, for a total value of $100,000. "Can't make whisky fast enough," a census taker commented that year. With $6,000 invested in the mill and $10,000 in the distillery, it was clear that distilling was no sideline. Their fifteen workers could produce 50,000 gallons of proof spirits annually. Unlike other Upper Canadian distillers who mashed wheat, Hespeler and Randall catered to a largely German population and used rye. They called their product Alte Kornschnapps (old rye).

Business was brisk, and by 1863, Hespeler and Randall had invited Randall's brother-in-law, William Roos, to join the firm. Hespeler likely had another motive to take on Roos, as in 1864 he left for an extended visit to Europe. Before leaving, he hired none other than twenty-three-year-old Joseph E. Seagram to look after his interests. This would be a life-changing opportunity for Seagram. Hespeler had invited him to live in his house, where he met Hespeler's niece, Stephanie Erbs. In 1869, Stephanie and Joseph were married. His impending nuptials had given Seagram the inside track when, earlier that year, Hespeler decided to sell his shares in the business. Thus, Joseph E. Seagram became a partner in the new firm of George Randall & Company.

By 1875, the firm was shipping whisky to Great Britain, New York, Cleveland, Detroit, Toledo, and Chicago. The United States would become its primary market by the end of the century. In 1878, Seagram and Roos bought George Randall's interests; then, five years later, Seagram bought out Roos. He conducted business as Waterloo Distillery, but registered the firm as Joseph E. Seagram Flour Mill and Distillery. In eighteen years, he had become the sole proprietor.

With a staff of almost forty men, his mill could make a hundred barrels of flour a day, as well as grinding grist for the distillery's million-gallon annual output of whisky. Seagram fed herds of hogs and cattle in sheds adjacent to the distillery and sold leftover distillery waste to local farmers. With his market now international, he renamed Alte Kornschnapps "Seagram's Old Rye" and began bottling a white wheat whisky for sale in Quebec. In 1887, to commemorate having bought the distillery outright, Seagram introduced the first whisky distilled and matured under his sole ownership. He called it Seagram's 83. The whisky had spent four years in thirty-seven-gallon sherry casks imported from Spain. He continued using sherry casks until supplies dried up with the start of the First World War in 1914.

OTHER WAYS TO SERVE THE PUBLIC

There was a recurring pattern in the lives of Canada's first distillers: parallel to their business careers and expensive hobbies, they were drawn to political life. Like JP Wiser and Henry Corby, Seagram ran for Parliament, where he sat on the Opposition benches from 1896 to 1908 as a Conservative MP.

Also like Wiser, and later LJ McGuinness Jr., Seagram indulged his passion for horses. One of his first actions on arriving at Granite Mills in 1864 was to negotiate care and keep for a horse as part of his remuneration. Within ten years, he was racing thoroughbreds, ultimately building a winning racing stable with the best British bloodlines. His son Edward later took the Seagram stable to the greatest heights in the annals of Canadian horse racing: a string of wins at the Queen's/ King's Plate beginning in 1891. By 1935, Seagram's stables had twenty wins, and six years later the distillery introduced the black and gold ribbons—his racing colours—that for decades decorated bottles of Seagram's V.O.

When he reached seventy, Seagram decided it was time to secure the future of the business. In 1911, he invited his sons Edward and Thomas to become partners with him, and renamed the business Joseph E. Seagram & Sons. Three years later, Thomas asked distiller William Hortop for a good barrel of whisky to celebrate his marriage. The blend Hortop prepared so impressed the Seagrams that they felt they had to bring it to market. When it was first introduced to the world in March 1917, Seagram's V.O.—the meaning of the initials has been lost to time—was a ten-year-old blend rich in rye spirit. It went on to become Seagram's biggest seller.

Although he drew little attention to it, Seagram gave generously to local churches and schools, and provided the land for the Kitchener-Waterloo Hospital. His grandson, JEF Seagram, later donated Joseph's sixty-five-room house for the town to use as an orphanage.

Following Joseph's death in 1919, at age seventy-nine, his sons, Edward F., Norman, and Thomas W., continued to operate the family firm, but found it tough going. The Ontario Temperance Act of 1916 had cut into their business, and four years later, when the US implemented Prohibition, the firm again suffered badly. The Seagram brothers turned to making furniture and running a cooperage, but still, times were hard, and in 1927 they decided to take the Waterloo Distillery public. A year later, they merged their firm into Samuel Bronfman's Distillers Corporation of Montreal. And though the Seagram brothers nominally retained their power and position, it soon became clear that Sam Bronfman was really in charge.

NEW BEGINNINGS

Samuel Bronfman was born on February 27, 1889, in Bessarabia, which at the time was part of Russian Romania and is now in the republic of Moldova. Shortly after Sam's birth, his parents, Yechiel and Mindel Bronfman, fled anti-Semitic pogroms in Bessarabia and arrived in Canada with their four young children in tow. The family made their first Canadian home on the

Sam Bronfman

prairies in Wapella, in what is now Saskatchewan. Yechiel had done well as a tobacco farmer in Bessarabia, but he quickly realized he could not grow tobacco in the harsh prairie climate. So in 1892, the family moved to Brandon, Manitoba, where Yechiel sold scrap wood, frozen fish, and later horses to support them.

When Sam's brother Abe was twenty-two and another brother, Harry, was eighteen, the family bought the Anglo-American Hotel in Emerson, Manitoba. It was a profitable venture, so they added the Balmoral Hotel in Yorkton, Saskatchewan, and Sam moved there to learn the hotel business from Harry. Then, when Sam turned twenty-two, Harry and Yechiel bought Winnipeg's Bell Hotel for Sam to run on his own. Meanwhile, as penance for his gambling, Abe was banished to the Mariaggi Hotel in Port Arthur (now Thunder Bay), Ontario. Abe's gambling habit earned him Sam's lasting contempt. Harry, meanwhile, found success as a hotelier and real estate investor in Yorkton.

The Manitoba Temperance Act brought liquor sales there to a halt in 1916, and business at the Bell Hotel dropped off. Every Canadian province except Quebec implemented prohibition at one time or another, but provincial laws applied only to sales within the province. The provinces did not have the power to regulate manufacturing or transport of alcohol or its sale outside the province. Shrewdly, Abe relocated to Kenora, Ontario, from where he could readily service the Winnipeg whisky market, then moved again, this time to Montreal, to sell whisky by mail order. At about the same time, Harry Bronfman set up a bonded warehouse in Ottawa and began selling imported Scotch by mail or forwarding it to Yorkton for distribution. From his headquarters in Winnipeg, Sam set out on the road, buying and selling whisky. While he covered the country from Ottawa west, Abe did the same in the east.

OPPORTUNITY IN ADVERSITY

For nearly two years, until the end of the First World War, it was illegal to manufacture alcohol except for industrial, medicinal, and sacramental purposes. So Harry opened a new business he called the Canada Pure Drug Company in a one-storey building he erected next to the Balmoral Hotel. Sam was now shipping whisky made in Scotland and eastern Canada to his brother in Yorkton, to the tune of about $50,000 a month. But this was just the beginning.

Harry and Sam then bought ten 1,000-gallon wooden vats and a bottling machine. Suddenly, they were distillers. With 100 gallons of aged rye whisky, 318 gallons of overproof alcohol, some flavour, colour, and enough water to top it up, Harry could produce 800 gallons of whisky a day. An assortment of labels turned a single batch into a variety of brands. Their first efforts were spoiled, though, when stray metal in the vats turned the whisky black. Quality was not yet a Bronfman signature, and Harry blended it away, little by little, in future batches. When he refused to pay for the defective vats, the supplier sued him. The proceedings revealed that Harry's medicinal whisky business was worth a cool $390,000 a month, and the court ordered him to pay for the vats.

Next, Harry opened warehouses, known colloquially as "boozoriums," along the Saskatchewan border to supply rum-runners from the northern United States. It was perfectly legal for Harry to sell whisky for export. It was the customer who broke the law when they carried it into the US. Similarly, Saskatchewan boozoriums on the Alberta and Manitoba borders exported whisky legally to those provinces as well. It was profitable, and even exciting— but everything changed on October 2, 1922, when masked gunmen robbed Harry's brother-in-law, Paul Matoff, of the night's take and shot him dead in the process. Harry never really got over Matoff's death. Shortly thereafter, the federal government closed all the export warehouses.

In 1923, the Saskatchewan government took control of liquor sales in the province, and the $390,000-a-month Saskatchewan adventure was over. But the adventure wasn't yet done with Harry Bronfman. Officials charged him—without grounds, it turned out—with bribing a federal customs agent, and by the time they dropped the charges, four years later, Sam had reduced his influence substantially. In 1930, Harry was acquitted of new charges of tampering with a witness, but he never again had a prominent public role in the family business. No, from that point on, it was always Mr. Sam.

STARTING OVER—AGAIN

In the early 1920s, as provincial governments across Canada took over the sale of alcohol, Sam and Harry had a new idea. In May of 1923, the brothers bought the

Seagram's LaSalle (Montreal) distillery.

Greenbrier Distillery of Louisville, Kentucky, and had it shipped in pieces for reassembly in LaSalle, near Montreal. Harry managed the construction, and, by virtue of his experience in Yorkton, took charge of operations. The brothers, together with younger brother Allan, named their new enterprise Distillers Corporation Limited. Thus began the Bronfman quest for quality. It had become more important to be known for excellence than to make a quick dollar, and when spirit began to flow, rather than selling it, the brothers put it in warehouses to age. As Sam told biographer Terence Robertson years later, "Respect walks arm in arm with integrity. Taken together, they, not money, not position, are the true measurement of success." This ethic would make family members billionaires many times over.

Meanwhile, to keep the cash flow positive, the brothers formed a partnership with the world's largest whisky corporation, the Distillers Company of Scotland, and began importing Scotch, gaining exclusive rights to several top brands. Following their 1928 merger with Joseph E. Seagram & Sons, they named their new entity Distillers Corporation-Seagram's Ltd. Bronfman saw Prohibition as an opportunity rather than an impediment, and instead of closing Seagram's distillery, as had seemed inevitable, he increased production. One hundred and fifty men made a million gallons annually of V.O., Seagram's 83, White Wheat, Canadian Rye, Paul Jones Bourbon, and Old Quaker American Rye for thirsty Americans still coming to terms with the Volstead Act. The Seagram Distillery was now firmly in Sam Bronfman's hands, and despite Joseph E. Seagram's many successes, its best days were still ahead.

Among the greatest assets of the new firm were the Seagram's brands 83 and V.O. Mr. Sam was acutely aware of the success Walker's Canadian Club was having in the US, and made V.O. and Seagram's 83 the keystones in his growing empire. Sensing that Prohibition could not last, he correctly predicted a huge market for well-aged blended whisky, and so expanded and upgraded the

Waterloo and LaSalle Distilleries. When Prohibition finally ended in 1933, Seagram's instantly—and legally—filled American whisky bottles with mature whisky for the first time in nearly fourteen years.

In the dying days of Prohibition, Bronfman had told Rosenstiel, "I have a hunch that the masses are going to go for light blends. Look at the shops today. There's lighter foods, lighter tobacco, lighter clothes, lighter shoes, lighter coffee, lighter tea. People enjoy things on the lighter side, and I'll stake everything I've got that they will enjoy lighter whiskies." His first new whisky, an American blend called Seagram's 7 Crown, came out of his plant in Lawrenceburg, Indiana, in May 1934. He had rejected permissive US regulations that allowed him to include cheap neutral spirits in the blend, and instead followed the Canadian practice of using aged base whisky. That September, ads in nearly 200 news-papers and magazines boasted, "Thanks a million, America! You've made us #1 in sixty days." Even now, there are those who believe Seagram's 7 is Canadian whisky, but of course it is not.

By the mid-1930s, Bronfman was looking to science to make his whisky taste even better. He knew, for example, that yeast influenced the flavour. So he hired scientists to collect yeasts, then his staff tested each of the 240 strains for flavour. Most were unremarkable, but a few still contribute to former Seagram whiskies. Then, while competing distillers were working on squeezing more alcohol from their mashes, Seagram focused on flavour-rich grains, paying plant breeders to create new strains and directing his distillers to mash sorghum, unmalted barley, buckwheat, and other grains and report the results.

POMP AND CHARACTER

Even with his growing wealth, Samuel Bronfman yearned for a place in high society. An opening arose in 1939, when the three-funnelled *Empress of Australia* docked in Quebec City on May 17, and King George VI descended the gang-plank with his wife, Queen Elizabeth (later to become known as the Queen Mother). From there, they toured the country in a specially outfitted train pulled by a steam locomotive and provisioned with Crown Royal Fine De Luxe, a new whisky Bronfman had created just for them. Blended from whiskies as old as thirty-five years and billed as whisky fit for royalty, it was packaged in a purple flannelette bag hand-sewn by Bronfman's sister-in-law. While the royal couple did not comment publicly on the whisky, when the emir of the British protectorate Katsina later visited London, an aide was spotted paying his bills with cash dispensed from one of those bags.

One hundred cases of Crown Royal Fine De Luxe, shipped to liquor stores across Canada, sold briskly for $4.30 to $4.90 a bottle. This was when a top whisky such as V.O. cost $3.25, Seagram's 83 went for $2.95, and Seagram's Special Old a mere $2.50. When the royal couple returned home, Seagram's bought back any bottles the liquor stores had not sold, then re-released it in time for Christmas. It became a Canadian staple. Although Crown Royal showed up occasionally in commissaries at US military bases, and Seagram's released a batch of 18,000 cases in New York City for Christmas 1961, the firm waited twenty-five years before making it available across the United States. Bronfman wanted to be sure Seagram's had enough long-aged whisky to meet demand without sacrificing quality. He may also have been conflicted. Some of the same component whiskies used for Crown Royal were also needed for his sentimental favourite, V.O., which already had strong sales in the US. Crown Royal is now the bestselling Canadian whisky in the world, the second-bestselling whisky of any kind in North America, and it outsells the next six top-selling Canadian whiskies combined—none of which, incidentally, were ever Schenley's.

A SILKEN GOWN

During Prohibition, Bronfman had taken pains to make sure that Seagram's whisky bore no resemblance to others' Prohibition hooch. The success of Seagram's 7 only made him more determined to put Prohibition-era instant whisky behind him. His need to erase any memory of his Prohibition beginnings became an unrelenting obsession to establish a new reputation based not on himself, but on the quality of his products. To him, V.O. became "a silken gown," to be admired by carriage-trade consumers for its uncompromising attention to detail—not just the whisky, but its packaging, too. But the liquid was what mattered most. Working out of Waterloo, Seagram's chief blender, Roy E. Martin, maintained the flavour profile from batch to batch, blending component whiskies from Waterloo and LaSalle, with a bit from Amherstburg and New Westminster. Volumes were huge, and growing, so Martin had the components and the current formula sent to LaSalle, Waterloo, and New Westminster for blending and bottling.

As Martin's protege, and later Seagram's chief blender, Art Dawe, explains, they weren't held to a set number of whiskies to use in V.O. "We had a flavour we wanted to maintain. If it took forty, fifty whiskies, so be it," he says. "Mr. Sam always took a deep interest in V.O., no doubt in my mind; Edgar, too." Edgar, who was Sam's eldest son and ultimately his successor, was initiated to the specs of V.O. in October 1952, when, as a twenty-three-year-old learning his father's business, he was sent to work with Roy Martin. They were in LaSalle, ramping up for the busy Christmas season, when Edgar, thinking Martin looked very ill, called Sam in New York and suggested he send Martin home to recuperate; Edgar would handle the blending. Then, to his horror, Edgar discovered that a 25,000-case batch of V.O. did not match the standard. He immediately called Sam, who simply told him to fix it and hung up. Edgar shut down the bottling plant and, after a weekend spent unravelling the problem, had it ready for Monday morning bottling. Sam never forgot his son's initiative.

THE BRONFMAN EMPIRE

Although ownership was shared, Sam Bronfman was the president of the company, and on the force of his personality, Distillers Corporation-Seagram's Ltd. rapidly became his personal enterprise. He alone made almost all the important decisions, including buying up distilleries in the States. He started in 1933, with the Rossville Union plant in Lawrenceburg. Next came the Maryland Distillery in Relay, Maryland, where they were bottling raw alcohol as Lord Calvert American blended whisky. Bronfman put a quick stop to that practice, shipping well-aged Canadian whisky to Relay to bolster the blend until supplies of mature US-distilled whisky became available. The acquisitions continued until Seagram's owned thirteen distilleries in the US.

Late in the 1930s, Bronfman acquired the Jordan Wine Company. That was the beginning of even greater diversification to come. Over the next few years, the distillery acquisitions continued, the best-known being Kentucky's Frankfort Distilling Company (Four Roses), in 1943. At about the same time, he purchased the Reifels' British Columbia Distillery Company, and with that came the Amherst distillery in Amherstburg, Ontario, and, later, United Distillers Ltd. (UDL) of Vancouver. By 1945, the Amherstburg distillery was the home of the Calvert Canadian and V.O. brands. Still thirsty for blending components, in 1955, Seagram's bought the Montmorency Distillery in Beaupré, Quebec, and expanded its maturing capacity.

To increase shelf space in liquor stores and competition within the company, Bronfman introduced the Thomas Adams brands, headquartered at UDL in Vancouver, under the leadership of his other son, Charles. Meanwhile, Edgar took the lead with the Calvert line. To differentiate them from the other Seagram brands, which had distinctive bourbon notes, Adams featured rye, while Calvert was a synthesis of the two.

Seagram's fortunes in the United States called for a landmark building there. When Sam shared the early plans with his hard-headed and creative daughter, Phyllis Lambert, her withering dismissal convinced him to turn the entire project over to her. In 1952, the company engaged architect Mies van der Rohe to design and build a headquarters suitable for the House of Seagram. The stunningly beautiful thirty-eight-storey, bronze-clad tower he built sits amid pools and fountains at 375 Park Avenue in New York City. The interior and the decor, also under Lambert's control, made an equally favourable impression on all who entered the building, reflecting the same aura of quality that Sam sought in his whiskies.

Success in the US was overshadowed by tensions back in Canada when, in 1953, Bronfman decided to replace the Waterloo Distillery and Amherstburg-based Calvert Distillery with a single new plant in Oakville, Ontario. The atmosphere was charged when Bronfman, the feared, heartless businessman, eventually visited the old Seagram plant in Waterloo and fell in love with it. In the late 1960s, when Seagram's finally built a new modern distillery in Gimli, Manitoba, to make V.O., it continued making Crown Royal in Waterloo. Despite propping up the deteriorating Waterloo plant, in 1965 Seagram's became the first Canadian company to clear the billion-dollar-a-year sales hurdle.

Seagram's also expanded internationally, branching into foreign-made vodka, gin, rum, wine, and other products. By 1970, the firm was a publicly held corporation with 20,000 shareholders and 15,210 employees. The company owned a total of thirty-nine distilleries around the world, seven of them in Canada. In addition to Crown Royal, V.O., and a host of other Canadian whiskies, their brands included the Glenlivet and Chivas Regal Scotch whiskies, Mumm Champagne, and a number of other household names. Later, in 1987, Seagram's bought the French cognac maker Martell & Compagnie for $1.2 billion.

Although he remained president of the parent firm until the end, in 1957 Sam appointed his son Charles as president of Seagram's in Canada, while his other son, Edgar, became president of the US operation. When Sam Bronfman died in 1971, full leadership of the company passed to Edgar, who proved to be a steady hand, and profits continued to grow. In 1975, Edgar changed the business name to the Seagram Company.

In the 1970s, the company's original Waterloo Distillery remained a going concern, paying $4 million in wages to some 250 employees. It spent $6 million on supplies and processed 650,000 bushels of Ontario Essex County corn annually to generate an annual income of $60 million, on which it paid over $800,000 in local business taxes. In 1978, there were 570,493 barrels of whisky ageing in its warehouses, but the old distillery needed repair and the city was encroaching on all sides. When the bottom fell out of the international whisky market in the late 1970s and early 1980s, it forced Seagram to consolidate most of its operations in Gimli and close other plants.

Waterloo was on borrowed time even as the company struggled to keep the historic plant in operation. In 1990, amid declining sales, high taxes, and limited expansion opportunities, the axe fell. The last barrels rolled off the Waterloo line in November 1992, and not ten months later, the silent distillery was razed by fire. A community icon was gone. All that remains today is a rack house, now used for offices, and a few other warehouses converted to condominiums.

In 1994, Edgar Bronfman passed the company to his son, Edgar Jr., in a move that was the beginning of another kind of end. Sam Bronfman had a prophetic saying: "Shirt sleeves to shirt sleeves in three generations." Edgar Jr., who had been raised in luxury, had no passion for the spirits business. Rather, he had his sights set on Hollywood. In the 1980s, Seagram's had tried to buy an oil company, and ended up owning a major stake in the DuPont chemical company. When Edgar Jr. took control, DuPont was Seagram's largest profit centre. To finance his purchase of Universal Studios, MCA, PolyGram, Deutsche Grammophon, and several theme parks, Edgar Jr. sold Seagram's stake in DuPont for $9 billion. It was a death blow to the company, culminating in the year 2000 with the sale of the once-mighty firm to Vivendi. Pernod Ricard quickly took over the beverage division, marking the break with the Bronfman family and Seagram's. Still, certain brand names and several distilleries remain.

In 2001, Diageo acquired the Seagram name and portfolio from Pernod Ricard, and in 2008 it purchased the Valleyfield Distillery from US-based Constellation Brands and began distilling components for Seagram's brands there. Crown Royal is now distilled in Diageo plants in Gimli, Manitoba, and Valleyfield, Quebec, and by 2025 Diageo's fourth Crown Royal facility will be capable of producing 5.7 million proof litres a year, on 160 hectares in St. Clair Township near Sarnia, Ontario. Seagram's Crown Royal Fine De Luxe, the jewel in Mr. Sam's crown, is now simply called Crown Royal Fine De Luxe. The brand remains a leader in innovation, with regular high-end and connoisseur additions to the line and an innovation centre established in the enlarged Valleyfield Distillery.

Mr. Sam's volcanic temper would undoubtedly erupt to learn that Valleyfield, once owned by his friend-cum-archrival Lewis Rosenstiel, today makes Crown Royal. Sam ultimately came to detest Rosenstiel, accusing him, among other things, of stealing his trademark Seagram's "S." The former Calvert plant in Amherstburg now bottles Crown Royal, while fifty-millilitre minis are filled in Plainfield, Illinois. Special bottles and 1.75-litre "handles" see glass in Valleyfield.

THE LEGACY OF MR. SAM

The story of the Bronfman family, like that of so many families, has many layers. Sam, it appears, was the brains and driving force behind the family fortune, and over time Seagram's evolved to become "his" business. He could be foul-mouthed, cruel, and ruthless at times, yet he inspired loyalty, respect, and perhaps even love in those who knew him well. His brothers and sisters and their

Mister Sam
66.9% alc/vol | Old Montreal

Massive, dynamic, singular, venerable, grand. Lush and full, with sweet black fruit, roses, maple, mash, earth, tannic tugs, and chocolate, all from a cedar-lined oak humidor.

Seagram's 83
40% alc/vol | Old Montreal

Muted maple syrup, butterscotch. Bright, glowing pepper. Underlying citrus pith, herbal tones, and mild oak. Balanced and interwoven with toasted oak, flinty rye, soft caramels, candied ginger, and oak tannins.

Seagram's VO
40% alc/vol | Old Montreal

Floral, lush, with slight oaky pull, waves of peppery heat, ginger, cooked corncobs, freshwater plants, cedar, and oak. Slightly sweet, with blazing peppermint, grain dust, and classic grapefruit pith.

Seagram's VO Gold
40% alc/vol | Old Montreal

Lush feel underlies citrus pith, glowing cayenne, gingerbread, floral tones, grassy herbs, clean wood, burnt wood, and sponge candy. Fair complexity. Longish, drying finish with crispy oak.

families benefited financially from Seagram's success, and left to pursue business interests elsewhere; they, too, succeeded abundantly. Still, while solicitously loving to his wife and as unquestioningly supportive of his children as a mostly absent father can be, for a while, Sam grew distant from his siblings.

Without question, Mr. Sam was one of the most brilliant business-people Canada has ever known, and perhaps will ever know. Moreover, he was principled and determined, and above all, he really knew good whisky and how to make it. He created one of the best-loved whiskies of all time, Crown Royal Fine De Luxe, and was undoubtably one of the greatest whisky men who ever lived. Yet, despite this enormous success, his pride in hobnobbing with the elite and his dreams of a royal warrant—if not a seat in Canada's Senate—speak of man who still needed to be acknowledged by others.

Self-centred, yes, but never greedy or selfish, he was remarkably generous, particularly in Montreal's Jewish community, where he used substantial amounts of his own money to seed fundraising campaigns for Jewish charities and for the State of Israel. Various business ventures by family members, many in real estate, still keep the Bronfmans much more than solvent. In the whisky world, though, the family has become little more than the fading memory of a most remarkable saga, largely because his descendants let the business slip through their fingers. Nonetheless, to say Sam Bronfman's influence on Canadian whisky and its history is without match would please him, and it would not be an exaggeration.

Left to right: Three Reifel generations—George H., George C., and Henry Reifel at George C.'s home, Casa Mia in Vancouver.

(16)

THE REIFEL FAMILY:
VANCOUVER AND BEYOND

William Braid left his home in Kirknewton, Scotland, in 1872 and headed for Canada, arriving in Hamilton, Ontario, with two assets: a knowledge of the wholesale grocery trade learned from his father and remarkable personal stamina. Although known occasionally to show off his exceptional physical strength, the shy and unsocial twenty-year-old applied himself tirelessly to his work, eschewing a family life and friendships for business. Having travelled west several times, in 1892 he settled in the lively port city of Vancouver, where he sold groceries and later imported tea and coffee.

BRITISH COLUMBIA DISTILLERY COMPANY

It was May 1903 when a now-wealthy Braid and five well-to-do partners sought water concessions from the city so that they could build a modern distillery. With distilling equipment en route and still no water agreement, the investors lost patience in 1904 when the city requested yet another meeting. Giving up on Vancouver, they purchased 1.7 hectares in the Sapperton neighbourhood of nearby New Westminster, on Brunette Avenue between Pipeline Road (renamed Braid Street in 1909) and the Brunette River. Their British Columbia Distillery Company was producing pharmaceutical spirits by 1905. Nine years later, the plant processed nearly sixteen tonnes of wheat and rye daily and was maturing about 100 barrels of whisky on the side. From time to time, Braid would publicly remind Vancouver how much his distillery contributed to New Westminster's economy.

While the province had banned the sale of alcohol in 1917, production was still allowed until the spring of 1918, when Prime Minister Robert Borden, by order-in-council, effectively shut down beverage alcohol distillation across Canada. Borden's order expired twenty-one months later, on January 1, 1920, and by 1921 British Columbians had also given sober second thought to prohibition. Less than four years after the province of British Columbia turned off the taps, they were flowing again. But nothing is simple in public policy. Just as BC decided to end its dismal experiment with prohibition, the United States banned the manufacture, transportation, and sale of alcohol there. With their usual posturing, witless American legislators created an extraordinary business opportunity for Canadian distillers willing to turn a blind eye (or possibly not) to where their product might end up. Well-connected Canadian whisky distillers had had a year's notice, and they moved quickly to replace dwindling US supplies. However, Borden's order-in-council had put the BC Distillery into receivership, and because it focused on pharmaceutical and non-potable spirits, it did not have US contacts to help it join the bonanza.

William Braid had been a man of robust good health until he suffered a stroke in 1922. Still a bachelor, he vacated his lodgings at the Vancouver Club and moved to a suite at the Hotel Vancouver. His death on January 28, 1924, was not the end of the BC Distillery, though. The previous April, Braid had sold his idle plant to Henry Reifel and his sons, George C. and Henry F. (also known as Harry). But who were these Reifels?

THE REIFELS

The Reifel distilling legacy began with German-Alsatian brewmaster Heinrich E. (Henry) Reifel. Henry had not originally set out to make rye. Rather, as he had done in San Francisco and Portland, he began brewing beer in Nanaimo shortly after arriving in BC in 1888, and by 1933 he claimed 48% of Vancouver's beer market. His sons George and Harry were also prominent brewers until October 1917, when the government of British Columbia, yielding to temperance agitators, prohibited the sale of beverage alcohol in the province. In the shadow of uncertainty this cast over their business, the Reifels packed up their kit and moved to Japan to establish the Anglo-Japanese Brewing Company, making beer from rice. Japan is likely where they learned to convert grain starches to fermentable sugars using the *Aspergillus awamori* fungus. This process would later revolutionize rye distilling in Canada.

Having purchased Braid's plant shortly after they returned from Japan, the family seized the opportunity that government concessions on ageing afforded them. Before the year was out, the Reifels had the BC Distillery working again, making just whisky now and supplemented their stocks with alcohol recovered in their Vancouver Brewery while converting full-strength beer into 1% "near beer." Soon, they introduced the popular BC Double Distilled Canadian Whisky. (Reifel's Prohibition-era bottling had no age statement. Later, as spirits that had been distilled by Braid matured, it was released as an eleven-, then a twelve-, and, by 1936, a sixteen-year-old Canadian rye.) Working with British investors during Prohibition, they consolidated their operations into a holding company called Brewers & Distillers Ltd., and for the American trade, they formed a business called Pacific Forwarding that operated a fleet of ocean-going vessels. They delivered such BC Distillery–made brands as Coon Hollow and Old Colonel Bourbons and Old Pitt and Four Aces American Rye to American bootleggers through various transit points in Mexico, South America, and the South Pacific. Before long, Pacific Forwarding was also exporting whisky on behalf of Distillers Corporation-Seagram's Ltd. and Hiram Walker & Sons. During this time, they each amassed sizable fortunes supplying West Coast rum-runners in the service of "American drought relief."

Details are sketchy at best—the West Coast rum-runner's credo, "Don't never tell nobody nothin', no how," was rarely broken. However, in 1992, Fraser Miles, a hand on Harry Reifel's boat, the *Ryou II*, published a book called *Slow Boat on Rum Row*. In it, he describes delivering tens of thousands of cases of Vancouver-made whisky to buyers in American West Coast communities from Puget Sound to Baja California. Locals dubbed this area "Liquor Lane" or "Rum Row," just as people on the Eastern Seaboard did their coastal waters.

REIFELS IN AMHERSTBURG

Even as the Reifels were building their West Coast empire, they also wanted to tap into the lucrative trade in eastern Canada. As early as 1923, they hired thirty-year-old William Massey of the Windsor, Ontario, suburb of LaSalle as an agent for the BC Distillery. Massey later took a lead role in establishing their modern distillery on 6.5 hectares on the Detroit River in nearby Amherstburg. On June 12, 1928, the Reifels' lawyers announced that construction would begin within weeks on a $300,000 distillery with capacity to make 4,500 gallons of whisky daily. Until it was up and running, the Reifels shipped large volumes of BC Distillery whisky there for bottling.

Leslie Abbott, whom they appointed the construction engineer, had built Seagram's distillery in LaSalle, Quebec, six years earlier and knew that Prohibition meant not having to start from scratch. Instead, he purchased distilling equipment and three 8-storey metal warehouses from a closed distillery in Kentucky and brought in cypress fermenters from another in Illinois. He also had the Michigan Central Railway lay a spur line on the property and began digging a tunnel to deliver distillery waste to the St. Clair River and whisky to a portable steel dock. He abandoned the tunnel when it collapsed, killing a worker. The plant opened in 1929 with the name Pioneers Distillers (unsurprising, as the Reifel patriarch proudly regarded himself a Canadian pioneer) and a staff of fifty, including about thirty women, who bottled whisky shipped in from British Columbia.

The Reifels had planned to take advantage of Prohibition opportunities in the east, as they were doing already in the west. However, several events conspired against them. First, a 1928 Ontario provincial ruling closed the export docks integral to rum-running, putting many potential bootleg customers out of business. Then, the arrival of the Great Depression in 1929 further shrank the market for whisky. However, the US repealed Prohibition on December 5, 1933, and within a month, the distillery was shipping large volumes of BC-distilled American-style rye and bourbon to Peoria, Illinois, legally, for rectifying, blending, and bottling. Still, Amherst, as the plant was then called, did not achieve its distilling potential until after 1941, when Seagram's bought the Reifels' distilling interests and Amherst came with the package. Seagram's soon renamed the distillery Calvert.

BC Distillery Double Distilled
abv not stated | British Columbia Distillers (defunct)

Big, fruity rye spices, soft maple fudge, creamy and lush. White pepper, clean oak, and toasted fruitwood. Long-fading glow finishes slightly sweet and oaky, with classic bitter grapefruit pith.

United Distillers Old Rye
abv not stated | United Distillers (defunct)

Massive, bright, fresh, and exquisitely distinctive. Infinite fragrance. Burnt fruitwood, balsam, lumber, sweetest prunes and figs, tannic, well-tempered barrel tones. Long, peppery spice, nail polish, cooked corncob, monster rye.

Carrington
40% alc/vol | Alberta Distillers

Fudge, barley sugar, almost molasses, soft white peppers turning hot. Milled cedar, caramel, grapey fruit. Soon fades sweetly into pleasing pithy bitterness with fruit and oaky overtones.

Coincident with Seagram's takeover, wartime production of industrial alcohol had the distillery running at full capacity for the first time. However, Seagram's promising start was interrupted in July 1942 by a fire that consumed the distillery. Management rushed to rebuild, and had the business back in operation within six months. Disaster hit again in August 1950, when grain dust exploded, levelling the plant. This time, it was six years before full production resumed. By 1970, the distillery needed another bottling hall to keep up with US demand for Seagram's V.O. Nonetheless, declining whisky sales worldwide in the 1970s led to a seven-month layoff in 1977 before labour unrest affecting the distilling industry broadly during this era closed the facility entirely in 1979. Current owner Diageo now uses it exclusively to bottle Canada's bestselling whisky, Crown Royal.

Phenomenal demand for Crown Royal in recent years has finally given the Amherstburg plant an opportunity to shine. To keep pace with sales, Amherstburg site director Josh Reit added a night shift in 2020, and replaced two ageing bottling lines with a seventh capable of filling four million cases a year. Housed in a separate 3,700-square-metre building, as large as some distilleries, twelve operators, three warehouse workers, and two mechanics keep Line 7 running twenty-four hours a day, five days a week. "Our biggest constraint is mature whisky," says Reit. "The youngest whisky in Crown Royal, even the flavours, is at least five years old."

Notwithstanding that, between eight and twelve railcars and two to six tanker trucks arrive each day with whisky ready for final blending in one of thirty-four blending tanks. The tanks, incidentally, are sized to hold a railcar load at a time. Semi-trailers, 250 to 300 of them, bring in bottles and materials, and, after it is bottled, take packaged whisky to distribution centres across North America. Reit keeps at least 600,000 cases on hand, ready for shipment. It's hard to know who would be prouder of Amherstburg: the Reifels, who built it, or Sam Bronfman, whose whisky has demonstrated the plant's capabilities.

UNITED DISTILLERS LIMITED

And what became of the Reifels' BC plant? Distillers Corporation-Seagram's Ltd. purchased it in 1941 and continued producing Reifel's popular BC Double Distilled brand. They also began blending and bottling key Seagram's whiskies, such as V.O. Significant changes had been in store for both the New Westminster distillery and the industry at large, beginning with the 1925 establishment of United Distillers Ltd. (UDL), which the British Columbia Distillery went on to acquire nearly thirty years later.

UDL had arrived as a rumour in December 1924. Within six weeks, architects had let contracts to build a half-million-dollar plant on a 2.6-hectare Point Grey property. Early in April 1925, workers began driving foundation piles near the banks of the north arm of the Fraser River and outfitting the plant with distilling equipment from Kentucky distilleries forced to close by Prohibition. By November 1925, a staff of twenty-five had begun operations.

The owners invested another $1.5 million over the following four months to equip it to turn twenty tonnes of grain each day into American bourbon and rye (from mixed mashes), Canadian rye whisky (blended), and gin. Even then, the distinction between American and Canadian rye was well established. With its philosophy of BC first, Canada next, the firm purchased wheat and rye in British Columbia, bringing in malted barley from Alberta and corn from the US via its rail spur. Its spirits matured in oak barrels made at Sweeney Cooperage in Vancouver, and workers shipped them out via rail and from company docks on the Fraser. They also made enough feed each day for about 1,600 cattle.

Launched during American Prohibition, UDL could have expected some choppy waters, and president Russell Whitelaw was comfortable in that environment. President of Western Canners, a director and partner with Henry

Reifel and others in Consolidated Exporters, a director of various enterprises in warehousing and shipping, and an accused Pacific Rum Row bootlegger, Whitelaw spent his entire career two steps ahead of the law. Managing director Isadore J. "Hickey" Klein, vice-president George W. Norgan, and secretary-director AL "Big Al" McLennan had similar proclivities. Apparently, treasurer Nathan Bell did not.

Beyond the distillery proper, the campus soon filled in with a granary and elevators holding 760 tonnes, a dry house producing nearly 4.5 tonnes of cattle feed daily, three rack warehouses with room for 50,000 barrels in all, and bottling and shipping facilities. With 110 staff and business booming, in 1928, management purchased an adjoining 2.6 hectares to build more rack houses and a new distillery plant. By 1936, 130 UDL staff were turning twenty-five tonnes of grain into ninety barrels of whisky daily.

At UDL's annual general meeting on March 26, 1934, three and a half months after Prohibition ended, managing director Hickey Klein reported that the previous year had been a busy one. Sales were up 60% in Canada, and the firm had purchased John Dunbar & Co. Scotch blenders and bottlers of London, England, a 50% interest in Potomac Distilling of Baltimore, Maryland, and a New York City–based import company. As well, it had trademarked the letters UDL for whisky and gin in the US and planned to build a new 16,000-gallon-a-day plant, to be called Big 4 Distilleries, at Dundalk, just outside Baltimore. Clearly, UDL was surging, and within three years, it reported sales in such far-flung places as Ecuador, Fiji, Guyana, Hong Kong, Honolulu, Jamaica, Japan, Manila, Newfoundland, New Zealand, Shanghai, Trinidad, the United States, and Yukon. Expansion in Canada came in May of 1939 with the purchase of the defunct Dunrobin Distillery in Grimsby, Ontario.

BUYING DUNROBIN

In the forty years leading up to 1930, the nondescript two-storey building at the corner of Oak and Elm Streets in Grimsby, Ontario, had already housed, among other things, a hockey rink, a rubber company, and, briefly, a circus. So no one raised an eyebrow when George MacKay Sutherland outfitted it that year to distil brandy from Niagara Concord grapes and renamed it Dunrobin Distillery. Six years later, when the government reduced excise duties from $4 to $3 a gallon, general manager EC Walsh announced the firm would proceed with Sutherland's grand plans to enlarge the plant. Unfortunately, this was not to be. Instead, the firm entered bankruptcy in 1939 and a trustee sold it off in pieces.

McGuinness Distillery in Mimico purchased the distilling equipment and inventory, while United Distillers Ltd. bought the land and buildings. UDL then moved its Montreal-based eastern bottling plant into the Dunrobin building and began shipping large volumes of whisky from Vancouver and abroad to Dunrobin for bottling. By 1948, it was exporting whisky and gin to forty-eight countries.

The first real inklings of trouble at UDL emerged in 1952, when US tax officials claimed directors Klein, McLennan, and Norgan had parlayed a $4,000 investment into $20 million through "a mushrooming set of paper corporations, chartered in Cuba and Panama." The situation worsened when Netta Bell, the widow of former treasurer Nathan Bell, launched a suit against UDL, its three directors, and several subsidiaries for $2.5 million in damages. She claimed they had not disclosed the massive profit and used deception to persuade her husband's estate to sell its shares, then set up "a sham and dummy corporation" to protect the $20 million windfall.

On June 26, 1953, the board sold United Distillers of Canada, United Distillers Ltd., John Dunbar & Company, Duncan Harwood & Company, and the Dunrobin Distillery to BC Distillery, by then a subsidiary of Distillers Corporation-Seagram's Ltd. of Montreal. They valued the assets at between $8 million and

$15 million, with the final price to be set after an independent audit. Four days later, Mrs. Bell won a $3.5 million judgment against the company and its directors. Nonetheless, legal wrangling would drag the case through the courts, attracting two more claimants along the way, while company officials refused to answer questions that "might tend to incriminate the company, myself, or others."

By late 1957, the claim had ballooned to $7.5 million when the parties reached an out-of-court settlement of $1,123,000. The claimants withdrew charges of fraud or misconduct, and the company began steps to wind up its affairs. That would have been the end of it had a backbench politician not sensed an opportunity to grandstand, and demanded a probe by Canadian tax officials. His bid failed, but it put the windup in abeyance. During this delay, the estate of another shareholder

Dunrobin Rye Whiskey label.

launched a new suit and requested an injunction preventing UDL from distributing its assets. Six months later, still another shareholder sued, and in 1959, the two shared a $450,000 settlement. As if that were not enough, in October 1963, the US government obtained a federal court judgment against McLennan for $15,287,861. He denied the charges and fought them vociferously, though he declined to travel to the US. Big Al McLennan might have chuckled as he drew his final breath on May 26, 1968, never having paid a nickel.

Finally, on September 11, 1979, United Distillers (1953) Ltd. served notice that it would surrender its charter, direct its cancellation, and fix a date when the firm would be dissolved. The private and unsurprisingly taciturn enterprise had brought welcome employment to Vancouver and staggering wealth to the local businessmen who founded it, then had itself staggered, this time into oblivion, having failed to abandon Prohibition-era business ethics when Prohibition ended.

Meanwhile, the demise of the British Columbia Distillery became certain in May 1975 when, amid plummeting demand for whisky worldwide, the workers' union called a strike. Eventually, this led provincial liquor officials to withdraw Seagram's products from liquor stores. As a diversified company, Seagram's remained profitable despite falling whisky sales. However, many distillers had begun closing plants and consolidating operations. Management kept BC Distillery open, in part, by bottling Seagram's bestselling brands for western distribution. The downturn likely would have closed the distillery anyway, as eventually Seagram's consolidated its seven distilleries into three. Nostalgic workers later recalled high-paying jobs and pensions that had been among the best in the industry globally. BC Distillery had made beautiful whisky, and, under Seagram's management, had developed a robust export market. Nevertheless, a last-ditch revival effort in 1978 failed, and the final barrel rolled off the line on January 24, 1979. The distillery never reopened for regular production and was largely demolished in 1981.

THE REIFELS' ALBERTA REPRISE

What of the Reifels throughout all this? After America repealed Prohibition, the US government charged several family members with tax evasion, and their nervous British shareholders insisted the family divest itself of its interests in Brewers & Distillers Ltd. Then, in 1941, the firm sold the Reifels' distilleries to Sam Bronfman's Distillers Corporation-Seagram's Ltd. Meanwhile, the Reifels shifted gears, investing generously in corporate Vancouver, building a theatre and donating land on West Georgia Street for the city's first art gallery and in the Fraser delta for a migratory bird sanctuary. However, when Calgary came calling in 1946, the family opened its knowledge banks and its chequebook to establish Alberta Distillers, with George C.'s son, George Henry Reifel, taking the lead—more on that in chapter 19.

In 1964, US-based National Distillers bought the distillery and appointed George Henry to its board as director of Alberta Distillers—before learning that George served its products in a restaurant he owned in Palm Desert, California. Perceiving this as a conflict of interest, they insisted he sell the restaurant. Dismayed that his long-time colleagues on the board did not come to his aid, Reifel resigned in a bitter departure. Charlie Wills took over the chairmanship of the distillery, and a third generation of Reifels retired from whisky.

But this is still not the end of the Reifels and whisky. In 2022, current Alberta Distillers owners Beam Suntory contacted the eldest son from a fourth generation of the family, a man named (what else?) George C. Reifel, for permission to restore the family crest to their packaging. George smiles when he recalls the heady aromas of mash and his father approving spirits samples. The Reifel family did not ask for payment. Instead, Beam Suntory quietly made a donation to the George C. Reifel Migratory Bird Sanctuary near Vancouver.

Red Wheat Whisky was long Royal Distillery's leading brand.

(17)

LOST DISTILLERIES

ROYAL DISTILLERY, HAMILTON

Every generalization about Canadian whisky has its exception. Take Benjamin E. Charlton's Hamilton Distillery Company, for example. Unlike almost all of Canada's early distillers, who began as millers, brewers, or both, Charlton started out making vinegar.

BE Charlton was born in Brant County, Ontario, on April 12, 1835, the son of English and American immigrants. His paternal family was prominent in English society, leading to Benjamin's education in Toronto to become a teacher and, at thirty-two, celebrate Canada's 1867 Confederation as the well-heeled mayor of Hamilton, Ontario. By 1883, he had established the Hamilton Vinegar Works; its prosperity led to an extension that became known as the Royal Distillery.

Perhaps because alcohol distilled for vinegar benefited from a lower tax rate than that made for drinking, the exact date Charlton switched to whisky is uncertain. However, the distillery reported nearly 90,000 gallons of spirits produced in the year ending June 30, 1888, and as early as 1893, the Hudson's Bay Company offered Royal brands in barrels and bottles across Canada, from Quebec to BC. Royal claimed at the time that its Maple Leaf, Early Dew Maple Leaf, Royal Old Rye and Malt, Royal Special Old Rye, and Grand Jewel, and its leading brand, Red Wheat, had been fully matured in barrels. It was August 1894, though, before Charlton changed the name of his vinegar works to the Hamilton Distillery Company, thus capturing the move to distillation. With unrelated distilleries named "Royal" operating in Ireland, the US, and Scotland, the more mundane "Hamilton" seemed prudent, although he maintained the Royal branding. Following Charlton's death in 1901, his successors, faced with a trademark dispute initiated by Meagher Brothers of Montreal, dropped their Maple Leaf whisky brands and updated the brand portfolio to include Royal

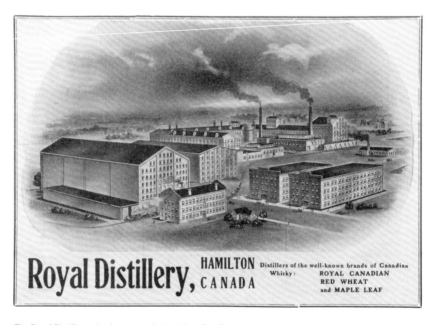

The Royal Distillery, also known as the Hamilton Distillery, was originally built to make vinegar.

Reserve (styled to resemble Canadian Club) and Royal Canadian brands. Neither had much success. Nor did their 1907 efforts, as part of a consortium of large distillers, to launch a new distillery in Winnipeg.

The original shareholders had been prominent Hamilton businessmen, well known to each other socially. However, as they died, rapid turnover in ownership to successors with no interest in distilling led to the distillery's demise. In January 1918, they put the plant up for auction as a going concern with capacity to distil thirteen tonnes a day, rack warehouses for 900,000 gallons of whisky in barrels, and 300,000 gallons of tank storage. Its owners described it as a modern, convenient, well-equipped grain spirit and whisky distillery in good condition, served by a private switch connecting to the Grand Trunk Railway. The sale included everything except materials, supplies, and manufactured products on hand, which the proprietors planned to store in the rack warehouses. With that, the Royal Distillery and its brands evaporated from public view until March 1922, when the distillery buildings finally sold for $140,000. However, American Prohibition arrived in 1919, and perhaps coincidentally, when Jimmy Barclay's brand-new distillery emerged, just down the road in Niagara Falls, it had plenty of mature whisky for sale, some of it sold as Barclay's Special Old Rye, a former Royal brand. Today, the original distillery office, a grey-painted, two-storey brick building measuring 8.5 by 9.8 metres at 16 Jarvis Street, hosts karaoke. Much as Royal Distillery has faded from memory, so, too, recollections of Red Wheat and the other Royal whiskies Benjamin Charlton distilled in his Hamilton Distillery are limited to amateur archaeologists who occasionally unearth their broken bottles.

MELCHERS, BERTHIERVILLE

It was a beet sugar refinery and abundant local grain that drew Jan J. Melchers to Berthierville, about eighty kilometres downstream from Montreal on the St. Lawrence River. His family, gin distillers and exporters in Schiedam, Holland, since the 1830s, had sent the twenty-three-year-old abroad to see about building a distillery in North America. Quebec was a rich market for genever gin, and in 1896 the family formed Melchers Gin & Spirits Distillery Company Ltd. of Canada, with Jan Melchers at the head. One of their local investors, Senator JM Wilson, was a partner in the prominent liquor import and distribution firm Wilson & Boivin.

Within two years, Melchers had built a distillery in Berthierville and installed distilling equipment he brought in from Holland. Rather than importing distillers' yeast from the US, as others were doing, Melchers used beet molasses to propagate a Dutch yeast culture for fermentation and sale. An avid entrepreneur, Melchers quickly extended his distilled spirits port-folio beyond gin, and established a lucrative European trade in Quebec lumber. In 1914, a key yeast customer, Fleischmann's Canada, purchased the distillery and, in 1926, began distilling bourbon and American rye whisky there, primarily for the Canadian market.

When Fleischmann's divested its interests in 1928 and the distillery went public, three brothers from a family called Marchand, who had worked for Melchers, took over as majority shareholders. Leading the business was the Hon. Victor Marchand, who had been a partner in Wilson & Boivin. The recently modernized facility occupied thirty-three hectares and could produce two million gallons of spirits annually, with warehousing for 1.6 million gallons. It also made other saleable by-products of distilling, including yeast, which Fleischmann's bought under contract. Liquor boards in eight provinces

Melchers Rye, distilled in Berthierville, Quebec.

stocked Melchers gins and spirits. In 1929, Melchers launched a three-year-old whisky, primarily in Canada. (By the mid-1960s, 60% of sales were to the US, and mostly whisky.)

Sales increases brought expansion during the 1940s, and by the 1950s, Melchers was producing three bourbons, one American rye, and four brands of Canadian "real rye," ranging from three to eight years old. Each of these was made from imported corn, and rye grain grown in nearby Joliette. By the time JJ Melchers died in his Montreal home on December 2, 1960, the world could not get enough Canadian whisky.

LES DISTILLERIES MARCHAND, QUEBEC

With growing sovereignty sentiments in Quebec came opportunity, and in 1964 Melchers launched Les Distilleries Marchand, an independent marketing company headquartered in Quebec and owned exclusively by French-Canadians. Marchand sold genever gin distilled and bottled by Melchers, and three of Melchers' directors sat on Marchand's board. Melchers also arranged for Potter to blend and bottle Melchers products at its distillery in Langley, BC, thus reducing shipping costs to western markets significantly. Recognizing a trend towards lighter flavours, Melchers launched a white rum, and, for the first time, began referring to some of its whiskies as "light." Ahh, marketing.

In 1967, Senator Paul Desruisseaux generated new enthusiasm when he bought out Maurice and René Marchand to take a controlling interest in Melchers. With him came a loan of $7.5 million for expansion. Melchers increased its production capacity by 90% in 1969 after investing $5.2 million in the Berthierville plant and purchasing an idle distillery in Manitoba.

CANADA'S MANITOBA DISTILLERY, MINNEDOSA

In November 1967, about ten months after Seagram's revealed its intention to build a $10 million distillery complex at Gimli, Manitoba, a group of Manitoba investors led by former media magnate and provincial Liberal leader Izzy Asper announced a $4 million investment of its own. Supported by a government grant, they would build a distillery three hours away, in Minnedosa. To be called Canada's Manitoba Distillery, the $2.5 million plant would use 12,700 tonnes of grain a year—all grown in Manitoba, of course—to produce 1.5 million proof gallons of Canadian whisky, which they would ship in bulk to the United States. Officially opened in September 1968 by the local member of the provincial legislature, the plant sat mostly idle until Melchers assumed ownership in January 1969. The words *sale* and *sold* were never uttered. Rather, the businesses were "merged," but the Minnedosa distillery was now a wholly owned subsidiary of Melchers. Manitoba management enthused that this allowed them to start making whisky four years sooner than expected. In fact, Melchers dipped into its own stocks to bottle Plainsman Canadian Whisky for Manitoba Distillery, and also shipped bulk whisky there to mature.

By 1970, its warehouses held the equivalent of 13.5 million bottles of whisky, though Canada's Manitoba Distillery had used just 1,260 tonnes of grain in 1969. The following year, citing oversupply, management put the distillery on a voluntary temporary shutdown. Production was sporadic from that point until 1973, when Melchers accepted that the Minnedosa plant was unviable and closed it. Melchers had touted Minnedosa as a bridgehead to the Canadian west, but distilleries worldwide were suffering from declining interest in whisky. The early 1970s became very difficult for many of them, including Melchers. Despite brave faces, logical explanations, and promises of good prospects, Melchers suffered one loss after another. Desruisseaux sold his interests in 1973.

Adams Private Stock Aged 6 Years (1975)
40% alc/vol | Seagram/United Distillers (defunct)

Caramels, burnt sugar, crumpets, toasted oak, baking spices, searing heat, cloves, ginger, grapefruit pith. Such skill to blend twenty-nine whiskies into one so discrete, yet complex, hearty, and distinguished.

Bush Pilot's Private Reserve 13 Years Old, Single Cask
43% alc/vol | Robert Denton

Pink caramel corn, varnish, crisp and clean. Oaky foundation with slippery, oily feel. Breakfast cereal/porridge, soothing hot embers pulling grapefruit pith. Elegant, austere, ethereal, and classically Canadian.

Canadian Masterpiece
40% alc/vol | Seagram/Calvert (defunct)

A whisky colossus. Fragrant wood, apricots, dried black currants, then grape skins, roasted nuts, and digestive biscuits. Softly smouldering spices, dark fruits, red wine, and bitterish walnut skins.

Captain's Table
40% alc/vol | McGuinness (defunct)

Molasses, butterscotch, NOLA pralines. Peppery swells sweep forward, bringing hints of oak, then citrus pith along. Simple, though round, mouth-filling, and pleasing. Short, cleansing, pithy finish. Genie's bewitching bottle.

Early in January 1977, Melchers accepted an offer from a group of twenty-three Manitoba businessmen to purchase the Minnedosa distillery. However, two months later, when a grant from the Department of Regional Economic Expansion for a bottling plant failed to materialize, the group withdrew, leaving Melchers with an expensive albatross around its neck. Eleven days later, on March 14, 1977, Melchers declared bankruptcy.

A trustee was appointed to keep the Berthierville distillery operating until a buyer could be found. Nine months later, a consortium of rival distillers calling itself Melcan came forward. Members included Calvert of Canada (Seagram's), Corby Distillers, John de Kuyper & Son (Canada) Ltd., and Meagher's Distillery, all of Montreal, and the American Distilling Company of New York. Almost certainly, their sole objective was to prevent the Quebec Liquor Corporation, which had expressed an interest, from buying the plant to bottle brands of its own. Melcan kept the plant open while it bottled and sold through existing spirits stocks.

Finally, in November 1984, Seagram's bought out the other partners and announced that the Berthierville distillery would close. Angry threats of a town hunger strike eventually reached the ears of the local member of Parliament, who arranged government transition funding to save jobs. By November of 1985, demolition workers were on site, levelling the plant. Seagram's had deeded the property and buildings to the town, which hoped to use the empty warehouses for an industrial park. In just over a year, threats of closure became wholesale obliteration of what had, for eighty-seven years, been Berthierville's largest employer.

Melcan sold the idle Minnedosa plant to H. Corby Distillers, which specialized in unpotable alcohol and cologne spirits, and in 1980, Corby sold it to Mohawk Petroleum to make fuel alcohol.

MCGUINNESS, TORONTO

A plaque near the Warehouse Lofts on Toronto's Manitoba Street commemorates the distillery that LJ (Larry) McGuinness founded nearby at what was then 2 Algoma Street. Beyond that, if spirits lovers remember McGuinness at all, it is likely from an extensive line of liqueurs bearing his name and now produced by Corby Spirit & Wine at the Hiram Walker Distillery in Windsor, Ontario. But in the first half of the 20th century, McGuinness was a trailblazer in Canada's whisky industry as a whisky merchant, distillery founder, and owner.

Lawrence Joseph McGuinness was born on December 6, 1883, in Port Hope, Ontario, to Patrick and Mary McGuinness. Patrick, then age twenty-nine, had immigrated to Canada via the US from Cootehill, Ireland, working at various jobs, including a stint at Cosgrave Brewery in Toronto. By 1901, the family was settled on Withrow Avenue in Toronto, where Patrick worked as a stable hand and Lawrence, who went by Larry, as a shipper. Within four years, Larry owned three liquor stores in Toronto.

In 1914, Canada joined Britain in what would become the First World War. Two years later, the government of Ontario enacted prohibition and required all working distilleries in the province to make industrial alcohol for military use. Although the war ended in 1918, prohibition remained in force in the province until 1927. However, this did not deter McGuinness from operating his business. In 1917, he opened a mail order office in Niagara Falls, New York, selling liquor legally into Ontario. Larry's childhood friend and next-door neighbour Frank "Red" Gallagher, who travelled to the US regularly to train competitive boxers, would bring Larry along to attend to his liquor business. By January 1920, when America declared Prohibition, McGuinness had established a strong distribution network south of the border. On June 24 of that year, his son Larry McGuinness Jr. was born.

BARCLAY DISTILLERY, NIAGARA FALLS

McGuinness's liquor business generated enough income that, in 1923, he joined partners Harry and Herb Hatch to purchase Toronto's failing Gooderham & Worts Distillery and, three years later, the Hiram Walker & Sons Distillery in Windsor. McGuinness soon brought legendary Scottish whisky entrepreneur Jimmy Barclay into the fold. Barclay established James Barclay & Company as a Canadian sales agency selling whisky made at his distillery in Niagara Falls, Ontario, and elsewhere. The raffish Barclay dealt directly with ruffian Prohibition-era "distributors" in New York, as scars on his body later testified. Barclay sold his Canadian distillery to Hiram Walker-Gooderham & Worts in 1931 and transferred ownership of Barclay Canadian whiskies, including the popular Royal Canadian Rye, Special Old, Gold Label Rye, and De Luxe Canadian Rye, to Hiram Walker's in Walkerville. Walker's introduced the new Barclay Square brand in the early 1960s.

Barclay was a free agent until 1938, working for competitors Hiram Walker & Sons (Scotland) Ltd. and Sam Bronfman of the Distillers Corporation-Seagram's Ltd. at the same time. He acquired the Glasgow firm Robert Brown Ltd. for Seagram's in 1935. Barclay maintained whisky business interests in the Bahamas and Nassau, as well as producing several American blended whiskies. In the 1970s, Hiram Walker moved production of Barclay's whiskies to its short-lived new distillery in Winfield, BC.

Barclay, McGuinness, and their wives remained life-long friends, visiting socially in Florida, where McGuinness spent his winters. To Maxwell Henderson, Seagram's treasurer and later auditor general of Canada, Barclay was "one of the greatest whisky entrepreneurs ever to graduate into the respectable era from the bootlegging days." Nevertheless, he is best remembered now for his global success selling Chivas Regal and Ballantine's Scotch whiskies.

MIMICO

McGuinness, who had built a lakefront mansion in the tony Mimico neighbourhood of Toronto, where he lived with his wife and children, enjoyed a wide and influential social circle. He was close friends with Ontario premier Mitch Hepburn, for instance, and on May 5, 1937, McGuinness and his wife sailed from New York to London to attend the coronation of King George VI.

McGuinness Sr. and the Hatch brothers made a good team in the slick hooch hustle of the Prohibition era. McGuinness took pride in a quality product, while the Hatches' specialty was sales. However, when the US finally repealed Prohibition in December 1933, McGuinness sold his shares and split amicably from his partnership with the Hatches. In 1934, he bought a modern, four-storey, 540-square-metre plant with room for expansion, just down the road from Walker's in Riverside, and began making fruit liqueurs using spirits purchased from Walker's. Mimico was home, though, and by 1938 he had bottling operations in Toronto. Then, early in 1939, he bought land to build a three-storey blending, bottling, and warehousing facility in Mimico, with plans to add a distillery.

Luck favoured McGuinness that same year when Dunrobin Distillery of Grimsby, Ontario, went into bankruptcy. McGuinness bought all of Dunrobin's inventory for about $35,000 and, not long after, purchased their distilling equipment and moved it to Mimico to create LJ McGuinness Distillery Company. The distillery was so successful that, early in 1942, McGuinness moved his headquarters to Mimico and put the Riverside plant up for sale.

In 1946, Larry McGuinness Jr., age twenty-five, returned from service in the Second World War and took over management of the firm from his father. Both father and son were personable, nice guys, and their genuine interest in their employees served the company well. "Quite unconsciously," a McGuinness manager said in 1964, "Larry McGuinness (Jr.) has instilled a real loyalty to the company in our people. It's a pretty happy place to work, and people stay around." An era of expansion for the already thriving distilling company began around 1948, when Larry Jr. announced plans to extend the Mimico operations with a 750-square-metre addition that included a basement and two mezzanines above the main floor. Sadly, in the midst of so many triumphs, on February 3, 1951, while friends and family awaited his winter arrival in Miami, Florida, LJ McGuinness Sr. died in Elgin County, Ontario. He was sixty-seven.

ACADIAN DISTILLERS, BRIDGETOWN

Later that same year, as Larry Jr. prepared to open a new distillery in Atlantic Canada, government requirements that diverted steel to Canada's Korean War effort intervened. So McGuinness purchased an Annapolis Valley apple processing facility on thirty hectares in Bridgetown, Nova Scotia, and converted it into Acadian Distillers, a bottling plant for imported rum. By 1961, with government restrictions lifted, Acadian Distillers finally began to distil its own spirits.

Initially, the sixty employees fermented juice from unsaleable Annapolis Valley apples to make gin, vodka, brandy, and liqueurs. Soon, they added western rye for whisky, and manager John Affleck successfully encouraged local farmers to grow rye as well. Acadian also purchased a herd of cattle, which they fattened on spent grains from the distillery to encourage local beef farmers to buy distillery waste.

In addition to producing some McGuinness spirits for sale regionally, Acadian sought markets for its own products across Canada. By 1968, liquor stores in all Canadian provinces except BC carried them. Next came America, and Acadian's 1975 foray into the US market was ingenious. The original Acadians had come from Nova Scotia's Annapolis Valley, so the firm launched a new "Frenchly

Canadian" brand called Acadién. A major advertising campaign targeted the Acadian heritage of US citizens in Louisiana, Vermont, and Upstate New York, and boasted that the prospering distillery now employed 137 people. It was not to last.

Late in 1966, McGuinness had expanded its Mimico site once again, opening what it claimed was Canada's most modern distillery, with such recent innovations as CIP (cleaning-in-place) sanitation. At six storeys, the automated 2,800-square-metre distillery included new grain handling equipment, mills, cookers, ten new stainless steel fermenters holding exactly 25,008 gallons, and both column and pot stills, all run by just twenty people. The previous year, McGuinness had added 2,800 square metres of storage space as well as a 3,700-square-metre expansion to the existing plant. Even still, McGuinness planned for additional barrel warehousing, case warehousing, and bottling facilities.

McGuinness celebrated Canada's 1967 centennial with the release of its premium Old Canada whisky. Its label featured the historic Cornelius Kreighoff painting *Bilking the Toll*, painted around 1861 at Longueuil, Quebec. McGuinness had been ageing its whiskies for up to sixteen years, but Larry Jr. had a nose for change, and, inspired by his success with white rum, was convinced that lighter whisky would sell well. In 1968, the Liquor Control Board of Ontario allowed producers to display just four whiskies on its shelves. So McGuinness pulled its second-best seller and replaced it with an aged white rye whisky made by filtering aged rye through charcoal, then adding a bit of mature rye back in to flavour it.

The Mimico and Bridgetown distilleries were both going concerns on June 13, 1970, when McGuinness sold the burgeoning company to US food giant Standard Brands for over $20 million. His accountant had advised him this was the best way to protect his equity from capital gains tax. Between them, the McGuinness and Acadian Distilleries had a total production of twenty million litres annually, with retail sales nearing $80 million, including sales to export markets. As per his father's request, McGuinness obtained the concurrence of all family members before selling. When all was said and done, Larry's share was $4 million, while the rest went to his mother, brother, and sister.

Although McGuinness protected his fortune from the tax department, the sale turned into a disaster when he invested his profits in the Canadian mining sector, only to see mining stocks plunge. In November 1977, Larry McGuinness Jr. declared bankruptcy. He later retired and joined his son and brother in Florida, where he died on December 22, 2017. Still, his legacy lives on. When he became a mining executive in 1972, Larry Jr. quietly began subsidizing Toronto's transit system so that revellers could get home safely on New Year's Eve. His bankruptcy brought that practice to an end in 1976, but Corby Spirit & Wine recently revived this forgotten gesture.

CENTRAL CANADIAN DISTILLERS, WEYBURN

The McGuinness family had made distilling, in all its aspects, a hugely profitable business, driven by hard work, quality products, and insightful decision making. To Standard Brands, though, it was just another profit centre in an expanding international foodstuffs conglomerate. At first, distilling suited their profit-hungry management team well, and in 1974 they greedily and foolishly took control of Central Canadian Distillers of Weyburn, Saskatchewan.

Where there is booze, there is government, and where there is government, there are vote-buying grants. As its turbulent history reveals, the Central Canadian Distillers plant, on the northwestern edge of Weyburn, should never have been built. Despite politician after politician extolling its potential for job creation and economic spinoff, then pumping in government subsidies, the ill-fated distillery pinballed from one disappointment to the next as still more politicians offered new hope—and, of course, new dollars.

First word came late in 1969, when Saskatchewan premier Ross Thatcher announced a $3 million distillery that would employ sixty-five people and buy eight tonnes of local rye each year. It took just a few hours for the nearby city of Moose Jaw to object, claiming it needed jobs more. Thatcher preferred Weyburn, though, because its hospital was closing, and he wanted a good-news story. Along with federal and provincial subsidies, the town offered tax incentives, too.

Federal cabinet minister Otto Lang joined Thatcher for the formal announcement a few months later. Local businessman (and later mayor) Tom G. Laing, a director of the company, said the biggest benefit would be a new market for agricultural products. Nonetheless, some wary farmers needed further encouragement to grow rye, and within two years, the distillery was offering a premium of $330 a tonne for Cougar and Frontier varieties.

In May 1971, with 1,000 people watching, Premier Thatcher declared the distillery open as he flipped a switch to unload a truckful of rye. Along with everything else, the province had taken an equity position of 12.5% and lent the distillery $450,000 to purchase mature whisky to sell while its own matured. And to remind voters of the province's monopoly on liquor sales, Premier Thatcher remarked, "I wish the principals of this operation every success. I hope they make a lot of profit, for we get 52% of it."

The spectacle of politicians at three levels of government tripping over each other to launch a distillery in grain-rich Saskatchewan did not sit well with the eleven members of the Association of Canadian Distillers. Among other things, they worried that the conflict of owning shares in the distillery and having a monopoly on sales might lead the province to give them less shelf space. They did not mention, though, that while Saskatchewan's liquor board carried products from every distillery in the country, the Weyburn Distillery had secured just a single product listing in the rich Ontario market. The association reminded all who would listen that distilling is heavily taxed and raised the prospect of religious Saskatchewan citizens being offended to learn they owned a distillery. Finally, they called for a study of the economic viability of operating a distillery in Saskatchewan. You mean, no one had done that already?

In June 1973, manager John Affleck (formerly of Acadian Distillers) reported that sales were climbing. The Weyburn plant had produced 31,700 barrels of whisky the previous year and added two new warehouses, although disposing of waste stillage was not going as well as hoped. Farm animals thrive on this protein-rich stillage, so Weyburn's management had offered it free to people willing to establish a feedlot with a minimum of 2,000 head of cattle. Several feedlots, including some newly created, had taken advantage, but not enough to absorb the thirty-four million litres produced annually.

Late in 1973, the company collected the final instalment of its government grants, and three months later, on February 15, 1974, the owners sold their 87.5% share to LJ McGuinness and Company—i.e., Standard Brands. The province kept its 12.5% stake. Strongly criticized for letting the distillery go to a US firm, government officials said the plant would continue at capacity production. They had given the grant to provide jobs in Saskatchewan, they said, and those jobs would remain. And besides, the firm's commitment that the plant would stay in Canadian hands had ended with the final payment.

All looked good in July 1976, when a tanker truck loaded with 20,000 litres of bulk blended whisky rolled out of Weyburn for Fleischmann Distilling's bottling plant in Plainfield, Illinois. Distillery management gloated, saying it was the first of 76,000 litres of whisky bound for Fleischmann's, with double that projected for 1977. In anticipation, Weyburn management had launched a $4.5 million expansion. However, by May 1977, it was clear that something was wrong. Weyburn had much more whisky than it could sell, and its warehouses were filling up.

Management decided that, although bottling would continue, distilling would shut down for four months while they sold excess inventory. Other distilleries, they said, were also facing declining demand. If it was a tough blow for distillery workers, it was even more so for feedlot operators, who suddenly lost their feed source. When the distillery finally reopened three years later, the province of Saskatchewan had doubled its interest to 25%. Meanwhile, waste disposal had become even more difficult. Cattle farmers were reluctant to feed distillery waste with no guarantee that the plant would remain open. Finally, on January 23, 1987, the problem became moot when the Weyburn Distillery closed for the final time, its Lord Simcoe and No. 1 Hard Canadian whiskies fading into memory.

As Larry McGuinness had predicted, the market wanted lighter flavours, and drinkers were switching from brown spirits to white. Despite much protestation (the president of Corby disparaged vodka as a communist drink that should not be sold in Canada), inventories of unsold whisky continued to grow industry-wide in the 1980s, causing major disruptions in Canada and around the world. In January 1987, Acadian Distillers also became one of the casualties as McGuinness closed the plant for good. The loss of an industry often has far-reaching effects in small communities. However, Bridgetown residents lamented nothing more than the end of the used whisky barrels they had bought eagerly, and legally, to make "swish." By filling discarded whisky barrels with hot water and rolling them around, purchasers could extract up to forty bottles of liquor from the used wood.

In December 1987, Corby purchased McGuinness Distilleries and, a month later, moved McGuinness's operations to Corby's then-silent distillery in Corbyville. "The whole industry has been operating at low capacity, 50% and less," an analyst commented. "This will bring Corby back to pretty good utilization." Sadly, that judgment proved faulty in 1991, when management closed the Corby Distillery and centralized its operations at Hiram Walker & Sons in Windsor. In 1989, most of the McGuinness Distillery was demolished. A few McGuinness brands still live on, though, produced now at Walker's and other distilleries.

MONTMORENCY DISTILLERY, BEAUPRÉ

Details on the establishment and early products of La Distillerie Montmorency, about sixty-five kilometres downriver from Quebec City in Beaupré, Quebec, are slim. When American firm National Distillers Products built the facility in 1946, president Seaton Porter would only say that the distillery would produce "a variety of the distilled spirits for which Canada is well known." However, when the distillery broke ground for a two-storey, 1,200-square-metre concrete-and-brick rack warehouse, it confirmed rumours that Porter wanted a Canadian rye to compete head to head with market leaders Canadian Club and Seagram's V.O. A bottling hall followed in 1950. The distillery released Montmorency Canadian Whisky later that year, with its namesake Montmorency Falls pictured on the label. The better-known Dominion Ten Canadian Whisky followed in 1953, with distribution in Canada and the US.

A global trend for distillers to accumulate and dispose of distilleries touched Beaupré in August 1952, as Distillers Company Ltd., a US subsidiary of Scotland's own Distillers Company, purchased shares in Montmorency. Then, in 1955, in a $6 million, three-distillery deal that saw it acquire Old Overholt Distillery in Pennsylvania and Baltimore Pure Rye Distillery in Maryland, Seagram's purchased Montmorency. Its former Scottish owner told shareholders somewhat laconically, "On the other hand, we have disposed of our interest in the Canadian whisky concern, Montmorency Distillery Ltd."

With Seagram's whisky sales flourishing, it put the distillery, renamed Beaupré, to work supplying blending components for some of Seagram's fast-growing brands, including the highly regarded Canadian Masterpiece. By 1968, Seagram had added another rack warehouse to increase maturing capacity from 100,000 barrels to 125,000. While Seagram's key brands of Canadian, American, and Scotch whisky weathered the whisky downturn of the 1970s and

1980s, as the overall demand for whisky declined, Seagram joined other distillers in closing branch plants, and in September 1989, that came to include Beaupré.

POTTER DISTILLERY, VANCOUVER

After serving with the Canadian forces in Europe during the First World War, a young man named Ernest Potter returned to his native Vancouver with a new-found love for apple cider. However, Canada's liquor laws stymied his hopes of opening a cidery. So instead, in 1958, he and sausage maker Karl Wimmer established Potter Distillery. In 1961, they rented space on Annacis Island in Delta, BC, and began making liqueurs using spirits they purchased from Alberta Distillers of Calgary. By September, their products were available in BC liquor stores.

Their success caught the eye of a prominent local entrepreneur and sea captain, HJC "Cap" Terry, who bought Wimmer's share and took financial control. Terry's two sons joined him in the partnership, and Potter Distillery became a Terry family business. Under their direction, sales skyrocketed, and in 1963, Potter, which by now had begun distilling grain spirits, added Canadian whisky and gin to the lineup.

By 1964, Terry was planning a 930-square-metre distillery and two warehouses on six hectares in Langley, BC. Efforts to sell 25% of the business to Melchers Distillery of Montreal to finance the expansion became a $300,000 loan, on the agreement that Potter would warehouse, blend, and bottle Melchers whisky for the West Coast, while Melchers would do the same for Potter in the east.

When the $600,000, fully automated distillery opened in 1967, Canadian rye was the fastest-growing type of whisky in the massive US market, and demand for Canadian whisky was huge. With stockbrokers predicting that

Canadian distillery stocks would be among Canada's best performing investments, Potter looked forward to a bright future, and that's how it began. Of course, Potter Distillery no longer exists, so we know that dark clouds lurked beyond the horizon. However, in 1967, along with sales of Potter's Special Blend and Potter's Special Old, the firm projected annual exports of 1.5 million gallons of bulk whisky to the US and offered 325,000 shares for sale to the public to raise funds.

Growth in Canada, the US, and overseas nearly doubled sales in 1968, leading to rapid expansion of the Langley plant and rumours that Potter Distillery was for sale. Instead, the firm paid its shareholders a dividend. By 1970, Potter was selling in Germany, Portugal, Switzerland, Great Britain, Hong Kong, Singapore, and South America, with plans for distribution to every US state. Potter already sent its Crown, Special Old, Western, and Charter Canadian whiskies in bulk to Louisville, Kentucky, and to Hood River Distillers of Oregon, to be bottled for the US market, a practice that saved transportation costs and US taxes.

Whisky distillers follow one of two philosophies: some convert grain into whisky, while others convert whatever they can lay their hands on into money. In 1971, Terry inked deals to produce and bottle whiskies in western Canada for Montreal gin and liqueur maker Meagher's, and more prophetically, to distribute London Winery products. Soon, the Terrys were courting other domestic and foreign winemakers. It was the first of many diversifications into wine, beer, and non-alcoholic mixers.

Late in 1975, Potter opened an 1,100-square-metre bottling plant in Portland, Oregon, to supply up to a million cases of spirits to the western US and Southeast Asian markets. A year later, the firm announced plans for a distillery in St. Catharines, Ontario, to serve eastern Canada and eventually replace Potter's Chicago operations, which served the eastern US. But by the end of the decade, the cost of expansion and declining sales were taking a toll on profits. Potter declared a loss in 1979 and just modest earnings in 1980, though it bravely predicted a return to profitability in 1981.

The St. Catharines distillery seems to have been put on hold, although the firm opened a brewery there some years later. Steadily increasing interest rates kept pace with growing sales, and company profits remained lean in the early 1980s. "We are such a small company, the only way we can go is up," company president Frank Terry told shareholders in November of 1982. He later announced that Potter would build a winery on its Langley property for its subsidiary Beaupré Wines Canada (no affiliation with Beaupré Distillery). Earnings and a share issue in 1983 allowed Potter to pay down some of its debt, and Terry accurately predicted a profitable 1984.

Although 1985 was still profitable, the firm needed to reduce costs, and in January 1986, it sold its Oregon operations to General Western Industries. A few weeks later, financial analysts in Toronto declared the distilling industry stagnant, noting a consumer trend away from whisky. By 1986, the Potter Distillery could no longer stand on its own, and General Western bought a controlling interest in the firm. The Terry brothers, who had inherited Cap Terry's shares on his death in 1984, became minority shareholders. Although the Terrys had five-year management contracts and some continuing influence, the new owners soon appointed TM Sterling, a twenty-five-year brewing industry veteran, as president and CEO of Potter.

Later that year, Potter merged with another General Western subsidiary, Pacific Western, to form a new company: International Potter Distilling. Although the firm bore the distiller's name and continued to blend whisky, it suspended distilling in Langley, and most of the new company's profits came from the brewing side. Financial analysts noted that even the largest distilleries were suffering, and any profitability came from holdings outside the drinks industry. Meanwhile, the president of Potter's/General Western's Oregon distillery (a bottling plant, really) said what many must have been thinking: to boost profitability, they were cutting whisky prices and would begin bottling imported vodka. Whisky makers blamed punishing taxes, drunk driving campaigns, and healthier lifestyles, but white spirits were clearly in ascendance.

Back in Canada, International Potter Distilling was rapidly expanding its operations in beer, and in 1989, it bought Kelowna, BC–based Calona Wines from its US-based owner, Heublein Inc. With more than half of Potter's profits now coming from Calona Wines, and the Langley plant silent since the mid-1980s, whisky, although still important, had become a side gig for Potter. In 1989, the company made this official by selling the Langley distillery and moving its remaining staff and distilled spirits to Kelowna. Although Calona bottled whisky and other spirits from Standard's McGuinness, Acadian, and Central Canadian (Weyburn) Distilleries and had at one time operated a small brandy still, Potter no longer had facilities to distil whisky. Instead, Potter Distillery had become a winemaker, brewer, blender, and drinks distribution company, operating from a cavernous wine warehouse in the BC Interior.

With its debts mounting, in 1990, Potter sought financing from Danco Investment, a Swiss firm. Eventually, Danco took a controlling interest in Potter, then went under itself, leaving the pieces to portfolio managers EBC Zurich. EBC sold all remaining US distilling interests for cash and put the St. Catharines brewery on the market. In 1995, EBC renamed the firm Cascadia Brands, dissociating it from liquor production and sales. And, in a final act before selling the firm to Andrés Wines, it realized Ernest Potter's original dream: it made apple cider, for sale in Japan.

Potter's days of whisky glory were past long before that final day in 2006 when Highwood Distillery carted away the last 10,000 barrels—eighty truckloads of ageing whisky—from the non-distilling Potter Distillery in the former Calona

Wines building in Kelowna, BC. Whether Potter distilled any of that whisky is doubtful. It had been buying spirits from Consolidated Distilleries (Corby) and maturing them in Kelowna, but the business had shifted almost entirely to wine. For sure, though, none of it came from Calona's tiny brandy still.

CN Tower (1974)
40% alc/vol | McGuinness (defunct)

The big butterscotch, billowing, spicy heat, and wonderfully grippy green tea that epitomized this era's whisky. Soft fruits, grapes, cinnamon, oaky tannins, leather, and golden sugar. Comforting simplicity.

McGuinness Old Canada
40% alc/vol | McGuinness (defunct)

Closed nose hints at vague oak and spice. Sweet caramel, peppery spices—hot like ginger root—fade into drying tannins. Some complexity. Pithy, herbal, sweetish. More finesse than might.

Silk Tassel Aged 7 Years (1972)
40% alc/vol | McGuinness (defunct)

Butterscotch and blistering heat, sharp kiwi fruit, slight oiliness. Short, sweet whispers of an era past fade quickly to green tea and barrel tones with a beguiling, lingering, soft glow.

PARK & TILFORD, VANCOUVER

Joseph Park and John Mason Tilford likely were not thinking of Canada when they opened the doors to their Manhattan grocery store for the first time one sunny October morning in 1840. Nor could they have imagined that, as their now-public enterprise approached its 110th birthday, its stockholders would rename it Park & Tilford Distillers to better reflect its core business. Despite once-nationwide US sales of packaged foodstuffs, perfumes, medicines, and imported luxury goods, they now focused on distributing imported liquors and wines and whiskies they distilled themselves.

In 1954, Canadian Schenley built four ageing warehouses on an eleven-hectare property in North Vancouver and began sending train tankers filled with whisky and spirits there from its plant in Valleyfield. Meanwhile, in 1955, Schenley Industries (US) bought control of US-based Park & Tilford. Then, in 1959, Canadian Schenley announced it would complete its North Vancouver distillery, to be called Canadian Melrose Distillers, and make whisky there for sale in Canada and the US. A month later, management changed the distillery's name to Canadian Park & Tilford.

By mid-1960, 115 people worked in distilling, bottling, quality control, storage, shipping, and sales. Demand for Canadian whisky was booming, and Canadian Park & Tilford whiskies were soon selling strongly across Canada and the US. Repeated plant expansions more than doubled distilling output, increasing warehousing to accommodate 150,000 barrels and quadrupling bottling capacity. At the same time, lighter, less expensive blends began to dominate the market. While US Park & Tilford could advertise that its American whiskies now contained up to 70% grain neutral spirits, that flexibility was, by law, denied Canadian whisky makers. So Canadian Park & Tilford took a different tack, bragging that they offered greater value by including older, mature whiskies in their blends. They also lightened their whisky by distilling some of it from starch-rich milo (sorghum), which gave a more neutral flavour than other grains and was less expensive.

Promoting whisky in Canada required ingenuity in the 1960s, as provincial government monopolies on sales included tightly held authority to approve advertising and promotion. In 1967, Canadian Park & Tilford CEO Don McNaughton announced that the firm would invest $500,000 to create seven ornamental gardens on a large, weedy lot next to the distillery. When McNaughton conceded the gardens would draw attention to Park & Tilford's operation, he learned that the British Columbia Liquor Control Board had to consent. Happily, it did, and the Park & Tilford Gardens remain a destination for more than 300,000 visitors a year.

When Lewis Rosenstiel retired in 1968, he sold his interest in Schenley to the Glen Alden Corporation, which, in turn, merged into New York–based Rapid-American in 1972. Signs of trouble appeared in 1978 when Rapid-American ordered a management shakeup at Canadian Schenley. They demoted several Park & Tilford executives and merged management with that of Schenley's Gibson Distilleries. Late in 1981, Rapid-American sold Canadian Schenley outright to the Byrn family of Vancouver, and eighteen months later, the Byrns sold it on to Penfund, a Toronto pension fund acting on behalf of anonymous investors. It did not bode well when Canadian Schenley's president commented that the spirits industry was in the doldrums, with production hitting its lowest level since 1976. He blamed recession, escalating taxes, and changing consumer tastes without mentioning massive overproduction by Schenley Industries (US) in the early 1950s. In 1984, Penfund closed Park & Tilford Distillery altogether and consolidated operations in Salaberry-de-Valleyfield, Quebec. It was the end of twenty-five glorious years.

Park & Tilford's five Canadian whiskies had sold well. Still, once redevelopers demolished the distillery, none of Gold Medallion, Royal Command, Three Lancers, 1840 Reserve, or Three Feathers Rye was remembered or sought by collectors. No, when it closed in 1984, Park & Tilford left behind little but warehouses, now converted to movie studios, and a shopping mall with an ornamental garden that still bears its founders' names—not in Manhattan, their home, but in Vancouver, a foreign city on the other side of the continent.

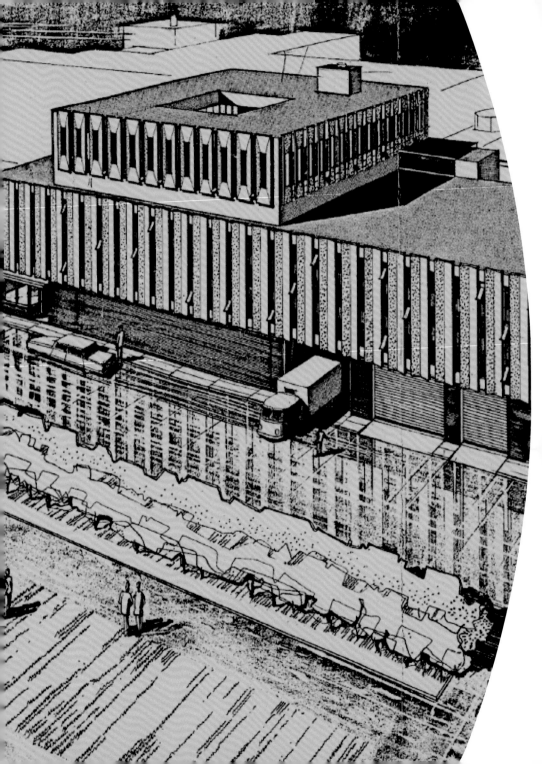

(18)

RENEWAL AND GROWTH

The 21st century has witnessed a dramatic rise in fortunes for Canadian whisky, with each of Canada's large legacy distilleries ramping up production of old brands and introducing new ones. More than that, Canada's most successful brand, Crown Royal, is investing a quarter of a billion dollars in expanding its facilities. Meanwhile, for the almost forgotten Meagher's Distillery in Montreal, reduced in less prosperous times to a bottling plant, this renewal has brought new life as a full-production distillery.

MEAGHER'S DISTILLERY

In 1873, two brothers (and former figure skaters) opened what would eventually become one of Canada's largest liqueur makers and importers and distributors of spirits and wines. Joseph G. and John Meagher Jr. (pronounced ma-HAR or mar) left their glissades and barrel jumps behind to found Meagher Brothers Distillery in Montreal. Their father and two of his brothers

Old Montreal Distillery today.

had also tried their hand at whisky distilling in Napanee, Ontario, not far from their home in Kingston, and while they didn't have much luck, this second Meagher Brothers Distillery was a success from the start. John (who also worked as a lawyer) ran the business while Joseph took charge of production, creating their first line of liqueurs and gin. As the business grew to become an industry leader, they brought their younger brother George A. (also a former skater) into the firm.

John Meagher Jr. died on May 9, 1909, followed two years and a day later by Joseph G., leaving John's son John Joseph Meagher to run the business. By the 1920s, Meagher's liqueurs and their Boulton London Dry Gin were big sellers in Quebec and across Canada and the firm needed space to grow. So in 1930, it bought three adjacent lots with 2,300 metres of street frontage and buildings dating from 1873. The previous owners, hardware dealer McArthur Irwin, had imported, manufactured, and sold glues, oils, and paints, and, somewhat oddly from a 21st-century perspective, they also sold glass and whisky. The Britannia Street property, not far from the Lachine Canal, was in a working-class neighbourhood called Victoriaville and better known as Goose Village. Nearly a century later, while preparing for Expo 67, the City of Montreal declared the area an eyesore and razed all but the distillery to make way for the Autostade stadium. The city also reconfigured the roads, so the distillery is now located on Chemin des Moulins.

DUTCH PARTNERS

In the 19th century, Dutch distiller De Kuyper discovered a strong demand for genever gin in Quebec. By the beginning of the 20th century, the firm was shipping much of its production there. Then Canada imposed high import duties, and in the 1920s De Kuyper engaged Canadian Industrial Alcohol (which owned Corby) to blend and bottle De Kuyper products in Canada. Unhappy with the arrangement, around 1928, De Kuyper began exploring other options, and in 1932 bought a 70% interest in Meagher Brothers. Early in 1933, Meagher's added a four-storey brick warehouse, 7.6 metres by 30.5 metres, on the site at 1161 Britannia Street. Since genever gin is made from malt spirit rather than the neutral spirits used for most gins, De Kuyper installed a malt distillery and sent Henry de Kuyper over from Holland to run it. By 1937, they had extended the plant again and increased malt distilling by 50% to meet growing demand. Two divisions operated under one roof: Meagher's made liqueurs and sold imported wines and spirits, while De Kuyper specialized in genever gin.

In April 1963, Meagher Brothers & Company merged with wine and spirits distributors Gillespie & Company to form Meagher's Distillery. At the same time, they negotiated a twenty-five-year agreement to make genever gin for John de Kuyper & Son. Then, in April 1973, Meagher's acquired wine distributor William Mara and became Canada's largest liquor importer. Corby purchased Meagher's in 1978, so in 1987, when Allied-Lyons bought Hiram Walker & Sons, which itself owned Corby, Allied became a 51% shareholder in Meagher's Distillers. In turn, Pernod Ricard bought out Allied in 2005, and in 2011, sold Meagher's decommissioned distillery to the Sazerac Company, one of America's oldest family-owned, privately held distillers and a strong player in the global spirits market.

Robert (Bob) Maillé joined Meagher's Distillery in 1977, when De Kuyper still owned the plant. Bob remembers mashing malt in six African walnut–wood fermenters and distilling malt spirit in two stills, to make De Kuyper genever gin. A year later, Corby took over. "We stopped making gin after Corby bought us," he recalls wistfully. "Whisky came with Sazerac." For Corby, the distillery was strictly a bottling plant.

SAZERAC, SEAGRAM, AND OLD MONTREAL DISTILLERY

When Mark Brown, president and CEO of Sazerac, learned Meagher's history, he sought to recapture the extraordinary quality he sensed in it. Sazerac began by installing an eleven-metre copper column still, charmingly named Sam (after Seagram's Sam Bronfman), and a hybrid pot still with a five-plate copper column above. Refitted in 2018 with a new stainless steel cooker and four fermenters, Meagher's Distillery began operations again as the renamed Old Montreal Distillery. Today, mature whisky pours from barrels as they roll, one by one, over a metal-lined wooden dump trough recycled from the original African walnut fermenters.

For a whisky lover, the greatest excitement comes from Sazerac's role as custodian of the Seagram whisky legacy. "You can't own history," a tour guide at the refitted distillery explains, "but we are the guardians of Seagram's history." In 2018, Sazerac bought Seagram's V.O., 83, and Five Star brands from Diageo, with a ten-year agreement that Diageo would produce them at Valleyfield, on contract. It was more a reunion than a takeover. A global organization with origins tracing back nearly four centuries, Sazerac had first joined forces with Seagram's in the 1940s to distribute Seagram brands in the United States.

Sazerac's long-term vision to elevate Canadian whisky making and showcase the art of blending is fitting, given that Sazerac's master blender, Drew Mayville, is a twenty-three-year veteran of Seagram's blending program. It was Seagram's that pioneered what has become known as the Canadian multi-component approach to blending. Mayville consulted with his Seagram's mentor, the legendary Art Dawe, on Sazerac's plans to restore the Seagram's VO (dropping the periods from the name) and 83 brands to their former glory.

After all, these were the top Seagram whiskies when Canada's historic whisky colossus, Mister Sam Bronfman, was at the height of his career. Bronfman had made Montreal the centre of Canadian whisky it once was, and V.O. had been his favourite tipple—not to mention Canada's bestselling whisky in the 20th century. Only when Seagram's broke up in 2000 did Crown Royal soar above, as sales of the other Seagram's brands declined due to inattention. During a multi-year transition, Sazerac is actively directing and overseeing the blending and bottling of these whiskies at Valleyfield to ensure they follow Sazerac's quality and consistency standards. As well, in a salute to the master, Mayville has blended forty-five old Seagram whiskies from Canada and the US to create one of the most outstanding whiskies of all time, a sensuous, voluptuous dram aptly named Mister Sam. "Making new whisky for sophisticated palates," Mayville calls it.

Today, Old Montreal Distillery is one of the few legacy distilleries fully set up for public tours and sampling. Along with their whiskies, the samples include the ever-so-malty De Kuyper genever gin, which, in partnership with De Kuyper, they have put back into production. Of five production lines, the artisanal Line 5 is the most interesting. There, a hand-operated, six-spout bottling machine fills bottles of Caribou Crossing and Mister Sam before workers hand-label and package them. Sazerac has also introduced a "Single Barrel Select" program for customers who want to buy their own full barrel of the flavourful Caribou Crossing.

Caribou Crossing Single Barrel
40% alc/vol | Old Montreal

Cracker Jack popcorn, soft peppery spice, creamy, and vaguely oaky. Citrus tones and soft oak tannins. Balanced and focused on luscious, mouth-filling luxury.

ST. CLAIR DISTILLERY

With sales of Crown Royal growing by as much as a quarter annually, and plans for expansion beyond North America, brand owner Diageo announced early in 2022 that it would build a new $245 million distillery. Commencing operations in 2025, the plant is located on 160 hectares in St Clair Township, near Sarnia, Ontario, with capacity to distil up to twenty million litres of absolute alcohol annually, along with maturing and blending operations.

Like Diageo's Valleyfield Distillery and other Crown Royal facilities, plans for the St. Clair plant include technologies to minimize waste, using 100% renewable energy to make the plant carbon-neutral, and sending zero waste to landfills. The new distillery, which will concentrate on making base whiskies, is an addition to the current Crown Royal operations in Gimli, Manitoba, Valleyfield, Quebec, and 150 kilometres due south of St. Clair, in Amherstburg, Ontario.

Old distillery, new stills, including a column still named Sam.

5

LEGACY DISTILLERIES
AND NEW ARRIVALS

Calgary investors and his grandfather
supported George H. Reifel in building Alberta Distillers.

(19)

ALBERTA DISTILLERS

Calgary sits amidst vast expanses of prime Canadian grain fields, so it is no surprise that in 1946, when the Alberta government offered subsidies to stimulate the struggling economy, someone thought of making whisky. Calgary businessman Frank McMahon, a wealthy petroleum man even before the 1947 Leduc discovery turned him into an oil baron and transformed Calgary from a backwater to a bustling metropolis, saw opportunity in those grain fields. So did Max Bell, a rancher and newspaper publisher, and together they developed the idea of establishing a distillery in Alberta. Although McMahon and Bell certainly knew how to make money, they had none of the skills required for whisky. They needed a partner who could build the plant and run the operation—and make quality whisky. Who better to turn to than BC's Reifel family? Although they had retired from distilling after Prohibition ended, whisky was still in their blood. So when McMahon and Bell approached them, the family quickly jumped back in, helping George Henry Reifel establish Alberta Distillers

Ltd. (ADL) on a sixteen-hectare plot of vacant land in what George Henry's son, George C. Reifel, then a child, recalls as "the boonies." At the time, Calgary was home to barely 100,000 people, less than one-tenth of its size today. George C.'s earliest memories include the fragrance of newly dumped barrels.

In 1963, an American firm, National Distillers, launched the Canadian whisky brand Windsor Supreme, relying on Alberta Distillers for its supply. Windsor was so successful that, just a year later, National bought Alberta Distillers to ensure it would always have a reliable source. In the process, this acquisition put a third generation of Reifels into retirement. Windsor Supreme, now called Windsor Canadian, is still among the most popular whiskies in the United States. In 1987, Fortune Brands (now Beam Suntory), bought the distillery and all its brands. Now, in addition to what they bottle in Canada, Alberta Distillers ships carloads of finished whisky, including Windsor Canadian, to the Jim Beam distillery in Kentucky to be bottled for the American market.

THINK LOCAL, BUY LOCAL

ADL, the oldest distillery in western Canada, has not changed much in appearance since the early days: remnants of polished hardwood floors still recall its proud beginnings. However, continual process improvements have kept it at the leading edge of rye distilling. With so much rye grown locally, that makes sense. Alberta Distillers is the only Canadian distillery to make both base and flavouring whiskies entirely from rye grain. The firm remains the largest purchaser of rye grain in the west, generating millions of dollars annually for local rye farmers. Although Alberta Distillers makes most of its whisky from 100% unmalted rye, from time to time, it also mashes corn, wheat, unmalted barley, and triticale. In all, it can store 3.2 million tonnes of grain in eight towering silos. Except for some corn, all this grain comes from western Canada. Alberta is not corn country, so the distillery brings in what it can't buy locally from the American Midwest. This variety of grains contributes to a host of different whiskies, each with distinct characteristics. For instance, Alberta Premium is always 100% rye, while Alberta Springs may differ from batch to batch.

Unique among today's Canadian distilleries, in the 1970s, Alberta Distillers switched from using malt for the conversion process to broad-spectrum microbial enzymes it grows on site. According to retired distillery manager Rob Tuer, a trained microbiologist, commercial enzymes are made for corn: "Sure, they'll work on rye, but our own enzyme also attacks the cell wall components, which deals with the viscosity problems. Our enzymes make sure the starch is available and doesn't gum up the works."

ALBERTA DISTILLERS SPECIFICS

Distilling whisky is a generic process, yet each distillery approaches it a little differently—one reason each distillery's whisky is unique. So just how does Alberta Distillers convert "small prairie grains" into big Canadian rye whiskies? Twenty times each day, workers load grist into one of three batch cookers and mix it with water and natural enzymes to make a mash. Once it's cooked, they hold the mash in a drop tank until a fermenter is available to receive it. Alberta Distillers uses a continuous batch process, meaning that its eighteen fermenters, each covered to prevent infection, are in constant use. While some are fermenting, workers are emptying, cleaning, and refilling the others. Each fermenter holds three or four cooker batches, so every day, operators cook twenty batches to keep all eighteen fermenters going on a three-day fermentation cycle. As soon as a fermenter contains enough mash to cover the agitator, workers begin adding yeast. Then, when the mash has fermented, they pump it into a beer well—a reservoir—to wait until it goes to the beer still. Maintaining a reserve of fermented mash allows the distillery to run its only beer still 24/7 without having to stop and restart between batches or if there's a glitch somewhere in the process.

Alberta Distillers uses three different distillation processes to make spirit for its flavouring whiskies. They may fill the high wines directly into barrels as soon as they come out of the beer still, or they may redistil, or "double," them in an 84,000-litre stainless steel pot called a batch kettle. They call this process "doubling" because the still removes approximately half of the water without losing any congeners or spirit. A third distillation approach uses the batch kettle like a traditional pot still. Copper demisters in the beer still and other columns keep sulphury off notes out of the new spirit.

ADL uses new wood and ex-bourbon barrels to mature flavouring whisky, then reuses these barrels for base whisky. They use both pallet and rack warehouses, up to nine barrels high, to mature the whisky, so maturates from different parts of the warehouse are noticeably different. At any time, more than 450,000 barrels of whisky are maturing in ten on-site warehouses. Given Calgary's dry climate, the raw spirit that they dilute to about 78% alc/vol before filling it into barrels loses water as it ages, coming out of the barrel at about 81%. The spirit also penetrates further into the staves than it would in a more humid climate.

TASTING THE NASCENT WHISKY

Alberta Distillers' base spirit—called Canadian Whisky Spirit, or CWS—smells sweet and almost oily when first distilled. Kathy Pitchko, retired spirits quality assurance manager, calls this "a pretty neutral product, probably the most neutral in the west." She agrees, though, that it retains a rye character and is generally smoother and rounder than vodka. A sip reveals hints of dry grain with promises of peppery rye spices. Maturation changes the spirit quickly, and after three years in the barrel, the so-called neutral base whisky shows whisky-like woody notes, which enhance its native rye spices on the nose. Meanwhile, the palate has become soft, and the dried-grain flavours more pronounced. At this point, it's whisky, and ready to ship out in bulk to some commercial customers. However, time rewards those willing to wait just two more years, with a base that is very

ADL quality assurance manager and chief blender Maria Palafox.

Alberta Premium Cask Strength
63.5% alc/vol | Alberta Distillers

Lush, fruity sweetness, lively spices, barrel tones, pear, ripe orchard fruit. Vibrant, then fading peppers. Big, mouth-filling, and fragrant. Oak tannins, herbs, nose tickle, then a peppery, oaky finale.

Reifel Rye
42% alc/vol | Alberta Distillers

Potent, bold rye with broad swaths of gingery pepper forged into a complex unity. Sweet butterscotch. Creamy, fruity, and floral, with earthy undertones and that finishing crescendo of bitter rye.

Windsor Canadian
40% alc/vol | Alberta Distillers

Crisp, floral, rye-spiced aromas. Feels lusciously creamy until caramels greet bracing gingery peppers, and a pithy grapefruit cleanse follows. Sweet enough to shoot, hot enough for ginger ale.

Alberta Premium
40% alc/vol | Alberta Distillers

Maple syrup, mild oak, crisp, clean, searing white pepper. Soft sweet flowers, flash of spirit, and dry grain. Bracing heat and pithy citrus peel fade into oaky tannins.

much rye whisky, loaded with sweet and peppery spices. And that's without the flavouring whisky blended in. After ten years in the barrel, the base whisky has picked up a range of crisp woody notes—not dry, tannic wood, but fresh and spicy oak with hints of vanilla and a touch of maple syrup. Though understated, it now tastes like fully mature rye whisky. "This is the substrate, or platform, on which we add the rye flavouring whisky for Alberta Springs," says Pitchko.

"For a three- or four-year-old product, the age of the whisky is pretty consistent," she continues, "perhaps varying up to three months." Maturation is not an exact science, though, and the whisky in some barrels matures more slowly than in others. As a result, a bottle of ten-year-old whisky may include some older whisky that the blender held back a couple more years to mature properly. Nevertheless, the age stated on the label is always the age of the youngest component. Alberta's rye flavourings really come into their own after about six years, perhaps explaining why ADL's younger whiskies sometimes include rye flavouring that is a bit older than the rest of the blend. While technicians use scientific instruments to check for flaws and see if the spirit is within standard, a tasting panel assesses the flavour. Blending master Maria Palafox explains: "There are some things, such a sweetness, richness, and other things, that the nose and palate can pick up that instruments can't." Seven parts per billion is the threshold of the gas chromatograph, about a thousand times less sensitive than a trained human nose. After they have blended each batch and the quality panel approves it, the blenders send it for re-barrelling so it can marry and smooth out any variations in colour and flavour.

THINK LOCAL, SELL GLOBAL

Each year, Alberta Distillers produces about 20 million litres of whisky and bottles about 5.75 million litres of it at the plant in Calgary. It's quite an operation, with two bottling lines that combine state-of-the-art computer processing with low-tech, but highly effective, human quality control. Machines invert the empty bottles, wash them with compressed air, flip them back over, fill them with whisky, put on the caps or corks, and affix the distinctive labels. Then workers inspect each bottle and pack it by hand into one of the more than 640,000 cases they will fill.

With over 200,000 cases sold each year, Alberta Premium, first released in 1958, has become the world's bestselling all-rye whisky, even though most of it stays in Canada. Despite its success at home, the distillery's name remains largely unknown to consumers elsewhere. This will change as a new business model sees them releasing more branded product while reducing bulk sales by up to 70%. ADL had been exporting more than fourteen million litres of whisky each year, most of it sold in bulk to others who put their own brand names on it. This practice allowed ADL to maintain the integrity of its brand. The bulk whisky ended up in as many as fifty-five countries, including South Africa, Malaysia, Japan, Britain, Sweden, and France. In recent years, independent bottlers in the United States particularly found Alberta Distillers a reliable source of the best American-style straight rye whisky.

Calgary is no longer the struggling city in one of Canada's struggling provinces that it was when Bell, McMahon, and the Reifels founded Alberta Distillers. Vast oil discoveries have changed the province forever. The Alberta government, which supported the early growth of the distillery back in 1946, became the first in Canada to end its monopoly on the sale of alcohol and the selection of whiskies when, in 1993, it announced the privatization of Alberta's retail liquor business. One hundred and twenty Albertans work at ADL now, and, although it may be in foreign hands, the distilling philosophy at Alberta Distillers remains: "Homegrown, grassroots, and local."

(20)

BLACK VELVET

n today's economy, the fortunes of distilleries follow not only global sales trends but also the strengths of their owners. So it was no surprise when, on November 1, 2019, Heaven Hill Brands of Bardstown, Kentucky, purchased the Black Velvet Distillery of Lethbridge, Alberta. It was a natural fit: Heaven Hill specializes in very-large-volume brands, and Black Velvet has the second-highest sales of all Canadian whiskies, most of them in the massive US market that Heaven Hill calls home.

The story of Black Velvet whisky goes back to 1946 and Gilbey Canada's Toronto gin distillery, where manager H. Crosbie Hucks and distiller John S. (Jack) Napier had begun toying with the idea of making whisky. By 1951, Hucks and Napier had developed several blends, including Old Gold, Special Old, Very Best, Red Velvet, Gold Velvet, Royal Velvet (their favourite), and, of course, Black Velvet. Bulk sales to the US soon made Black Velvet the leading spirits brand for Gilbey Canada and a strong favourite for highballs and cocktails at home and abroad.

The early 1970s were a heyday for Canadian whisky, and when global markets began demanding lighter whiskies, Canada's practice of blending mature base and flavouring whiskies made for an easy transition. Along with other Canadian whisky brands, Black Velvet was riding high—so high that the Toronto distillery could hardly keep up with demand. So Gilbey Canada, which in 1962 had become a division of International Distillers & Vintners (IDV)—which, in turn, later merged into Diageo—decided it needed a second Canadian distillery. They would build it about 3,500 kilometres to the west, on a 10.5-hectare site in Lethbridge. From there, they could supply the western US and Canadian markets with Black Velvet, Palliser Reserve, Colony House, and Golden Special Canadian Whisky, and Gilbey Canada's other hugely successful product, Smirnoff Vodka.

The southern Alberta town of Lethbridge straddles the banks of the Oldman River, not far from a rattlesnake-infested desert called the Badlands. IDV named its new plant Palliser Distillery for John Palliser, one of the first people to explore the area. When the $12 million distillery opened in 1973, general manager James W. Almond said Gilbey had chosen to build it in Lethbridge because the area had the energy, good water, and workforce needed, and nearby farms to provide high-quality grains.

However, markets can be fickle, and soaring whisky sales soon slumped globally. In 1990, Gilbey Canada announced it would close its Toronto distillery and move all production to Lethbridge. Thus, while many other Canadian distilleries disappeared, Palliser prospered, giving it the distinction of being the only branch plant to survive as a full-service distillery in the aftermath of the 1980s consolidation of the Canadian distilling industry.

Nevertheless, the inevitable churn of corporate amalgamations and takeovers brought new owners to Palliser in 1999, when Diageo sold the distillery and its brands to Canandaigua Brands, now known as Constellation Brands. Whisky sales were strong, but Constellation's primary focus was wine, and in 2009, the firm sold off most of its value-priced spirits, keeping just its high-volume, mid-premium brands, including Black Velvet. At the same time, it moved production of its Schenley whiskies from the Valleyfield Distillery to Lethbridge. Thus, two Schenley brands with strong ties to Quebec—Golden Wedding and OFC—came to be made in Alberta. The distillery also produces the MacNaughton and McMaster's brands. Constellation moved Schenley's head office from Valleyfield to Lethbridge and designated the Black Velvet brand a division of Schenley. Although Constellation renamed Palliser the Black Velvet Distillery, Black Velvet whisky itself slowly faded from the Canadian market as the parent firm focused on the US and Europe—and on wine.

So Black Velvet management and staff welcomed the family-owned Heaven Hill warmly in 2019. Heaven Hill's multi-generation presence in the whisky industry and strong distribution links brought new optimism, notably when Heaven Hill raised the likelihood of reintroducing Black Velvet to Canadian liquor stores. The acquisition, incidentally, made Heaven Hill the fourth-largest spirits supplier in the US at thirteen million cases a year.

Gratefully, Heaven Hill's focus on high-volume brands does not rule out new premium versions of Black Velvet. However, unlike past beauties such as Danfield's ten- and twenty-one-year-olds and Red Feather Saloon, new releases will sport "Black Velvet" labels to support the core brand. "We have some gems in the warehouse," notes distillery manager Jonathan Goldberg. He has also begun experimenting with distilling high wines in Gilbey's 1930s-vintage, heavy-duty 10,000-litre pot still made by military equipment manufacturers Canadian Vickers of Montreal.

Black Velvet Reserve Aged 8 Years
40% alc/vol | Black Velvet

Big, juicy butterscotch, hints of molasses, piri piri, distinct new lumber, flinty rye, grapefruit zest, and pith. Dark fruits and blackstrap round it out.

Danfield's Limited Edition 21-Year-Old
40% alc/vol | Black Velvet

Sweet, fragrant wood with sawdust and racy citrus zest. Cinnamon and ginger, both seething-hot. Tart berries, hard rye, wet slate, vague sweet pickles. Dry, aromatic nail polish, clean oak.

Schenley Golden Wedding
40% alc/vol | Black Velvet

Sweet, light session whisky with vanilla, vague pickles, dusty rye, and clean dry grain. Sweet and heat with red fruits, floral tones, and blistering chilis.

Proof and Wood Good Day 21-Year-Old
52% alc/vol | Black Velvet

Apple juice, barrel tones, buttery corn on a dusty cob. Candy floss, vanilla, lilacs, gentle wood. Orange Creamsicle quenches torrid cayenne. Wonderfully mastered wood. Freshwater plants. Grippy green tea.

WHISKY FORTS

When IDV arrived in 1973, Lethbridge already had a long whisky history as the site of the notorious Fort Whoop-Up (its official name was Fort Hamilton), a trading post brazenly established in 1869 by American traders from nearby Montana. In finagling buffalo hides from local Blackfoot people, these traders' primary currency was called whisky, although, really, it was raw alcohol shipped in five-gallon cans and mixed on site in various recipes to give it colour and flavour. This unscrupulous trade gave Fort Whoop-Up and other predatory American trading posts the nickname "whisky forts." Unconscionable exploitation of the Indigenous population by the traders, and the ensuing lawlessness, led to Canada's first declaration of prohibition and the formation, in 1873, of the North West Mounted Police (today's Royal Canadian Mounted Police). Those original Mounties established Fort Macleod a short distance away, but Fort Whoop-Up continued as a trading post until it was finally abandoned in 1893. A hundred years after the Mounties arrived to end the whisky trade, the Palliser distillery began producing Black Velvet Canadian Whisky, a libation with absolutely nothing in common with the damning firewater concocted at the original Fort Whoop-Up.

BLACK VELVET SPECIFICS

Today, operations in Lethbridge are automated, with a distributed control system running the process from the time the grain arrives until the final spirit goes into barrels. This automation has cut production staff from eight people per shift to two. The distillery operates two twelve-hour shifts per twenty-four-hour day, seven days a week, fifty weeks a year, employing sixty people. A few part-timers work on three bottling lines, one of which specializes in 200-millilitre and 50-mililitre mini bottles.

Despite 24/7 operations and substantial production volumes, railway tracks leading to the Black Velvet granary await the day when rail companies can guarantee on-time delivery. Meanwhile, each week trucks bring the equivalent of eight to ten railcars of corn to the distillery. Why corn when Lethbridge is on the western edge of the prairies? Because Toronto is right in the middle of southern Ontario corn-growing country, so that is what Hucks and Napier distilled when they developed the recipes. However, getting corn in Alberta has been an unexpected trial from the beginning. Even with promises from the distillery to purchase as much as a million bushels (25,500 metric tonnes) a year and generous provincial incentives to Alberta farmers to grow corn, it was not to be. As a result, Black Velvet Distillery buys its corn, including non-GMO varieties for the European market, from grain dealers in Montana. The malt, and approximately 1,500 metric tonnes of rye grain used annually to make high wines, come from local farms in Alberta. As Goldberg explains, they distil corn for alcohol and rye for flavour. "We are asking very different things of these grains." As a result, he rejects hybrid rye, which produces much more alcohol, but lacks character. He also resists the regulation that allows Canadian blenders to add other spirits to their whisky. Of necessity, Black Velvet uses them to take advantage of hefty tax breaks that make Canadian whisky competitive in the US market, but not for whisky sold in Canada or abroad. "We are proud of the *whisky* we make," is how he frames it.

After cleaning, the grain drops into one of two 100-horsepower hammer mills, where it hits the rotating hammers and shatters into small bits. Next, in a slurry tank, the system adds water, backset, and either enzymes (for corn) or malt (for rye) before injecting steam into jet cookers that cook the mash under pressure for three minutes. Then the mash moves on to a flash vessel, where a sudden drop in pressure causes the starch granules to burst like popcorn. After adding more conversion enzymes, then holding the mash for half an hour, the system cools it down to fermentation temperature, sends it to one of eleven fermenters, and adds dry yeast. Twenty-four hours later, the corn mash reaches about 8% alcohol; by the end of fermentation, that has climbed to 13% or 14%.

Black Velvet mashes and distils rye grain for three-week periods each May and September. Rye cooks at 64° Celsius, a low temperature that avoids burnt notes and maintains grain flavours. Rye mashes contain no corn but do include 10% barley malt in place of most of the microbial enzymes. The distillery uses specific yeasts to ferment base whisky, corn high wines, and rye high wines. Base whisky ferments for three days, while rye and corn for flavouring go longer to allow more time for congeners to develop. And, in a truly Alberta twist, when production moved from Toronto to Lethbridge, Gilbey began using glacier-fed Rocky Mountain water to make Black Velvet.

Fifteen Black Velvet employees, all trained as tasters, are responsible for daily quality review analyses of the plant's various products. "Sensory is a lot more sensitive than a gas chromatograph," explains Goldberg. They may have automated operations at Black Velvet, but the quality process requires the human touch. As a result, a minimum of twelve tasters sit on each quality panel.

Black Velvet distils its base whisky in a modern, four-column continuous still composed of a beer column, a high-pressure extractive distillation column, a fusel column, and a rectifying column. Sacrificial copper in each of these ensures no sulphurous off notes remain in the spirit. Water added to high wines coming from the beer still make impurities more volatile for extractive distillation. After fusel oils are removed through a draw (exit) low on the fusel column, the balance of the spirit travels to the rectifying column, which concentrates it up to just under 95% alcohol.

Black Velvet does not use mature flavouring whisky for blending. Rather, the system diverts corn high wines and heads cuts produced in the beer still into holding tanks, and then fills them into once-used barrels. Two years later, workers add newly distilled rye high wines and base spirit in a process dubbed "blending at birth." This blend of "old and new" enters used barrels at 77% alc/vol, where it spends at least another three years before bottling. Blenders at Black Velvet believe the flavours integrate better if they spend a long time together in the barrel. Once they dump the matured high wines, workers feather the once-used bourbon barrels back into the system. Beginning with premium iterations, Heaven Hill intends to switch gradually to using barrels from its Bardstown bourbon distillery as those from former supplier Buffalo Trace wear out. Chill-filtering the final whisky before shipping it avoids cold-induced precipitates in whisky intended for the US and the Baltic states, although, by tradition, Black Velvet does not chill-filter whisky earmarked for Canada and abroad.

As is common in many Canadian distilleries, Black Velvet stands its barrels on end on pallets for maturation. This means filling and dumping them through a bunghole in the barrel head rather than the side. Because summers are very hot in Lethbridge and winters bring biting cold snaps, they heat the warehouses to keep them above freezing. Shifts in the seasonal temperatures benefit the whisky maturing within. On average, the angels' share amounts to about 3% annually, with larger losses in new or dry barrels, which soak up a lot of spirit. Inventories taken at the time of sale to Heaven Hill showed 367,429 barrels, stacked five and six pallets high, resting in three warehouses, including a new 58,000-barrel warehouse added in 2015.

Each year, 100 rail tanker cars of Black Velvet travel to California and Kentucky for bottling. Transportation is such a large component of the cost of making whisky, and the United States is such a large consumer of Black Velvet, that it makes good economic sense to ship it there in bulk. Black Velvet destined for Canada and other non-US markets worldwide makes up about one-third of production and is bottled right in Lethbridge. Today, Black Velvet Distillery produces about 18.5 million litres of beverage alcohol annually, all of it Canadian whisky, and most of it the ever-popular Black Velvet.

(21)

COLLINGWOOD DISTILLERY

The quaint stone storefronts and treed streets of Collingwood, Ontario, population 22,000, get a lot of traffic from visitors who ski the nearby Blue Mountain in winter and lounge on the wide, flat sands of Lake Huron in summer. Spring, summer, and fall see fly fishers on the Pretty River, which tumbles down the Niagara Escarpment to slip through hardwood forest and fertile farmland into the lake's Nottawasaga Bay, just north of Collingwood Distillery.

Collingwood, with its deep harbour, developed as a shipbuilding town serving the Great Lakes in the 1850s, and later as a port with massive waterfront grain elevators. In the 1960s, Kentucky's Barton Brands was working with the now-defunct Melchers Distillery in Berthierville, Quebec, to develop a Canadian whisky tailored to American tastes. It was so successful, Barton decided to build a dedicated plant to keep up with demand. With its pure Georgian Bay water and easy access to the US market, Collingwood was a top contender for the location. And it didn't hurt that the government was offering incentives for businesses to locate there.

It took just five months to bring this distillery, which Barton called Canadian Mist, into production in 1967, and ever since then, its whisky of the same name has been one of the bestselling Canadian whiskies in the US. In the 1970s, this success made the distillery a prime target for takeover: in 1971, venerable drinks company Brown-Forman, also of Kentucky, purchased the plant from Barton Brands; then, in 2020, the US-based, family-owned Sazerac Company added the distillery and its brands to its four continent–wide distilling network, renaming the plant the Collingwood Distillery. Today, Canadian Mist is Canada's fourth-bestselling whisky.

With its broad global network, Sazerac has many resources at its fingertips, including strong managers and specialist production staff. When former distillery manager David Dobbin retired in May 2022, the firm tapped Georgetown native Dave Sands to assume the role of master distiller and general manager. With pertinent degrees from the University of Guelph and the University of California, and more than two decades of brewing experience, most recently as vice-president of operations at a brewery in Collingwood, Sands's background aligns with that of Kentucky-based Danny Kahn—Sazerac's master distiller and distillation and ageing operations director—to whom he reports. Plant manager Tom Hartle, whose summer job at the distillery has lasted thirty-eight years, worked in the shipyard as a teenager. He now oversees two control room operators and nine production staff who make the whisky. In all, the plant employs forty-two people.

Though Sazerac has brought improvements to consistency, capacity, and experimentation, the plant, equipment, and machinery remain much as they were in 1967. "Some variability is good, though," Kahn comments, "as it allows for blending opportunities and new discoveries." While Canadian Mist is formulated for just one market, Collingwood Distillery makes other whiskies and so produces a variety of corn and rye flavouring whiskies. In 2011, Brown-Forman showcased the distillery's versatility with an upscale whisky fittingly called Collingwood. One of those flavouring whiskies, released in 2014 as Collingwood 21-Year-Old Rye, won Canadian Whisky of the Year at that year's Canadian Whisky Awards. Rumour has it that delays in bottling kept this sensational whisky in barrels long past its twenty-first birthday. Sazerac's plan to inject new vitality into the Canadian whisky category will benefit from other well-aged rye and bourbon-style flavouring whiskies in the Collingwood warehouses.

COLLINGWOOD SPECIFICS

Collingwood's base whisky begins with 100% Ontario dent corn. In the early days of Canadian Mist, corn would arrive by laker from the American Midwest. That was before crop breeders had developed varieties more suitable for Ontario's short growing season. The shipbuilding is gone now, the lake terminal up for redevelopment, and corn, much of it grown locally, arrives at the distillery by truck.

The base whisky—creamy, sweet, and mouth-coating when it first comes off the still—develops delicate cereal notes after a day in stainless steel tanks as it waits to be put in barrels. Although it is high in alcohol, only the deadest palate would call this spirit neutral. During three years in barrels, the base whisky gains a white-wine colour. Flavours of fruit and spices float on aromatic undertones of dried grain in a unique mix of vanillas, creamy corn syrup, more obvious cereal tones, and an unexpected dash of chocolate. Blenders at Collingwood combine this base whisky with a single rich, flavourful rye to make Canadian Mist.

Collingwood
40% alc/vol | Collingwood

Vanilla, creamy toffee, grapey dark fruit, maraschino cherries, floral tones, mulled cider, blasting chilis, then buttery. Fresh-cut lumber, hints of leather, tobacco snuff, and earthy cooked corncobs. Finishes sweet.

Collingwood Double Barrelled
45% alc/vol | Collingwood

Clover honey, clean oak, earthy rye spices, cherry chocolates, peonies. Slippery mouthfeel. Long finish with bracing peppery glow, orchard fruit and baking spices fading to citrus pith.

Collingwood 21-Year-Old Rye
40% alc/vol | Collingwood

Massive, robust, cedary tannins, yet velvety. Creamy, peachy, malty, almost nutty butterscotch. Torrid spice, cloves, cinnamon, ginger. Black fruits, lilacs. Long, oaky finish. Simply magnificent.

Canadian Mist
40% alc/vol | Collingwood

Barley sugar, vanilla, hints of mashed barley malt, hot peppers, rye spices, cooked corncobs, oak, and cleansing citrus pith. A dash of dark fruit and mild spirit.

Production begins when two large hammer mills pulverize the corn so it can pass through three-millimetre screens for operators to mix with water, thin stillage (backset), and enzymes in a slurry tank at 54° Celsius. "This avoids any lumps; it's like making gravy," plant manager Hartle explains jokingly. When the slurry resembles a well-mixed porridge, they pressure-cook it at 121° Celsius at a rate of about 255 litres a minute in a stainless steel jet cooker to gelatinize the starch. Next, they flash-cool the cooked mash to 63° Celsius and add malt and unrefined natural enzymes in a stainless steel conversion chamber. Using unrefined enzymes increases the complexity of the final whisky. Finally, workers pump the resulting mash into one of twenty 60,589-litre stainless steel fermenters and add commercial distiller's yeast. By adding protein-rich backset during mashing, and lowering fermentation temperatures when the yeast's natural protease enzymes are most active, Collingwood keeps the yeast healthy and ferments all of the starch in the mash without adding chemical nutrients. Precursors in the backset also increase the number of interesting aromas and flavours the yeast generates. Just as the temperature has to be right for fermentation to proceed properly, it also affects every stage of the process, including drying the grain. Overdried grain is less fermentable if its starches have caramelized in the dryers.

Conveniently, it takes sixty-two hours to empty and refill all twenty fermenters. Convenient because the base whisky ferments to completion in sixty-two hours. Flavouring, which continues fermenting over the weekend, takes ninety-two hours to develop its full flavour potential. Most Canadian distilleries ferment flavouring whisky longer than base whisky. Thus, three to five days after it enters the fermenter, operators send the fermented mash to a large holding tank called a beer well. From there, they triple-distil it in two stages. For a primary distillation, they send the fermented mash, including its grain residues, to the beer still and doubler (Americans might recognize it as a thumper). This produces a bourbon-like spirit at 72% alc/vol (this varies for some whiskies), which they may fill directly into barrels to mature into corn flavouring whisky, or send on for secondary distillation into base spirit. Solid residues from the grain exit the bottom of the beer still with the alcohol-depleted beer. For base whisky, they dilute the spirit to 14% alc/vol, then distil it to 94.7% in two adjacent columns called a clarifier (or purifier) and a rectifier.

Since fusel oil does not mix with water, the clarifying column removes it in what is called an extractive distillation. A final distillation in the rectifier further refines the distillate, removing undesirable congeners and the excess water added in step 2, before pumps transfer the new distillate into stainless steel holding tanks, ready to be put into barrels.

Stainless steel is rugged, long-lasting, and easy to keep clean, but it lacks a critical component for making whisky: copper. So workers coil long copper rods into short copper helixes and place them in the vapour section of the beer still to do their magic, removing sulphur notes and smoothing out the delicate spirit. "Copper is most effective in the vapour phase," says Kahn. Collingwood also uses a copper doubler, copper in the condenser tubes, and copper piping, just to be sure.

For flavouring whisky, Collingwood uses a mixture of unmalted rye, malted barley, and corn. It's all Canadian rye nowadays, much of it grown in Ontario, with a bit brought in from western Canada. Sourcing Canadian barley malt is another story, because American maltsters hold contracts for most of Canada's crop. While the malt they use at Collingwood is likely from Manitoba, since it comes via the US, its origins are not always certain. Sourcing local malt is difficult, as the barley varieties that thrive in Ontario's climate are less suitable for malting.

Collingwood relies on commercially produced enzymes and yeast for its base whisky, but not for its flavouring whisky. Instead, they ferment proprietary mash bills using the distillery's own strain of yeast, which they have specialists grow and dry according to strict specifications. Collingwood provides the yeast culture to the grower and verifies the DNA fingerprint of each batch to ensure consistency. Straight off the still, the new distillate for one of the flavouring whiskies is already rich in malty, mashy notes, with hints of butterscotch that will complement caramel and vanilla drawn from the barrel.

Before they fill it into charred white oak barrels to mature, workers dilute new distillate with water from Georgian Bay. The water in the bay and its Nottawasaga inlet is so clear, it draws divers from around the world to explore its many shipwrecks. Once-used bourbon barrels are much in demand these days. Fortunately, Sazerac, which owns the Cumberland Cooperage, produces a steady supply at its Buffalo Trace and Barton 1792 distilleries. As they become exhausted, Collingwood is phasing out its Brown-Forman barrels. Meanwhile, Sazerac has sent Collingwood workers to other plants to learn basic coopering skills so they can repair leaky barrels.

As well as distilling several different flavouring whiskies, Collingwood takes advantage of flavour differences between once-used and subsequent-use barrels to expand the range of flavourings. Extracting flavour from barrels is just one way to make flavourful spirits. Oxidation within older barrels gives blenders an entirely different range of flavours to work with, some of them quite delicate. As a result, part of the company's blending secret is how it uses a mix of these different barrels.

Warehousing, too, plays an important role. Collingwood winters are so cold that the warehouses are heated enough to keep the pipes from freezing. One warehouse also has the capacity to allow heat cycling for flavour development. Unlike the tall rack warehouses used by some distillers, at Collingwood, the warehouses are six metres high and accommodate just five ranks of barrels on pallets, so there is not much of a temperature gradient or variation within them. Rather than keeping an entire batch together, forklift drivers distribute each season's whisky among warehouses to guard against disaster and average out any unseen differences. Each warehouse holds up to 38,000 barrels, and at any one time, there are well over 100,000 barrels on hand. With the distillery now operating three shifts, seven days a week, the warehouses have reached 95% capacity, so management is building up to three more, contingent on approval from the town. They also mature some whisky off site. Blending whisky from different warehouses brings all the little variables together, explaining both the consistency and the range of flavours in Collingwood's whiskies.

The biggest market for the Canadian Mist brand continues to be the United States, which tells us why blenders add a dash of American blending wine to each batch. After blending it, workers pump the high-strength whisky into tanker trucks and send it to Kentucky for bottling. Waiting to dilute it at the bottling plant saves the cost of shipping water to Kentucky. Workers there filter the whisky before bottling, to remove any little bits of wood, charcoal, or other unwanted particles. While some distilleries chill their whisky and filter it before bottling, Collingwood uses gentler carbon-filled pads to preserve the integrity of the spirit.

And finally, a note on that whisky named Collingwood. A premium blend, it begins with a higher proportion of older rye whisky than Canadian Mist. And then they add another twist. Once they have blended it, the blenders hold it in marrying vats for almost a year with toasted maple-wood barrel staves floating on its surface. The toasted maple imbues the mature whisky with a rare fruitiness unique in Canadian whisky. If this sounds like innovation, it is, and it only makes whisky lovers more eager for the new whiskies Sazerac has in store. "From an experimental standpoint," says Sazerac master blender Drew Mayville, "we have some great whiskies developing and many more exciting projects to come."

(22)

FORTY CREEK

As you wind down the steep road from Forty Mile Creek to the distillery below, Toronto's skyline, fifty-five kilometres away, glimmers across Lake Ontario. Here the creek scuds over the same Niagara limestone from which the world's best-known waterfall plunges sixty-five kilometres (forty miles) to the east. Since the turn of the 21st century, Forty Creek Distillery's Niagara whiskies have become quiet ambassadors for this unique geography, until now known best to honeymooners, hikers on the Trans Canada Trail, and residents of Grimsby, Ontario.

Here, in 1970, Swiss mechanical engineer Otto Rieder accomplished something that no one else in Ontario had in decades. He, along with twenty-nine private investors, secured a distilling licence. Rieder had worked doggedly to do so since a 1954 drive to Niagara Falls opened his eyes to Niagara's bounteous orchards. Rieder's disbelief that no one made eau-de-vie from the generous harvest likely diminished each time he trod the tortuous halls of officialdom in pursuit of that licence. Yet he persevered, and by November 1972, his fruit spirits had found markets in Ontario, Quebec, and Alberta. Today, Rieder's dream has become one of Canada's most respected whisky distilleries: Forty Creek.

On July 27, 1987, a young winemaker named Bill Ashburn walked through the doors of Rieder's distillery and began making spirits. Rieder took a shine to the lad and, together with distiller Gerhard Cohn, taught him the trade. Having lived through the distillery's near bankruptcy, two changes in ownership, and stints at every production job in the plant, Ashburn today leads the way as Forty Creek's chief tastemaker, flavour guru, and blender. As he explains, "My responsibility right now is only to the liquid." The firm is slowly raising Ashburn's profile, but as a working master blender, he has little time for appearances, PR engagements, or social media. Once a year, he comes front and centre at Forty Creek's annual Whisky Weekend.

In 1992, a pivotal force entered the distillery's evolution in the form of veteran winemaker and drinks executive John K. Hall. Rieder had hired Hall to wrap up the business. In twenty years, it never made a nickel. Most distillery expenditures came in the fall, most sales at Christmas, and then, months later, government liquor boards eventually paid their accounts. The cyclical nature of this cash flow puzzled Rieder's bankers, making investment funds expensive to borrow. Nonetheless, Hall saw what the banks could not, and, rather than closing the distillery, he bought it. Ashburn, as both men joke, "came with the furniture." Rieder and Cohn built the distillery, and Ashburn has remained a constant thread throughout, but John K. Hall was the visionary who founded Forty Creek.

A chemist by education, a winemaker by trade, and a whisky maker by passion, Hall grew up in Windsor, not far from the Hiram Walker Distillery, where he had set his sights on a career. But that was not to be. For a while, he tasted spices and botanicals for Campbell Soup, then joined John Labatt's wine division, Ridout Wines, as an assistant winemaker. If the aromas of Hiram Walker's fermenting mash captivated his boyhood nose, and his quality control responsibilities at Campbell's disciplined it, making wine nurtured his creative curiosity. In 1989, when Labatt's decided to focus its business on beer, Hall helped lead a management buyout of Ridout, assuming the role of vice-president and general manager of Ontario sales and marketing for the newly created company Cartier Wines. It was a smart business move, confirmed when Cartier evolved into the wine conglomerate Vincor, the fourth-largest wine producer in North America and eighth-largest in the world. Fortunately for whisky lovers, by then, Hall had met Otto Rieder.

When Hall bought the distillery, Rieder supported its eau-de-vie business by distilling a little whisky and bottling and selling bulk vodka and whisky it purchased elsewhere. For a short while, it also bottled Canadian Mist under licence for sale in Canada. "It was a good distillery," Hall insists, "but no one in Canada was drinking eau-de-vie." Falling back on his winemaking skills, Hall obtained a provincial winemaking licence and, in 1993, converted the distillery into a winery he called Kittling Ridge. However, he did not abandon distilling. Instead, he installed a column still and began making vodka, just as today's start-up distilleries often do to generate quick sales. At the same time, growing consumer interest in bourbon and Scotch, as well as his natural curiosity, inspired him to begin distilling whisky. He also noted that the distillery had more bottling capacity than it was using, so he sought opportunities to bottle products for others, a practice called co-packing. Most of his bottling clients were wine or spirits makers, though Ashburn laughingly recalls a contract to bottle Plax mouthwash.

When it finally came on the market just before the turn of the century, Hall called his whisky "Forty Creek." The cult of Forty Creek is broad in Canada today, but just as Canadian musicians and actors often launch their careers in America, Forty Creek got its first real recognition south of the border. Forty Creek Barrel Select was a major hit in Texas right from its introduction there in 2003. Then, when it became the fastest-growing brand in Canada, making serious inroads in the US market, too, Hall sold the wine business and renamed the distillery itself Forty Creek.

Hall's strategy, to make his whiskies approachable and a little bit more flavourful than competitively priced brands, gave his first two releases, Barrel Select and Triple Grain, a lot of traction. He had to make a choice—split his attention between the two or focus on just one of these to build a solid brand. He chose the latter approach and dropped the still-lamented Triple Grain in favour of Forty Creek Barrel Select. To this, he added an annual special release, blended and priced for connoisseurs and introduced at the distillery's Whisky Weekend celebration, still Canada's whisky event of the year. He later added the most popular of these special releases to the regular range. Over time, Forty Creek built a massive loyal following in and beyond Canada. "He's a breath of fresh air for the industry," commented one competing distiller. "He's really done a lot for us."

In 2014, Gruppo Campari, a global spirits company based in Italy, paid $185.6 million to acquire the tiny eau-de-vie operation that John K. Hall and his team had successfully transformed into a Canadian whisky powerhouse. It is a just reward for his pioneering role in today's Canadian whisky renaissance that Hall, the force behind Forty Creek, can enjoy the fruits of his labours with his family. Campari has since invested significantly in the brand, upgrading and automating equipment to handle increased demand without having to expand, and adding a welcoming Brand House visitors' centre for drop-in visitors and organized tours. With global sales and distribution channels, Campari has all the resources to take Forty Creek to the world, as it plans to do once plant modernization, brand familiarization, and updating are complete. Nevertheless, with its origins in eau-de-vie and winemaking, Forty Creek Distillery and its whiskies remain as distinctive as the Niagara neighbourhood they call home.

Forty Creek Master's Cut
48.5% alc/vol | Forty Creek

Old blends redistilled, then rematured, turn soft and creamy before bursting with peppery spice. Stewed fruit, vanilla, citrus tones, nutty grain, and crisp oak. Big whisky, true innovation.

Forty Creek Barrel Select
40% alc/vol | Forty Creek

Creamy sweet toffee with raging Canadian ginger root. Dusty, earthy rye, ripe red fruits, sherry, sweet-and-sour sauce, floral tones, citrus zest. Finishes soft and clean and craving another.

Forty Creek Confederation Oak Reserve
40% alc/vol | Forty Creek

Lush, creamy butterscotch, vanilla, toasted oak, golden raisins, cereal tones, dry grain, rough caporal tobacco, balsam, soft tannins, and crisp wood, while a peppery finish fades into citrus pith.

Rieder Canadian Company
40% alc/vol | Rieder, now Forty Creek

Sweet caramel, burnt fruitwood, white pepper with a gingery feel, freshwater plants, mildly herbal, with a late-arriving glow. Pleasant, simple, and begging for ginger ale.

A 5,000-litre pot still at Forty Creek.

FORTY CREEK SPECIFICS

Since Rieder's originally made eau-de-vie, it did not have a mill. Rather than building one, Forty Creek continues to contract out its milling. Workers mash and ferment three mixed-grain mash bills in eight 25,000-litre and three 40,000-litre closed fermenters that Hall had used to ferment wine. Each has a circulating pump to prevent sedimentation. Workers add microbial enzymes rather than malt for conversion. While brewer's and distiller's yeasts predominate here, as in other distilleries, Forty Creek also adds wine yeast to certain mashes to generate specific profiles and capture the natural essences of the grains.

Depending on the mash, the season, and the yeast, five to seven days of fermentation produce beer with about 8% or 9% alc/vol. They distil this in the two small, original, steam-heated copper eau-de-vie pot stills that came with the plant. The larger of these, at 5,000 litres, has a short rectifying column up above to encourage reflux for a richer spirit. The other still, a bare 500 litres, can only be described as mini. After two distillations, the fermented mash reaches between 62% and 70% alc/vol, so there is no need for dilution before barrelling, and a rich complement of congeners remains in the new spirit. Spirit from the 5,000-litre still is softer than that from the 500-litre one, so they produce different spirits from the same mash. In practice, Ashburn generally uses the smaller still for his experimental runs. As most distillers do, he routinely discards heads and tails.

Barrel selection is paramount at Forty Creek Distillery, and because each barrel is unique, tasters sample the whiskies as they mature. For the most part, Forty Creek uses American bourbon barrels from another Campari distillery, Wild Turkey. But some years ago, when Hall found arborists thinning a grove of local oaks, he bought the logs and had a Missouri cooperage make them into custom-toasted barrels. Long, cold winters ensure that Canadian oak is denser than its American counterpart, and the harsh Canadian climate imbues it richly with vanillins. Although the barrels had been seasoned carefully, after a year in Canadian oak, the whisky was so loaded with intense aromas that Hall feared he would end up having to redistil it. But patience was rewarded as time smoothed it out, creating an exciting Confederation Oak special release that was awarded Canadian Whisky of the Decade at the Canadian Whisky Awards in 2020. Ashburn still matures Confederation Oak in Canadian oak barrels.

For the distillery's flagship whisky, Forty Creek Barrel Select, Ashburn mingles whiskies aged in a mixture of light- and medium-toasted and heavily charred white oak barrels, then reracks it into barrels used first to age sherry. He takes the same approach with Forty Creek Double Barrel Reserve, but instead of six months in sherry casks, he marries the blend in first-fill Wild Turkey barrels.

Whisky makers know that consistency is as important as name recognition and is one of the keys to successful whisky brands. Volumes are such that Forty Creek has some of its base whisky distilled off site to its specifications, then fills it into barrels at Forty Creek for maturation on site. And while they strive to maintain the distillery profile, some batch variation occurs, so Ashburn holds the mature base whisky in solera systems and blends it to a standard before adding flavouring whiskies. Fortunately, with handmade whisky, he can tweak each blended batch a little to accommodate any differences.

Forty Creek is a growing enterprise with sixty production staff in an 18,000-square-metre distillery, including still house, barrel ageing cellars, stainless steel storage and fermentation tanks, grain handling equipment, finished goods warehousing, and three automated bottling lines, plus a manual line for small batches. Compared to some other Canadian distilleries, this scale of operation is small.

NIAGARA WHISKY

The region of Niagara called "The Forty" is typical of the Ontario farmland where many early Canadian settlers distilled local grain in tiny backyard stills. The land above the ridge is flat and fertile, and Grimsby's harbour provided ready access to nearby York (Toronto). But if other Canadian distilleries promote their long heritage, tradition, and history, Forty Creek makes much of its recent origins and unique geography. Unencumbered by, but respectful of, tradition, Forty Creek has emerged as a centre of innovation for Canadian whisky. Ashburn's whiskies, flavourful yet elegant, originate with the simple question: "What can we do differently?" For instance, he subtly incorporated flavours from local flora in a botanical whisky called The Forager, inspiring other brands in Canada and abroad to do the same.

Discreet splashes of wines, drawn from Kittling Ridge–era barrels, occasionally anoint some surprisingly complex blends. For one Ashburn masterpiece, aptly dubbed Master's Cut, he blended some of the distillery's oldest whiskies, then redistilled and rematured them. Collectors take note: the result is both stunning and singular. Just as it was with John Hall, Ashburn's re-reinvention of the Canadian whisky wheel not only breaks new ground, it gives us one world-class whisky after another. Scientific instruments help Ashburn determine if a whisky is within standard and meets legal requirements. However, for flavour, he employs the most sensitive instrument in the distillery—his nose. Ashburn's recent switch from single-grain component whiskies to mash bills may end connoisseurs' quest for a single-grain release, but it has only enhanced the levels of innovation at Forty Creek.

Back in the 1960s, when Hall was a kid looking for a job, Walker's chose not to hire him. Isn't it ironic that many of today's connoisseurs look to Forty Creek for the latest innovations in Canadian whisky?

Gimli Distillery.

(23)

GIMLI DISTILLERY

n 1875, when the first wave of Icelandic settlers arrived in what would become Gimli, on the western shores of Lake Winnipeg, they slept in tents and broke boards from their flatboats for flooring. The 7,000 people who call the Gimli area home today give no hint of their ancestors' hardship, but gravestones in the small Icelandic pioneer cemetery speak softly of epidemic and misfortune. It's still a long way from almost anywhere else: Montreal and Toronto are another time zone away, while 1,500 kilometres of prairie grain fields lie between here and Calgary. Gimli, however, is a short ninety kilometres north of Winnipeg. As the straight, divided highway approaches the southern outskirts of Gimli, row upon row of warehouses signal arrival at the large, block-like distillery, now officially known as Diageo Global Supply, Gimli. Within these fifty-four warehouses, 1.6 million barrels of whisky sit quietly maturing.

In the late 1960s, sales of Crown Royal and V.O. had grown well beyond what Seagram's Waterloo Distillery could comfortably supply. Seagram also owned six

Crown Royal Noble Collection Winter Wheat
45% alc/vol | Diageo

Sweet vanilla, soft, dry grain, nutty, and creamy. Dried dark fruits, chocolate-covered bananas, sweet pipe tobacco. Punchy spice and crisp barrel tones. Hugely complex and simply radiant.

Crown Royal Fine De Luxe
40% alc/vol | Diageo

Bourbon-esque vanilla with buttery mouthfeel. Floral, gentle fruits, and hints of Canada balsam. Dry barn board, dusty grain, sweet baking spices, and hot chilis. Complexity rewards patience.

Crown Royal Black
45% alc/vol | Diageo

Toffee-ish, rum-soaked plum pudding. Creamy vanilla, sizzling pepper, ginger, dark fruit, orange bitters, bourbon. Charcoal, smoky oak, and floral tones. Vague pickles, dry grain, and brown hay.

Crown Royal Northern Harvest Rye
45% alc/vol | Diageo

Sweet apples, pears, and berries with vanilla custard. Mild floral tones, smouldering spice, cloves, cinnamon, ginger, spearmint, balsam, dry wood. Fades into reviving peppers, orange marmalade, and grippy pith.

other distilleries in Canada, each busy with its own brands. Business was booming, and building another one seemed the most practical way to meet demand. By 1969, their Gimli plant was on stream.

Seagram had planned for Waterloo to focus on Crown Royal, leaving Gimli to do the lion's share of distillation for V.O. Then plummeting sales and the growing popularity of white spirits in the 1980s created a glut of whisky. As a result, Seagram began consolidating operations in Gimli, and by 1992, having absorbed production capacity from other Seagram's plants, including Waterloo, Gimli was operating at capacity.

By the time drinks giant Diageo bought Gimli in 2001, the plant produced Seagram's entire lineup, making it the last Seagram facility to survive intact as a distillery. Under Diageo's leadership, sales of Crown Royal have skyrocketed, and though it still maintains a human touch, Gimli is one big machine. Several upgrades and expansions could not keep pace with sales, so Gimli now focuses on Crown Royal, while the Valleyfield plant makes Crown Royal components and other Diageo brands. But even that could not relieve the pressure, and in 2022 Diageo announced a new quarter-billion-dollar distillery near Sarnia, Ontario. Meanwhile, skyrocketing sales in North America keep hijacking Diageo's plans to take Crown Royal global.

GIMLI SPECIFICS

The giant distillery is not far from the clean, clear waters of the mammoth Lake Winnipeg. However, the plant draws its water from a vast aquifer deep below its property. Rich in magnesium, with a touch of calcium chloride salt added, this water is ideal for making whisky. Gimli mashes Manitoba corn for base and bourbon-style flavouring whisky and, as much as possible, distils rye flavouring whisky from Manitoba-grown rye. Workers use hammer mills—spinning metal plates that smash it into small pieces—to mill the grain. Separate mills ensure the optimum grist size for each type of grain.

Since 1983, Gimli has used high-pressure continuous cooking for one of its two base whiskies. A jet cooker heats the mash almost instantly to 125° Celsius, then sends it through cooking tubes to gelatinize the starch. Continuous cooking is all about volume and speed, and the whisky makers at Gimli aim for a cooking rate of about 8.5 tonnes of corn an hour. However, for flavouring whisky and a second base whisky, called batch base, they cook mashes in discrete batches, as the name suggests.

Once they have cooked and cooled the mash and converted all its starches to sugars in a dedicated conversion tank, workers pump it into one of their twenty-eight fermenters. Twenty of these, each holding the equivalent of three batches of cooked mash, are reserved for making base whisky. As soon as the incoming mash covers the bottom of the fermenter, a worker adds yeast and fermentation begins. After about sixty hours, with all the mash fermented into beer, workers pump it into a common holding tank to await distillation.

In addition to dry yeast for base whisky, workers propagate unique pure strains of yeast in a specially formulated grain mash, in a bank of nine yeast tubs that look remarkably like small fermenters. It takes two batches of cooked mash to fill each of the eight square stainless steel flavouring fermenters and seventy-two to seventy-six hours for the pure-strain yeast to imbue it with fruitier flavours. Although the mash enters the fermenter at 20° Celsius, there are no mechanical agitators, so the temperature climbs to 32° Celsius with the activity of the yeast. A small amount of bacterial "contamination" that is always present in the uncovered fermenters "drives the guys in the lab crazy," says former distiller Larry van Leeuwen, "but it's traditional to use open containers; the bacteria add something special to the flavour."

In all, Gimli produces five spirit streams. These include spirits for continuous base corn whiskies; batch base corn whiskies; typical corn-based bourbon, officially known as CBW (corn-based whisky); rye flavouring; and a rye batch whisky unique to North America—and, likely, to all the world. They distil this second rye whisky from exactly the same mash as the bourbon, but using Canada's only operating Coffey still, which came from Seagram's now-defunct LaSalle plant in Quebec. From these five spirits, they make dozens and dozens of different whiskies using various ageing regimens.

All these spirits begin with distillation into high wines in a beer still. Then, depending on which spirit they are making, the distiller sends the high wines to a continuous rectifier, a batch rectifier, a column and kettle still, the Coffey still, or straight into barrels. For example, they use a four-column distillation (the first column being the beer still) to make the spirit for Gimli's continuous base whisky, the core whisky in Crown Royal. This process ensures a relatively pure spirit with a subtle grain-like bouquet and almost no fusel oils, aldehydes, or esters. Base whisky goes straight from the fourth column, a rectifier, to holding tanks, from which they fill it into used oak barrels. Although copper plays a crucial role in making clean spirit, copper doublers are conspicuously absent. Instead, Gimli employs copper demister pads at the top of each still.

For batch base whisky, they redistil the high wines in a copper kettle and column still. A kettle and column work something like a Coffey still in that they collect condensed spirit in a receiver, then reboil it in a 53,000-litre copper pot, from which it enters the bottom of a column that sits directly above it. As with traditional pot distilling, they discard some heads (foreshots) and tails (feints), leaving the centre cut—the spirit distilled in the middle of the run—to mature into whisky. They recover any spirit remaining in the heads and tails in a continuous rectifier, for vodka.

Bourbon-style spirit goes directly from the beer still into a holding tank without a second distillation. Workers then fill it into brand-new charred oak barrels for ageing. Using new oak to mature flavouring spirit probably accounts for the distinctive high-vanilla, bourbon-like flavour of Crown Royal. For rye-grain whisky, the distiller uses a two-column continuous still. Fermented mash destined for the Coffey still first passes through the beer still and then loads into the bottom of the Coffey still.

Workers at Gimli use charred new white oak barrels or first-fill bourbon barrels, or they refill barrels for maturing new spirits, depending on anticipated blending needs. They keep about 19,000 empty barrels on site, most from Kentucky, ready to fill with spirit. Machines fill about 1,000 barrels, six at a time, each working day. For full barrels, they first pump out the mature whisky, give the barrels a quick rinse with water to ensure they recover all of the previous contents, then refill them, all in one operation. New barrels, of course, skip the first two steps. Gimli also has a small but special bank of barrels sourced from the Cognac region of France, which they use for a cognac-finished whisky called Crown Royal XO. It's a blend of mature whiskies that spends a short time in these cognac casks before being shipped off to Valleyfield for bottling. At Gimli, bonds usually consist of 540 barrels. A bond is equivalent to a batch, as the spirit is the product of a single run, using the same processes from start to finish.

Once the whisky has matured, machines "dump" it in batches of 400 to 600-plus barrels at a time. Pumps aspirate it from the barrels through a hole in the barrel head and ship it off in one of Diageo's seventy railcars to Valleyfield or Amherstburg for blending and bottling. Five different spirits, three types of barrels, and an infinite range of ageing times add up to many blending permutations. Thus, individual whisky brands may include upwards of fifty different whiskies mingled together, each one contributing its special something. To reduce shipping costs, once some of Diageo's non–Crown Royal brands are blended, workers ship them to Plainfield, Illinois, for bottling. However, other than miniatures, all Crown Royal, regardless of the market, is bottled in Canada.

Because they mature the whisky in 540-barrel bonds, a quality control team takes representative samples each year, beginning when the bond is three years old. Once blenders have evaluated the bonds, they adjust the formula for each whisky brand slightly to maintain a consistent flavour profile. But to all appearances, a modern distillery like Gimli is a factory, so why wouldn't the whisky be the same from year to year? Well, to begin with, grain is like grapes. Each year is a different vintage. "Take 2009, for instance," says former plant manager Kevin Rogers. "2009 was a good year for rye. It's very, very spicy." Gimli may look industrial, with much of the whisky-making process automated, but in the end, it's not a computer but the blender's nose that calls the shots.

During those early years of hardship, the first settlers in Gimli set up a local government (New Iceland), a school, and a newspaper. With the arrival of the railway in 1906, there would be no looking back. Today, many of their descendants still celebrate their Icelandic heritage in an annual festival, the Islendingadagurinn. But they are Canadians, one and all, and 365 days a year, they are the makers and custodians of Canada's bestselling whisky, Crown Royal.

(24)

HIGHWOOD DISTILLERS

S een from High River, the Rocky Mountains could be dental shards smashed from some gigantic jaw and scattered on the distant horizon. Streams fed by their snow-crusted peaks lurch towards gentler foothills below, then, seemingly exhausted, grow sluggish to wander across dusty Alberta prairie. Usually. In June 2013, two days of unimaginable rain brought more than 300 millimetres of water to the normally parched grasslands near High River. Snow thawing rapidly in the Rockies turned the lazy Highwood River brutal, forcing all 13,000 residents to flee, some plucked from their rooftops by helicopter, as the town and townships became a broad, deepening lake. About a kilometre from the river, the cement-block Highwood Distillery was devastated. It took a year to recover.

Highwood, Canada's last remaining privately owned legacy distillery, was established as Sunnyvale Distillery in 1974 by investors from Calgary who hired a German eau-de-vie distiller to help them build the smallish plant at walking distance from the heart of High River. The first raw spirit came off its unusual column

Ninety Decades of Richness 20-Year-Old
45% alc/vol | Highwood

Creamy butterscotch with maple cream, peppermint, hot peppers, nutmeg, cloves, and ginger. Cooked corncobs and sweet spices buttress sour fruit and marmalade. Clean, tannic oak and tobacco. Balanced complexity.

Liberator
42% alc/vol | Highwood

Caramel, rye spices, clean wood. Plush and creamy, then peppery hot with barley sugar, herbs, burnt sugar, flint, and citrus zest. Throat-warming. Slowly, sweetly, fades into cleansing dryness.

Ninety 5-Year-Old
45% alc/vol | Highwood

Butterscotch, vanilla, clean oak, raging Scotch bonnets, overripe dark fruit, and pipe tobacco. Cooked corncobs, some dustiness. Flavourful, though not complex. Rich and creamy, with a hot, lingering finish.

White Owl
40% alc/vol | Highwood

Lemon custard, citrus cooler, butterscotch, hints of oak, and dusty grain. Cool lemonade and hot cayenne, vague anise, creamy toffee, sweet baking spices, and bitter marmalade. To mix.

on April 1, and until the flood, not much changed except the ownership and the name. In 1985, new proprietors, seeking to distance themselves from legal problems that had forced the founders to sell, renamed the plant Highwood Distillers. Highwood remains independent, and since February 2022 has been under new ownership led by Jarret Stuart of Nova Scotia's Caldera Distillery.

With just thirty staff, the place has a friendly, family feel. "I guess everyone likes to think of their co-workers as a family," says company president Michael Nychyk. "Highwood is a small place, like a cottage industry, and we try to keep our employees happy." Working in the whisky business soon becomes a calling, a vocation of sorts, and it has been no different for Nychyk. A job with one of Canada's major food chains turned into a career in whisky when former distiller Glen Hopkins invited him to join the Highwood family in 2006 as the operations manager.

Highwood is unique among Canadian distilleries in that it mashes 100% wheat for its base whisky. Perhaps that is because wheat makes a fine, flavourful base, and, with a slightly different distillation process, becomes a light-flavoured spirit suitable for vodka. "We're not set up for corn," says Nychyk, "but we use a lot of it for some of our whiskies, so we buy corn spirit from other distillers and age it ourselves. We also have all the corn whisky we got when we took over Potter's."

HIGHWOOD SPECIFICS

Making whisky is strictly a batch process at Highwood. Each week, seven batches of wheat go through the cycle, from cooking to distillation. Seven cooker batches of wheat become two batches of fermenting mash, enough for a single batch of beer ready for distillation. To start the cycle, workers pressure-cook about 2,500 kilograms of soft winter wheat in 12,000 litres of water to create a 14,000-litre batch of mash. Although it is close to the Highwood River and connected to city water mains, the distillery uses a deep well for the clean, potable Rocky Mountain water it needs for cooking, mashing, and processing. Highwood's cooking process is unique in Canada. Rather than milling the wheat, workers send it whole to the cooker, just as the facility's original German distiller intended. There it explodes like popcorn in the heat, releasing its starch. The cooker then expels the hot cooked wheat under high pressure into a chiller. On the way, any remaining kernels slam against a hard surface called a bell, where they explode on impact. An inspection of the spent mash reveals that wheat kernels seldom make it through the process without bursting open.

Workers add enzymes and yeast to the mash in a cooler so that conversion and fermentation begin as soon as they pump the first batch into the fermenters. Over the next twenty-four hours, they add the other six batches to the fermenting mash as they become ready. The cooking/fermenting cycle takes about five days from the start until about ninety hours after the final cooked mash enters the fermenter. It's an accurate and easy-to-repeat cycle that ensures that processes do not change among batches—and, importantly, results in a consistent beer with 12% alcohol by volume. It then takes another day for the distiller to turn the beer into new spirit.

High wines come off the stainless steel beer still at about 70% alc/vol, and workers reduce them to about 40%, then run them through a custom-built kettle and column comprising a fifteen-metre stainless steel rectifying tower mounted directly on top of a stainless steel pot still. Vapours from the pot still rise up the tower, creating a purifying reflux and allowing fine control of the components and concentration of the final spirit. Steam in a three-inch copper line that resembles a giant spring heats the pot still and does double duty by removing certain off notes from the beer. The final product is a very clean spirit that is virtually free of fusel oil and, as a result, matures about one-third faster than corn spirit. A whisky that ages more quickly gives a faster return on investment. Nychyk figures wheat whisky is at its optimum at about ten years.

People unfamiliar with North American distilling practices sometimes look at stainless steel stills such as Highwood's and assume that the spirit does not interact with copper during distillation. However, beyond the copper heating coils in the pot still, condensers and alcohol lines are also made of copper.

Until about a decade ago, Highwood distilled rye flavouring whisky. Today, they purchase newly distilled rye spirit and mature it on site. As the spirit ages, its flavours undergo so many changes that, every couple of years, it seems like an entirely different whisky. Various ages of rye flavouring whisky thus contribute distinct flavours to the final product, so Highwood always has a good variety of rye flavouring on hand.

Highwood Distillery.

Highwood buys mostly single-fill Jack Daniel's and Jim Beam bourbon barrels, never using virgin barrels to age its distillates. The demand for bourbon barrels is high, so from time to time, workers repair rather than replace some of them. About 17,500 barrels filled with maturing whisky stand upright on pallets, six ranks high, waiting for the whisky to be ready for blending, a process that might take up to twenty-five years in the extremes of the Alberta climate. The warehouses have no temperature control except for a bit of heat in winter. But winter can be bone-chilling in High River, so come spring, residents watch the western sky for the telltale arc of dark clouds that signals a chinook. As these warm winds rush in from the Rocky Mountains, they raise temperatures by as much as 30° Celsius in just a few hours and signal an end to winter.

Powerful whisky aromas greet you as you walk into the Highwood warehouse. Although losses are significant in Alberta's dry climate, more water than alcohol evaporates during ageing, so whisky that went into the barrels as new spirit at 72% alc/vol may have increased to 75% by the time workers draw it out for blending and bottling.

Blending is an art that sometimes seems almost magical. As with every magician, it helps to know a few tricks. One revolves around rye, the primary flavour source for the final whisky. Control the rye, and you control the whisky. Highwood blender Jarrod Grant includes whiskies of different ages in each blend, starting with eight to ten batches of mature base whisky. Blending various batches ensures consistency and averages out any variation among batches. The most significant factor in selecting barrels for blending is flavour, although inventory is also a consideration. There is no dump trough at Highwood. Instead, operators pump the whisky out of the barrels and prepare the blend using a recipe that Grant may adjust later—a simpler form of magic. Grant keeps samples of all batches from the past several years on hand to ensure consistency, and the Highwood tasting panel compares the current batch with the last two or three blends, tasting each at 20% to reveal the flavours and any flaws.

SPECIALTY PRODUCTS

Highwood has developed several specialty whisky products, one of which, a sipping maple whisky made by blending Highwood wheat whisky with Quebec maple syrup, does land-office business as a souvenir in Canadian duty-free shops. Highwood has also revived a long-lost Canadian whisky style from Quebec called *whisky blanc*, and it has taken Canadian cocktail lovers by storm. The original *whisky blanc* was aged in copper tanks, ensuring it had no woody flavours. Highwood's version, called White Owl, is just the opposite—aged in wood. But how can a whisky so loaded with rye whisky flavours be as clear as water? White Owl is a blend of fully matured rye and wheat whiskies that have been filtered through powdered charcoal to remove any trace of colour. Of course, this process also removes some flavour, which is why they include substantial rye flavouring whisky in the initial blend. White Owl competes with high-end vodkas on price, and now, with four flavoured versions added to the original, it is a runaway success. "My biggest problem with White Owl," says Nychyk, "is keeping enough of the custom bottles and caps in stock."

Six to eight people work on each of two bottling lines at Highwood, where machines wash 150 bottles a minute with 40% vodka before filling them with whisky. Then workers inspect each bottle by hand to make sure labels, caps/corks, fill lines, and so on are right before boxing it. It's labour-intensive, but nothing like the miniature-filling station, where, in another display of the Highwood spirit, half a dozen employees hand-fill, cap, label, and pack miniatures, one by one, in what seems more like a relay than an assembly line.

OPPORTUNITY AND ADVANCEMENT

In November 2005, Highwood Distillers bought the 10,000-barrel inventory of Potter Distilleries of Kelowna, British Columbia, about a six-hour drive to the west. Potter had long since abandoned distilling to become a whisky broker, with a bottling line but no stills. Highwood transferred all of Potter's maturing stock to High River and has maintained some of Potter's brands and formulas. Alas, they have not revived Potter's much-storied Bush Pilot's.

As new owners often do, Jarret Stuart and partner David Walker have plans to build on Highwood's long success. "We'll likely refresh the packaging," Stuart says, "maybe see more expressions." It seems a cautious start, but under Stuart and Walker, both dedicated to environmental stewardship, Highwood has also taken a giant leap by introducing Canada to the ecoSPIRITS format for circular spirits technology. High-volume customers, such as bars and restaurants, can purchase Highwood spirits in 4.5-litre refillable "ecoTOTEs," which saves them money and eliminates unnecessary packaging and discarded bottles.

Tucked in behind a farm machinery dealer on the edge of a small prairie town, Highwood Distillery really is a hidden gem, all the more so because its whiskies are, for the most part, available only in Canada, and some exclusively in the western provinces. More's the pity, because some of these whiskies—the Ninety Decades of Richness 20-Year-Old, with its liberal dose of much older whiskies, and Century Reserve 21-Year-Old all-corn whisky, for example—really are worth seeking out.

(25)

HIRAM WALKER & SONS

E stablished in 1858, Hiram Walker & Sons was once Canada's largest distillery and remains the longest continuously operating beverage alcohol distillery in North America. All the same, most of the plant, as it exists today, was either rebuilt in the 1950s and 1960s or is part of a major expansion undertaken when the distillery began making Malibu Rum. Still, the Canadian Club Heritage Centre, a replica Florentine palace that Walker built in 1894, and assorted bits and pieces of the original remain as Walker knew them. Updates since the turn of the 21st century have introduced computer-automated operations intended to give a more consistent product.

A riverfront elevator with thirty-three silos holds a two-month supply of corn, almost all of which once arrived by ship but now comes by truck. A little more than two-thirds of this grows near the southwestern Ontario distillery, and the balance in the American Midwest. Transporting grain long distances is expensive, so several years ago, when farmers in the region began growing hybrid rye,

Walker's switched to modern hybrids to save transportation costs. As a side benefit, hybrid rye is rich in starch, so it produces more alcohol than traditional varieties. At the same time, Walker's has phased out malted rye for conversion, substituting commercial enzymes instead.

HIRAM WALKER SPECIFICS

When demand requires it, the Hiram Walker & Sons Distillery can run twenty-four hours a day, seven days a week, to produce fifty-five million litres of alcohol annually. Corn for base whisky passes through a continuous cooker and then into one of thirty-nine closed fermenters, where distiller's yeast and diammonium phosphate are added. Marketing staff have had these fermenters painted a creamy off-white colour to match the floors and emblazoned them with logos of the distillery's various brands. This Instagram-ready fermenting room is an unusual sight in an industrial distillery—and, somehow, a welcoming one. Walker's distils its base spirit to 94.5% in a series of column stills, then dilutes it to 78% for ageing.

Rye cooks in a traditional batch cooker, and then the system adds microbial enzymes for conversion. After fermentation with commercial yeast, the beer goes to a beer still, and then the distilled spirit is filled into barrels. A second flavouring whisky begins much like the first. Then, after passing through the beer still, the spirit enters a 12,000-litre traditional copper pot for a second distillation to focus and enrich some of the flavour precursors and lighten the spirit a little bit. This is the spirit of the ever-evolving Lot No. 40 brand.

Although the stills are made primarily from stainless steel, certain sections are copper, so there is no need for sacrificial copper at Hiram Walker. Copper, so essential in distilling, plays an active role in the distillation, so eventually, it wears out. When this happened to the original pot still at Hiram Walker, Ian Ross, the chemical engineer who managed the distillery, was very concerned. Coppersmiths craft pot stills by hand, and Ross took great care to ensure that the replacement still they made conformed exactly to the first one. If it didn't, he feared that flavours could change. He recruited Vendome Copper & Brass Works of Louisville, Kentucky, to do the job, and when the spirit started to come off the new still, the distilling team at Hiram Walker breathed a collective sigh of relief. Nothing had changed. The distillery has since added two smaller pots for experimental runs.

The barrelling operation at Hiram Walker was tailor-built for the plant. Barrels of mature whisky arrive on pallets at the automated dumping/filling station six at a time. First, machines drill out the bungs from the centres of the barrelheads, two by two. Then vacuum lines aspirate the mature whisky from the barrels, and within a few seconds the barrels move to a second station, where another set of lines refills them with new spirit and workers seal them with new bungs. Right away, a forklift

Hiram Walker built a replica Florentine palace for his office.

Gooderham & Worts Four Grain
44.4% alc/vol | Hiram Walker

Juicy and lush with barley sugar, fresh bread, nutty grain, hot cinnamon, and peppery spice. White cedar, barrel tones, stewed prunes. Glowing heat, wafting oak, and pithy orange peel.

JP Wiser's 18 Years Old
40% alc/vol | Hiram Walker

Clean wood, sawdust, nail polish, age. Barley sugar, peaches, fruity habaneros, dry grass, milled grain, earthy hints of cooked corncobs, bright brisk barrel tones, grapefruit pith. Wow.

JP Wiser's Legacy
45% alc/vol | Hiram Walker

Candied, rich, and peppery. Stewed prunes, baking spices, resin, and citric zest. Balsam needles, cigar box, toasted oak, sour rye bread, dusty grain, lilacs, and bitter lemon. Spectacular.

Lot No. 40 Dark Oak
48% alc/vol | Hiram Walker

Juicy caramels, vanilla, wine vinegar, pitchy oak, turpentine, menthol, raisins, ripe apples, smoky dry wood, clean grain, cherries, grapes, brisk peppers, and peppermint. Chewy, then drying with fading heat.

driver loads the pallets into trucks that take them back to the warehouses, some twenty minutes away, in Pike Creek. There, other forklift drivers stack them six high. On an average eight-hour day, the dumping/filling line processes eight truckloads of barrels, about 1,400 in all. In the Pike Creek warehouses, the angels are particularly active during the first year of ageing, taking approximately 6% to 10% of the volume. After that, losses drop to about 3% annually.

As much as 40% of the whisky distilled at Hiram Walker goes to make Canadian Club, its most successful whisky brand. The process for Canadian Club whiskies differs somewhat from other whiskies distilled at Hiram Walker. For Canadian Club, the component whiskies are blended before being filled into barrels. Because the plant also makes Wiser's, Corby's, Gibson's, and other whiskies, systems are in place to keep the barrels for different products separate and avoid any accidental transfer of flavours. Once the barrels become too leaky to be worth repairing, workers withdraw them from service.

Initially, after the mature whisky has been removed from its barrels, it rests in stainless steel holding tanks until needed for blending. One hundred and fourteen tanks in the tank room hold nine million litres of various spirits, but according to Ross, you can never have enough tanks for the blenders. Walker's blends and bottles much of its whisky on site and also sells fully one-third of its production as three-year-old bulk whisky to US-based producers. This versatile plant produces a broad range of other spirits as well as whiskies.

Just across the road from the distillery, in the Hiram Walker bottling plant, four modern bottling lines fill 300 to 400 bottles a minute, after sprayers first rinse them with 40% vodka. Bottles are bulky, so the distillery has instituted a just-in-time handling system in which bottles for the next day's run arrive at the loading dock at night, already packed, bottoms up, in their shipping cartons. Doing this eliminates any need to store excess bottles at the plant, though it can create vulnerabilities to external supply-chain disruptions. On the bottling line, machines flip the

Pike Creek 10-Year-Old
40% alc/vol | Hiram Walker

The sweetest rum, but not molasses. Maple sugar, vanilla, singeing ginger, stewed dark fruit, nutty cereals, dusty grain, and clean, mildly tannic oak. Citrus inflections.

JP Wiser's 10-Year-Old Triple Barrel
40% alc/vol | Hiram Walker

Very sweet with contrasting bitter tones, citrus fruit, crisp oak, nutty grain, vanilla, and lively peppers. Simple and very quaffable. Longish, satisfying, sweet, glowing fade to grapefruit pith.

Lot No. 40 Cask Strength 18 Years Old
56.1% alc/vol | Hiram Walker

Dark rye bread, milled grain, almost salty. Crisp barrel tones with heavenly nail polish. Neatly integrated and very much rye. Long-burning finish with crisp drying tannins. Of another world.

Hiram Walker Special Old Rye
40% alc/vol | Hiram Walker

Steely rye with hot white pepper, vanilla, sweet-and-sour, fruity overtones, Christmas pudding and brown hay. Vague oak, hints of orange peel on a long, drying finish. Session whisky.

cartons over and lift them off the bottles, which are then filled, capped, inspected, and returned—right side up now—to their cartons, ready to be shipped out. While these high-capacity bottling lines work well for spirits that sell in large volumes, the distillery also has a slower line for smaller-batch editions.

The bottling lines are fully automated for efficiency, but the retooling necessary to change from one bottle shape or size to another is costly, so they schedule production runs carefully. Some wholesale customers demand plastic (polyethylene terephthalate, or PET) bottles for environmental reasons, to reduce weight, or to keep costs down. The plant uses glass and plastic bottles more or less equally. They seldom use plastic for premium whiskies, and plastic is not allowed for products shipped to Europe. They chill-filter whisky with a high rye content before bottling, so that calcium oxalate crystals don't form in the bottle after a few years on the shelves. These tiny crystals do not affect the flavour or quality of the whisky, but in the past, consumers have returned bottles with the telltale haze they can create. It's a nuisance that makes filtering the norm.

But spirits are not the only product of distillation. Like most distilleries, Hiram Walker sells its spent grains as animal feed. Walker is a large distillery, and its DDG (distillers dried grains) operation is also significant, capable of holding up to 5,000 tonnes. Prices fluctuate, but at $100 a tonne, Walker converts a by-product that might otherwise become waste into revenues that almost cover the cost of corn.

Were Hiram Walker himself to return today, he might well recognize Walkerville, the town he built for his employees, though it is now fully contained within Windsor's city limits. A giant bronze statue, erected in Walker's honour in 2022, would likely point him to his former headquarters building, where, sitting at his desk, his portrait peering down behind, he might marvel at how abundantly his distillery has contributed to the growth of this vibrant city, known to locals as Canada's Rose City and automotive capital.

(26)

VALLEYFIELD

Twin spires atop the Basilique-Cathédrale Sainte-Cécile in the town of Salaberry-de-Valleyfield, about an hour southwest of Montreal, evoke nothing so much as *la belle province historique*. Its first settlers arrived here on Grande-Île, in the St. Lawrence River, as early as 1789. Today, within this typical old Québécois town, the historic site that is now the Valleyfield Distillery has employed six generations of townspeople as bakers, brewers, and, since 1938, distillery workers. Valleyfield's dedication to innovation—including becoming the first of Canada's distilleries to go carbon-neutral—is just one of the reasons it remains at the forefront of whisky making in Canada.

Quebec's language laws require that the sign on the building be in French, and inside, 230 staff converse freely in *la langue maternelle*, but, like the townspeople, they'll quickly switch to English to greet an anglophone visitor. However, they are proud to point out that Valleyfield is the only major distillery in North America to operate in the French language. It's an industrial, column-stilled plant, for sure, but set as it is on a long, narrow lot that dates to the days of seigneurial land distribution, there is something decidedly human about Quebec's last legacy whisky distillery. Somehow, the Valleyfield Distillery, now known officially as Diageo Global Supply, Valleyfield, looks like it belongs here.

In the first few years of the past century, one Anatole S. Piedalue built his bakery, Star Biscuits, on this site. Just a couple of years later, in 1911, Piedalue sold his biscuitry to Édouard Hébert, better known as *le gros Hébert*, who converted it into the Golden Lion Brewery. The plant continued to brew beer through the Depression years until 1938. What did change several times, though, was its name. In 1923, it was the Salaberry Brewery; then, six years later, it became the Maple Leaf Brewery. Salaberry-de-Valleyfield is only forty kilometres from the US border, and Prohibition kept the brewery particularly busy from 1920 to 1933.

In 1938, Hector Authier purchased the plant and formed Quebec Distillers Company to ferment potatoes, grain, and molasses into alcohol for industrial and military applications during the Second World War. Then, in 1945, with the war finally over, he sold the distillery to Lewis Rosenstiel's Schenley Distillers. Schenley completely rebuilt it as a whisky distillery. Rosenstiel and several partners had established Schenley in the United States during the early days of Prohibition, buying defunct distilleries and brands and operating one of the few American firms allowed to produce and sell alcohol for medicinal purposes during Prohibition.

By 1946, the Valleyfield Distillery was exporting alcoholic beverages into the US, and two years later, Valleyfield's first whisky, Golden Wedding, was ready for market. Rosenstiel had purchased the Golden Wedding name and an extensive stock of American-made Golden Wedding whisky from Pittsburgh's Joseph F. Finch Distillery during Prohibition. However, Golden Wedding was soon to become an enduring, high-volume, competitively priced Canadian whisky with impressive sales in the Canadian and US markets and around the world. During the 1950s, Schenley reincarnated several other American whisky brands as Canadian whiskies, among them the Old Fire Copper brand, better known as OFC (later called OFC—Original Fine Canadian), a very popular eight-year-old whisky at that time. In 1954, as demand for Schenley's products blossomed and the distillery grew, the firm announced it had received government approval for a new distillery to be built in North Vancouver. Regrettably, financial difficulties at the American parent company delayed completion until 1959, when Schenley finally broke ground on what would become the Park & Tilford Distillery.

AMERICAN BRANDS—CANADIAN WHISKY

By 1969, the Valleyfield plant had distilled over a million barrels of spirit from Quebec-grown corn and other local grains. They sold it as Canadian whisky, but the labels bore the names of formerly American whisky brands owned by Schenley. Today, some people might cringe at the idea of whisky brands crossing international borders. Memories can be short, and people take trade protectionism for granted now, but geographic definitions for North American whiskies have not always been as rigid as they are today. For at least a century and a half, such restrictions were non-existent, and at that time, Canada had a thriving bourbon industry. For example, Schenley filled early bottlings of Ancient Age Bourbon with whisky it distilled (or bought) in Canada. This was also true for Walker's Old Crow and many other well-known bourbon brands, despite their colourful and dearly held Old South legends.

When Vancouver's Byrn family purchased Schenley's Canadian operations, Gordon Byrn declared, naïvely, that the liquor business was "the most recession-proof and inflation-proof business there is," and the new owners quickly set out to modernize the Valleyfield plant. But as worldwide overcapacity problems became obvious in the 1980s, the new owners were not prepared to invest as much as Canadian Schenley needed. At some point, fearing their client was tee-tering into insolvency, the bank stepped in and found Penfund to take over the company. Valleyfield struggled through the mid- to late 1980s, yet managed to remain in operation even as others were forced to close.

In 1987, Rapid-American sold Schenley Industries (US) to United Distillers—not UDL of Vancouver, but a subsidiary of Guinness, the Irish beer company. Then, in September 1990, United Distillers bought the Valleyfield plant and its brands as well. Thus began a roller coaster ride of mergers, acquisitions, invest-ments, divestments, and reacquisitions. Since 2008, Diageo, the world's largest drinks manufacturer, has owned the distillery. Today, Valleyfield makes distillate for Crown Royal and also for the VO, 83, and Five Star brands it sold to Sazerac late in 2018.

GIBSON'S FINEST

Among the many American whisky brands owned by Schenley was Gibson's. Gibson's Finest is now a leading Canadian whisky brand, but its origins lie elsewhere. John Gibson began distilling in 1836 on the banks of the Monongahela River in western Pennsylvania. His whisky was a well-known Pennsylvania rye until Prohibition closed the distillery in 1920. In 1972, Schenley revived Gibson's as a Canadian whisky, using spirit distilled at Valleyfield. Although Gibson's Finest had become one of Schenley's most prestigious Canadian brands, in 2002, Diageo sold it to William Grant & Sons. Then, in 2009, when Diageo squeezed Gibson's out of its first Canadian home at Valleyfield, Grant moved production to Hiram Walker's distillery. Gibson's Finest remains one of Canada's most sought-after whiskies.

VALLEYFIELD SPECIFICS

With such a long and convoluted history, it is no surprise that Valleyfield has its production idiosyncrasies. For example, as distillery manager Martin Laberge explains, Valleyfield uses 100% corn mash to make two very different base whiskies, both of which they distil to the same alc/vol. For one of them, they pass the fermented mash through a beer still, and then through a series of continuous column stills to produce a crisp, clean, continuous base spirit, just as most other distilleries do. For batch base spirit, though, rather than sending a continuous stream of high wines from the beer still through the rest of the columns, the distiller condenses them, then reheats them in a copper batch kettle and redirects the vapours into a second copper column. This kettle and column process is akin to pot still distillation. Part of the heads and tails are discarded, while other parts with pleasing sensory profiles are kept in the final distillate with the centre cut and saved to make whisky. Rich in butterscotch caramel tones, with hints of camphor, mint, mild spiciness, and a slippery mouthfeel, this centre-cut spirit has plenty of interesting flavours even before they put it into barrels. There, it matures into the creamy batch base whisky that is the signature of Crown Royal.

Heads from the batch kettle taste a bit peppery and smell of caramel, butterscotch, and chocolate, much like a rum-and-butter chocolate bar. The tails are sweet and fruity on the nose, like bubble gum, but with odd elements of cod liver oil. Tasted, though, they reveal distinct blackberry notes, generic fruitiness, more pepper, and bubble gum. Remarkably, after one tastes the tails, the heads seem to have transformed into a rich hot chocolate fudge. These heads and tails, of course, are the extremes, but it is instructive to smell and taste them, as an ideal centre cut includes well-balanced elements of both. It also reminds us that the flavours and aromas of whisky can change depending on what you have tasted recently.

Crown Royal Aged 29 Years
46% alc/vol | Diageo

Fragrant, sweet, very complex, yet subtle with vanilla, powerful oaky tannins, piquant heat, and baking spices. Fruity undercurrents, red wine, sweet prune juice, peaches, icing sugar, nail polish.

Gibson Olympic Aged 16 Years (1960)
40% alc/vol | Schenley (now Valleyfield)

Maple cream, vanilla, toasted cinnamon buns, sweet nail polish, rummy molasses, fruitcake, crisp oak, searing white pepper and flint. Round, weighty, and complex. More wood, then tannic black tea.

OFC 8 Years Old (1952)
43.4% alc/vol | Schenley (now Valleyfield)

Bright, crisp rye spices. Icing sugar, dark fruit, cherries, halvah, dusty rye. A real sipper from an era when artistry trumped muscle. Barrel tones, roses, and a cozy, warm glow.

Gibson's Finest Sterling
40% alc/vol | PMA

Strawberry shortcake, spirit, mild but crisp oak, blazing cayenne with warm baking spices. Tropical fruits, Concord grapes, cooked orchard fruit. Pleasingly dry walnut skin finish.

In addition to base whiskies, Valleyfield also makes bourbon-style and 96% rye flavouring whiskies for Crown Royal and other whiskies. Flavourings are whisky's signature and are highly dependent on the stills, so it is no surprise that workers needed time to tweak the processes and modify reflux to match the Valleyfield profiles to the standard from Gimli—after all, as distillery manager Laberge says, "My job is to make the blenders' job easy."

As directed by the blenders, workers fill the new spirits into new and reused barrels. Although the most rapid changes occur in the first couple of years, whisky tends to age slowly and deliberately in used barrels. This produces a smoother whisky in the long run, but it takes eight to twelve years to reach a good balance between smoothness and the taste of whisky. This is why Diageo uses older whisky in all Crown Royal versions—including the flavoured ones, such as Crown Royal Apple, which helps explain why Apple sells over a million cases a year. About 950,000 barrels of quietly ageing whisky sit in fifteen warehouses on site, with another 500,000 in newer warehouses nearby. An equilibrium between dumping barrels and filling them allows Valleyfield to run at capacity for the forty-eight weeks it is in production each year. Valleyfield uses pallet warehouses and rack warehouses, and, uniquely among Canadian distilleries, former distillery manager Luc Madore decided to remove the racks in three of the five-storey warehouses and stack the barrels in pyramids. "We got the cost of handling a barrel down from $2.40 to $0.40 using this approach," he says proudly. But how do workers take tasting samples from stacked barrels without moving them? Simple: drill a small hole in the side of the barrel, withdraw a small amount of ageing whisky, then fill the hole with a tiny wooden peg. Even so, workers spread each bond among various warehouse types so that any initially unperceived differences will average themselves out.

Valleyfield uses a traditional mechanical dump line to empty barrels one by one before blending and bottling the whisky on site. At the off-site warehouse complex, machines dump and fill six barrels at a time on pallets. The team at Valleyfield blends and bottles VO, VO Gold, Seagram's 83, and Five Star on contract for Sazerac, and, with Coffey rye shipped in from Gimli, a number of Crown Royal versions. Five bottling lines each produce about 290 bottles a minute, with one line reserved for 1.75-litre bottles and another for canned ready-to-drink products. Before filling them, machines vacuum-wash each bottle to remove any dust from the packing carton.

The cost of running a distillery rises constantly, and distillers can pass on only part of this increase to consumers. Governments throughout history have taxed the production and sale of alcohol to the limit, so a tiny increment at the production level translates into a significant taxable increase in bottle price. Therefore, distillers are always looking for economies. Two to three million litres of absolute alcohol of Valleyfield's production is flavouring whisky, and the rest—between twenty-five and twenty-seven million litres—is base whisky, so a cut of one cent per litre in the base is huge. Improving yield by 1%, for example, gives another four litres per tonne. At Valleyfield, workers avoid chemical yeast nutrients used in some beverage distilleries and fuel alcohol plants. Instead, the yeast feeds on amino acids generated when protease enzymes break down proteins in dead yeast cells.

Big production changes continue at Valleyfield, where Diageo makes decisions based not just on cost, but also environmental impact. Valleyfield is Canada's first large carbon-neutral distillery—and Diageo's very first. As well as no longer sending its waste to landfill, and installing scrubbers to recover ethanol that would normally evaporate during fermentation, the distillery has significantly cut fuel and water use by tackling the fine details, right down to calculating the optimal size for the boiler. And since Quebec is a major source of hydroelectricity in North America, switching from four gas-fired evaporators to a single large electric evaporator also helped cut carbon emissions. Any shortfall is made up by purchasing carbon credits.

Recently, Diageo has designated Valleyfield as its Canadian innovation centre and added four more 230,000-litre fermenters as well as a new stillhouse with a copper column and doubler, to make an additional five million laa (litres of absolute alcohol) of whisky spirit. The original stillhouse runs 24/7 for forty-eight weeks a year; the new copper stills, two days a week. Copper gives a spirit that is rich in flavourful esters and aldehydes for a lighter, fruitier whisky, but the trade-off is that workers must clean these stills regularly with citric acid, which reduces their useful life to twelve to fifteen years. Well, flavour is what Crown Royal is all about. As well, Diageo has installed a copper rectifier for white spirits and a giant copper gin still brought in from Plainfield, Illinois, for possible future use.

A lot of Canadian whisky history has happened in the only remaining legacy distillery in French-speaking Canada, from biscuits to wartime alcohol to the resurrection of defunct American whisky brands. All the while, the distillery has maintained its solid reputation for quality, both within the industry and with whisky drinkers. And ever respectful of that history, Diageo has left a giant Schenley logo on its water tower. Today's commitment to environmental stewardship and continuous innovation, the pride of its staff, and the determination of whisky men like Martin Laberge ensure this reputation is safe.

(27)

NEW DIRECTIONS

lobal recognition and steadily growing demand have Canada's whisky industry surging with confidence just as renewed media attention, generated by a flourishing microdistilling sector, brings new enthusiasm to Canadian whisky. A logical outgrowth of the whole-foods movement, micro-distilled spirits hold a special appeal, particularly for young professionals who are willing to pay for intangible features such as authenticity and localness. Of course, in Manitoba and Quebec, Crown Royal is local whisky, as are Canadian Club in Windsor, Forty Creek in Niagara, and Collingwood in its hometown.

KILTED CANADIANS

Microdistilling began in Canada in 1990 when Bruce Jardine built Glenora Distillery, hoping to make Scotch-like single malts in Nova Scotia. After all, single malts commanded the best price and making them was easy, or so some early distillers thought. Working with Scotland's Bowmore, Jardine built a typical Scottish malt distillery in Cape Breton, the Gaelic heart of Canada. When his health began to fail unexpectedly, he sold the distillery to Lauchie MacLean, and though Jardine did not live to see his distillery's whisky in bottles, in 2015 MacLean celebrated Glenora's twenty-fifth year with a whisky from Jardine's earliest distillations. Time has shown that Canadian distillers do make excellent single malt whisky—distinct from Scotch, though every bit as enjoyable.

Meanwhile, across the country, it was 2004 when Okanagan Spirits came online. There, in British Columbia's celebrated fruit and wine region, former distiller Frank Deiter focused on fruit spirits. Once a year, he would buy beer from a local brewer and make a single barrel of malt whisky. Since Deiter left in 2011, the Dyck family own and run the distillery, launching an award-winning lineup of malts and bourbon-inspired mixed-grain whiskies.

In 2009, whisky buddies Barry Stein and Barry Bernstein established Still Waters Distillery near Toronto. Stein and Bernstein began by buying and bottling barrels of Scotch malt whisky. Their early distillations also focused on malt whisky and earned an excellent reputation in Canada and the US. The year 2014 marked a turning point for Still Waters, and Canadian microdistilling at large, when the distillery released its first 100% rye-grain whisky. Microdistilling was finally coming of age in Canada. Hardcore whisky lovers appreciated not only its distinctive flavours, but also that it was bottled in both 46% alc/vol and barrel-strength versions. For years, Still Waters was the clear leader on Canada's microdistilling landscape and in 2018, the prestigious Icons of Whisky Awards named it one of the three top microdistillers in the world. The 2017 Canadian Whisky Awards had already designated Still Waters as Distillery of the Year.

However, being first in Ontario was not necessarily an advantage. By the time government regulations allowed distilleries to serve alcohol, Still Waters was firmly established in an industrial complex with no room for a visitor centre. Newer distilleries with tasting rooms and restaurants offered a visitor-friendly experience that helped build reputations and brand identities and generate much-needed revenues. Still Waters, which had to rely on distilling alone, supplemented whisky sales with contract distilling. In 2021, Still Waters made the move to contract distilling complete by selling its popular Stalk & Barrel brand to the Canadian Iceberg Vodka Corporation. Still Waters continues to make whisky for the new owners and has increased its custom distilling capacity to include whisky, vodka, gin, and other spirits.

Since 2011, Distillerie Fils du Roy—located 650 kilometres northwest of Glenora in Petit-Paquetville, New Brunswick—has made *whisky acadien* from local barley malt, rye, and other grains. Distiller Sébastien Roy matures these in an assortment of barrels, some of them coopered nearby on the Acadian Peninsula.

That same year, Patrick Evans built Shelter Point Distillery on his 150-hectare farm in Oyster River, on Vancouver Island. His two copper pot stills made the long sea journey from Forsyths in Scotland, through the Panama Canal and then north to Vancouver. Shelter Point makes outstanding malt whisky from barley grown right on its farm. Dig a little deeper, and you'll find that Shelter Point distiller James Marinus has also been putting away barrels of rye spirit, and a blend of 40% malted barley and 60% unmalted barley, distilled three times to make a typical Irish-style pure pot whisky.

In Canada's north, it was success with beer that prompted Bob Baxter and Alan Hansen to add a pot still to their brewery in Whitehorse, Yukon. Unlike many small distillers, Yukon Distillery bottles its Two Brewers single malts as small batches blended from several barrels. Besides barley, they mash other malted grains, such as roasted malts and malted rye.

THE SECOND WAVE

Leaving Scottish traditions behind, a new wave of proudly Canadian micro-distillers are making whisky their own way. The map on the inside back cover of this book shows many of them. Here are just some of the standouts.

ONTARIO KICKS IT OFF

The 2016 release of Dillon's first batch of rye whisky confirmed what Still Waters, Ontario's first dedicated microdistillery, had already foretold: well-made all-rye whisky need not conform to people's flavour preconceptions to be delicious. In Ontario, Still Waters, Kinsip, and Dillon's all have 100% rye-grain whisky now. It helps that all-rye whisky is often ready to drink long before whisky made from other grains. Founded by Geoff Dillon and his father-in-law, Gary Huggins, Dillon's Distillery focuses on small-batch spirits made from locally grown fruit and grain. In 2021, Dillon's joined the Mark Anthony group, which also owns the brilliantly innovative Bearface. Some of that brilliance has rubbed off on Dillon's, as demonstrated when it distils one of its vodkas through oak shavings to add hints of wood character.

When the store in front of Coyote, their successful Ottawa climbing gym, became vacant, Greg Lipin and Jody Miall converted it into North of 7 Distillery. Bourbon was a strong influence, so it is no surprise they chose to make whisky from a mixed mash bill. Each year, their releases get a little older and their bourbon-style, very-high-rye, and single malt whiskies show it in the glass. Despite many awards, somehow North of 7 remains a bit of a secret.

Maria Hristova, Michael Waterston, and a flock of funky chickens took over Sophia Pantazi and Peter Stroz's 66 Gilead microdistillery on thirty-two hectares of groomed heritage farmland in Prince Edward County, and with it, a good supply of maturing malt and rye whisky. Today, as Kinsip House of Fine Spirits, they distil local fruit and grain and mature their Canadian rye and single malt whiskies in local oak. Kinsip has found remarkable success by leaving its whiskies in the barrel well past the legal minimum.

Don DiMonte and Mike Hook seem blithely unaware of how great their Vaughan, Ontario-based Last Straw whiskies taste. Working with rye, rice, malted barley, malted corn, wheat bran, and the occasional beer mash from a local brewery, they are flavour leaders in Ontario, though low volumes keep them off the broader market.

The former Gooderham & Worts complex, now called the Distillery District, houses Toronto's first entry to the Ontario craft distilling movement. Mill Street Brewery is best known for its popular beers, but its annually released single malt whisky is just as quaffable. Meanwhile, Perth, Ontario, pioneer distiller John McLaren would be proud to know he inspired the city's Top Shelf Distillery. If only their moonshine weren't so popular, Top Shelf would be able to increase production of its Perth Whisky blend. Whisky making has also returned to Prescott, Ontario, at King's Lock Distillery, where Rob Heuval and Laura Bradley distil carbon-neutral organic rye from grain grown near where JP Wiser once farmed.

Wayne Gretzky's distillery in Niagara-on-the Lake, Ontario, makes several whiskies, some from spirits they purchase and some distilled on site. Since August 2010, another former Edmonton Oiler, Colin Schmidt, and his wife, Meredith, have operated Last Mountain Distillery in Lumsden, Saskatchewan. There, they turn wheat, barley, malted barley, and rye, all grown in Saskatchewan, along with corn from elsewhere, into toothsome, well-crafted whiskies.

Every microdistillery reflects the personalities of its owners, and Eau Claire in Turner Valley, Alberta, is no exception. A long background in brewing beer helps in making good whisky, but what really sets Eau Claire apart is owner David

Farran's love of workhorses. Farran plants and harvests his grain using Percherons—up to a hundred of them at once when the weather makes timing critical. The distillery's location in a Depression-era theatre and dance hall (brothel) brings a special terroir to its single malt and blended whisky, one much appreciated by visitors to the Calgary Stampede, where Eau Claire is the official whisky.

In Montreal, the epicurious Paul Cirka runs a gin house in his Cirka Distillery as he waits for his whiskies to mature, while Distillerie du St. Laurent in the Rimouski region of Quebec makes one whisky from a bourbon-style mash bill, another like American rye, and a single malt, too, all from Quebec grain. The future looks bright for St. Laurent's mischievous distilling team, Jean-François Cloutier and Joël Pelletier. Meanwhile, over in River John, Nova Scotia, Jarret Stuart distils local wheat, rye, and barley, then blends it with whisky from larger distillers to produce his Caldera Hurricane 5 blend. Popular in Nova Scotia and New York, Caldera shares Stuart's attention with his other distilling interest, Highwood Distillery in High River, Alberta.

THE BC EXPLOSION

British Columbia became a primary incubator for Canadian microdistilling when dozens of new distilleries began taking advantage of tax incentives introduced by the province in 2013. Some of these distilleries have strong whisky programs. Most make malt whisky, several employ Heriot-Watt–trained distillers, and some are adjuncts of microbreweries. It has become virtually impossible to keep up with all the microdistilleries making whisky in BC, so here are some highlights.

At the base of the Okanagan Valley, in Oliver, BC, Grant Stevely patiently hand-built a microdistillery from the ground up. Dubh Glas (pronounced like Stevely's middle name, Douglas) makes single malt whisky reminiscent of the

Lowland Scotch malt sensations of the 1970s, 1980s, and 1990s. Each single barrel bottling is delicate, yet complex and mature. Stevely's Dubh Glas comes close to making Scotch single malt, without surrendering its distinctly Canadian character.

In 2013, Central City Brewers added a still and a distiller trained in the highly respected brewing and distilling program at Edinburgh Scotland's Heriot-Watt University to their Vancouver brewery. When that distiller, Stuart McKinnon, teamed up with brewmaster Gary Lohin, their Lohin McKinnon labels began appearing on bottles of malt whisky in British Columbia liquor stores. Often using specialty beer malts, the team has created a cereal-forward lineup of whiskies with power and subtlety.

Another Heriot-Watt graduate, Gordon Glanz, infuses traditional, science-proven distilling technology with a sense of wonder that has led him to turn Vancouver's Odd Society Spirits into a house of distilling innovation. Beer malts, beer-barrel finishes, time-lapse releases, unusual wood barrel inserts, and a sense of artistic flair have taken his whiskies in new flavour directions, each demonstrating his educated grasp of the whisky-making process.

James Lester and Richard Klaus opened Sons of Vancouver Distillery in 2015; then, in 2021, when the COVID pandemic seemed never-ending, engineer Klaus took a job in oil and gas, and the distillery welcomed a new face at the still. By luck, Lester learned that Winnipeg-based distiller—and Lester and Klaus's former student—Jenna Diubaldo was looking for an opportunity. Diubaldo was an instant hit: her first whisky, called Toasted Marshmallows by a Campfire, is that rare example of two singular flavours melding in balance and harmony—peated rye whisky that actually works. While Lester and Klaus distilled the whisky, it was Diubaldo who finished and blended it to near perfection.

Stillhead Distillery at the mouth of BC's Cowichan River makes a variety of spirits, including its top-selling vodka. Not a vodka fan? That's cool, but consider that its sales buy the time distiller Brennan Colebank needs for his whisky to mature fully. Early success with malt and mixed-mash bourbon-style whiskies prompted Colebank to try rye in an effort so scrumptiously successful, he has expanded rye production, including an explosive 80% rye grain/20% BC malt mixed-mash whisky that he finished for a year and a half in a port-style black-berry wine barrel. Stacks of local Garry oak across from the distillery await coop-ering into barrels.

And there's more. Booze returned to Rum-runners Central, aka Granville Island, in 2010, when Robert and Lisa Simpson began work on the Liberty Distillery. Meanwhile, steps from Vancouver's Fraser River, mad scientist Scott Thompson uses the whisky equivalent of sourdough to keep his mash fer-menting one batch to the next in his Mad Laboratory Distillery. At Tumbleweed Distillery, next to a bootleggers' trail in the Okanagan Valley, Darren Bowman, Mike Patterson, and distiller Lokesh Khismatrao make respectable whiskies from a variety of grains, including triticale, a rye-wheat hybrid.

Speaking of triticale, Josh and Jenn McLafferty have two rich, ripe versions at their Monashee Spirits in Revelstoke. Then there is Pemberton Distillery, where Tyler and Lorien Schramm have been malting barley on site since 2014, occasion-ally drying it with peat or wood smoke. And halfway up Vancouver Island, Arbutus Distillery's single malt and 100% rye are each worth the drive to Nanaimo. And that's just to name a few.

Will all survive? Probably not. Along with their creative ideas, the winners will be those with the best business plans. Meanwhile, may these final pages of tasting notes inspire readers to explore the whiskies this brave new generation of distillers has created. Then raise a hearty toast to their passion, dedication, and perseverance. They are propelling Canadian whisky forward with each new release.

Coopers Revival
42% alc/vol | Kinsip

Splendid spirit meets skilful blending in wild grasses, herbs, and flowers. Strawberries, gooseberries, ice cream, and sizzling spicy rye turn waxy, buttery, jammy, herbal. Dry grass, minerals, tobacco. Sweet lacquer.

Two Brewers Release No. 37 Classic Single Cask
58% alc/vol | Yukon Brewers

Soft, barely sweet, tropical-fruit nose with barley sugar. Light caramels, vanilla, tingling white pepper, green papaya salad, then brighter fruit and sweet cherry. Tobacco, spice, and gently pulling oak.

Ahoy!
44.4% alc/vol | Strathcona

That fragrant nose: sweet spirit, rum, brown sugar, dried apricot! Sweet, youthful, hot, and spicy. Powdered milk? Clean wood, bitter oak, and vague herbal tones winding up on black tea.

Strath Ancient Grains Wine Cask Finished
57.4% alc/vol | Devine

Huh? Wow! Chipped granite, distant wine, sweet pickles. Aha! Butterscotch, pungent spices, gorgeous weathered oak, almond skins, black tea, then flourishing Merlot. Syrupy, yet a bit drying.

Caldera Hurricane 5
40% alc/vol | Caldera

Caramel, vanilla, jalapeños, and gingery baking spices. Apricots, orange marmalade, buttery then soft barrel tones, black tea, peach pit. Hints of old leather and pipe tobacco.

Arbutus Canadian Rye
40% alc/vol | Arbutus

Fruity, with glowing ginger. Dark fruit, dandelions, a medicinal turn of ashes and earth. Fruit sugars, prune juice? Complex and whole and wonderfully, alchemically singular.

Taber Corn Berbon
45% alc/vol | Bridgeland

Buttery corncobs, sweet rummy toffee, mint, herbs, new wood, spirit, and vanilla. Sizzling black pepper, dry brown hay, cereal, and dry grain. Cherries and charred oak dance forever.

The Scientist
53.2% alc/vol | Burwood

Raw barley. Soft wildflower honey, spirit, sweet tobacco, then malt. Sweet with scorching heat, then herbal. Delicate lily of the valley. Late berries, then zesty heat and bitter almond skins.

Antifogmatic Bliss
42% alc/vol | Moon

Sweet caramels and the underlying tartness of quince jelly.
Macintosh apples and late kiwi influence. Fresh, becoming lush
and round with the mildest peppers and clean oak.

Cirka Premier Whisky Québécois
45% alc/vol | Cirka

Grain, dark fruit, raisins, dates, walnuts, chocolatey pecans,
NOLA pralines, and mild lilacs. Sweet with vibrant white pepper,
new harvest grain, barrel tones, and cleansing pith.

Last Straw Rye Cask 6, Whisky in the Six
60.5% alc/vol | Last Straw

Chicken-scratch feed, walnuts, flaxseed, oddly nutty. Very sweet
with brisk chilis, linseed oil, then mild tannins. Massive whisky with
many walnut reprises.

Willibald Greenhorn Colombian Rum Finish
59.1% alc/vol | Willibald

Sweet, weighty, and very hot. Palate exceeds the nose with ripe
fruit, pulling pithiness, and a blazing burn. Grain spirit signals
youth. Vaguely oily. Longish hot finish.

GrainHenge Elevator Row
58.2% alc/vol | Troubled Monk

Sweet fruit, minerals, and dry hay weave through booming malt. Subtle wine-cured pipe tobacco, hints of plum, chocolate echoes, nuttiness, and barley sugar. Robust, classic single malt.

Durham Home for a Rest
45.5% alc/vol | Durham

Dusty nose, then caramel, honey, growing peppery heat, distinct peaches, and soft fruit. Its budding round, medium weight, late-arriving ginger, clean oak, and longish finish promise more to come.

Mad Lab Single Malt Batch 2
40% alc/vol | Mad Lab

Malty, waxy, sweet, and full-bodied with distinct wood, fruit, barley sugar, grain, cereal, and petrichor. Very clean, vague milk chocolate, linseed oil, and rising hot spices. Soft and engaging.

Fort Beausejour Peated Single Malt
46% alc/vol | Fils du Roy

Earthy peat smoke meets sweet cereal and quickly develops a warming glow. Integrated, tightly balanced, first-class peated malt with hot spice and grain. Grainy halvah and no rough edges.

Glynnevan Double Barrelled
43% alc/vol | Glynnevan

Maple syrup, honey, vanilla, bracing jalapeños, crispy oak,
hints of spirit, ripe orchard fruit, earthy freshwater plants,
beeswax, and dill pickles, ending with a refreshing crispness.

Dubh Glas Wee Rock
68.6% alc/vol | Dubh Glas

Fabulous nutty, red wine aromas. Oaky for Dubh Glas. Rewards
water: grape skins, dry red wine, raspberries, brown sugar.
Tobacco-ish burn becomes an intense celebratory blaze.
Suede, clean oak, fruit.

Harris Beach Rye 51
45% alc/vol | Harris Beach

Sweet, burnt fruitwood, almost syrupy. Soft, glowing white
pepper. Easy balance, flash of menthol. The most wonderful
woody framework. Fragrant, complex, with fading heat and
interlacing tannins.

Sons of Vancouver Marshmallows over a Campfire
59.5% alc/vol | Sons of Vancouver

Hard candy, marshmallows, graham crackers, s'mores,
and vaguely oily. Blisteringly hot with gorgeous woody peat
smoke, vaguest hints of fruit, and lilacs. A harmonious union of
peat, sweet, and heat.

Dillon's Three Oaks Rye
43% alc/vol | Dillon's

Lots of oak, though restrained. Floral and fruity, with ebbing hot spices, hints of varnish, peaches, and oaky tannins. Tobacco? Orange blossom water, black tea, and peach pits.

Lohin McKinnon Single Malt
43% alc/vol | Central City

Solid traditional single malt. Creamy oatmeal topped with ground nuts and ripe bananas. Soft barley sugar, lively hot spices, soft oak. Wonderfully malty, sweetish, and mildly fruity (green grapes).

Monashee Triticale
45% alc/vol | Monashee Spirits

A fruity, spicy whopper. Seared grain, licorice flashes, dusty, earthy, and sweet. Grainy hints of cattle barn. Lingering pepper with bashful fruits and soft barrel tones.

Eau Claire Single Malt Batch 006 Aged 6 Years
48% alc/vol | Eau Claire

Gorgeous nutty malt and barley sugar, with vanilla, fleeting oranges, sizzling peppers, cereal, clean grain, and clear barrel tones. Mouth-filling. Longish, spicy, malty, and oaky finish. Traditional single malt.

Odd Society Wild Thing
46% alc/vol | Odd Society

Some will love, some admire the mischievous wizardry of this ever-so-earthy, so woodsy, almost nutty, mushroom-cloud umami blast. A mycophile's malty, sweet fumet, laced with fiery spice.

Stillhead Rye Porty Spice
50% alc/vol | Stillhead

Golden raisins, black currants, dark plum pudding, dried apricots. Creamy sweetness softens, pulling grapefruit pith. Gunpowder, hot-hot-hot spices, and toasted oak. Bitter herbs. Earthy.

158 SMWS Cask 152.1
64.5% alc/vol | Shelter Point

Fragrant. Nutty grain, halva, canned fruit cocktail, baby powder, cigar ash, and tobacco. Jalapeños seethed in toffee, pears, dry green hay, burlap, fireplace ashes, and marshmallows. Water amplifies all.

Raging Crow FN Rye
40% alc/vol | Raging Crow

Lemon, with vivid orange blossom tones and kewra water. Sweet varnish, ripest cherries, barn boards, resin, beeswax, honey, vanilla pudding. Pleasing cider-like acidity, pulling astringency.

Resurrection Spirits 100% BC Rye
42% alc/vol | Resurrection

Very fragrant and complex with soaring esters, overripe fruit, maraschino cherry, flint, and barrel tones. Sweet hints of bitter oak. A long spicy burn as stewed fruit gently ebbs away.

Wild Life Wheat
45.8% alc/vol | Wild Life

Brisk ginger with florist's blossoms and greens and sprays of grain. Sweet cherry, soft white pepper, tart gooseberries, and rhubarb until only heat and sweet fruit remain.

Junction 56 Rye
40% alc/vol | Junction 56

Soft powdered Turkish delight and a bright, excited glow. Simple, beguiling nose reveals corn syrup and linseed oil. Seaweed, clean hardwood, earth, river plants, and caramel on the palate.

St. Laurent Rye 3-Year-Old
43% alc/vol | St. Laurent

Beer mash, bold fruit, hot spice, Weetabix, beeswax, minerals, crushed stone. Tropical fruit (not sweet), meaty, herbal. At last, hot peppers fade into sweet, grain, and hints of oak.

Stalk & Barrel
40% alc/vol | Still Waters

Waxy, creamy, until a peppery burst brings tugging tannins and grapefruit peel. Caramel, vanilla fudge, hints of maple. Slowly, engagingly, turns hot and pithy.

Patent 5, Single Barrel, Release 1
44% alc/vol | Patent 5

Aromatic wood, citrus peel, green grapes, and fruity esters. Sweetish with dark fruit, strong oaky tones, pulling tannins, a warming glow, cereal, grain, straw, and brown hay.

The Beast Wildfire Whisky Aged 6 Years
58.3% alc/vol | Maligne

Fragrant wood smoke, peat, bitterish oak, malt, bananas, and nail polish. Meaty, chunky, medicinal, herbal. The sweetest cherries. Metallic ash. Water damps the blazing, purgatory-destined footprint of this howling beast.

Trust Ancient Grains
44% alc/vol | Liberty

Concord grapes, lemon meringue pie, lime soda. Honey, chai, blistering ginger, Cointreau, tangerine juice, quince jelly, mulled wine, and grape skins. Fades slowly on sweet flowers and spices.

Western Grains
40% alc/vol | Goodridge & Williams

Sweet vanilla, ice cream, caramel, peppers—blazing flames subside into oak tannins, brown hay, just-baked baguettes, mild spirit, then a final, gentle fade from spice to toffee.

Shelter Point Artisanal Single Malt Aged 10 Years
57.8% alc/vol | Shelter Point

Oak caramels, lovely fruit sugars, hints of maple. Pleasing hot spice swells without overwhelming. Beautifully integrated grain, dark chocolate, ripest fruit, kiwi. Medium-long denouement of fading grain, sweetness, and apples.

Downriver Small Batch
47% alc/vol | Moonshine Creek

Grainy, weighty, and puckering at first. Then floral balm, toffee, oak caramels, and vanilla deliver fruit, grain, straw, and cereal. Bright white pepper dissolves in a soft, quaffable burn.

Two Brewers Peated PX Sherry
(special bottling for Edmonton Scotch Club)
58% alc/vol | Yukon Brewers

Daunting power. Huge sherry, dark fruit, and sweet cherries on a carefully restrained peat-smoke foundation. Buttery mouthfeel soothes as raging peppers plead for water. Briny, oaky, fruity, intense, spectacular.

EPILOGUE

The story of Canadian whisky is a tale of the creative use of raw materials— grain and water—that are processed to meet the constantly shifting demands and opportunities of the marketplace. Even Thomas Molson's decision to move to distilling was a creative adjustment to his well-established brewing business. As settlers moved west, they brought with them not only the necessities of life, but expertise in distilling. Always frugal, they made their whisky from local wheat, using the leftovers from their milling operations. Turning waste into profit—and goodwill, too—soon meant that almost every gristmill also had a still. When settlers from western Europe suggested adding a bit of rye, the rudiments of a new whisky style began to emerge.

One of the unique characteristics of this emerging enterprise was that large commercial and home-based microdistilling operations existed side by side. As transportation links grew, though, the few enterprises that survived were those that were able to export significant amounts of whisky to the United States. People on both sides of the forty-ninth parallel understand the deep roots of this cross-border tradition. Since the early days of Confederation, Canadian whisky has been a favourite of American drinkers. In the 1880s, when Hiram Walker decided to capitalize on this interest with a systematic approach to advertising, the result was a seemingly industry-wide switch to calling whisky "Canadian" regardless of where it was really made.

The absence of competition from American distillers during Prohibition created the impression that Canada's production expanded to fill the gap. However, Prohibition was a mixed bag for Canadian distillers. Although the Bronfmans, Reifels, Lewis Rosenstiel, and Harry Hatch seized the opportunity, each in a different way, not all Canadian distilleries flourished. That said, Prohibition did reinforce the American predilection for Canadian whisky that had emerged three generations earlier.

The cocktail fad of the Roaring Twenties became the cocktail fashion of the 1950s and 1960s, with Canadian whisky as the mixer of choice. Then, in the sixties and seventies, people began to demand lighter whiskies and Canadian distillers moved nimbly to meet this demand. The Canadian practice of blending lighter and heavier whiskies together, along with good supplies of well-aged stocks, made that a relatively easy task. The resulting newer, lighter whiskies responded to and fuelled this trend.

Enter vodka. In the 1980s, increasing interest in vodka was difficult for whisky producers, leading to a period of corporate contraction and consolidation. Brands disappeared and distilleries closed. It was the beginning of three difficult decades. Today, it appears that era is behind us. Not since the 1970s has there been so much domestic and international interest in Canadian whisky. Sales are up at home and around the globe. New whiskies, some of them ultra-bold, others finely elegant, and each masterfully blended, have brought new respect to the category. Although sales figures tell us that, until the recent bourbon craze, Canadian whisky never really lost its place as the most popular whisky in North America, all through those years it certainly seemed that way.

Canadian whisky now has more than token space in connoisseur magazines and books, as authors and journalists forgo the myths and support their stories with something approaching hard facts. High-end restaurants and bars across Canada and the US are increasing their selection of connoisseur-quality Canadian whisky, and several Canadian bars now specialize in it. Slowly, but assuredly, Canadian distillers are revealing more about their whisky and the details that make it unique. The doors are opening, if only slightly. Three large distilleries now have visitor centres, and others welcome the occasional tour. The people once securely hidden behind distillery doors are becoming known, at least by name. The nature of making whisky requires constant attention that does not leave much time for public interactions, though that has not kept some marketing people from adopting production titles.

As the business of Canadian whisky experiences a renaissance, so too is whisky culture maturing in Canada. It's cool again to be seen sipping Canadian. Each January, a key industry gathering at the Hotel Grand Pacific in Victoria, British Columbia, hosts the Canadian Whisky Awards. There, following blind judging by a rotating panel of ten independent spirits critics, the Canadian Whisky of the Year is revealed. Over the following two days, the Victoria Whisky Festival, a joyful whisky love-in, hosts A-list whisky ambassadors from Asia, the United States, Scotland, Ireland, and—yes—Canada.

It's not only on home turf that Canadian whisky features front and centre. At New York's Whisky Fest, one of America's top whisky shows, people line up each year to taste Crown Royal. At Whisky Live Louisville, in the heart of Kentucky's bourbon country, people stand shoulder to shoulder to sample Canadian Club 100% Rye and Crown Royal Hand Selected Barrel. Oh, yes, Crown Royal has done the unthinkable and introduced a sensational line of single barrel, high-alc/vol releases. And farther south, in New Orleans, at Tales of the Cocktail, America's most prestigious cocktail convention, Canadian whisky talks, dinners, and seminars routinely sell out. Canadian whisky is certainly back.

THE GOLDEN GOOSE

This is not to say that the category is without its challenges. Distilling has thrived because of its ability to change, and this industry has changed remarkably since Thomas Molson fired up his father's dusty old pot still. Today, multinational corporations control the liquor business—and most of the distilleries worldwide. Distilling in Canada remains a multi-billion-dollar business, kept alive by a single product: Canadian whisky. In Canada, there is a huge market for vodka, gin, rum, and other spirituous beverages, but the link between these and their place of production grows ever more tenuous. Distillers in Canada make them, but only because their distilleries are already in operation making Canadian whisky, the only spirit that must be produced in Canada.

According to Spirits Canada, Canadian whisky makers contribute $5.8 billion annually to Canada's gross domestic product and sustain more than 8,500 Canadian jobs across the country. Distillers source most of their grain in Canada, so many of those jobs are on farms. Canada's whisky makers generate the highest value-add on goods made from Canadian agricultural products, yet despite their whiskies' growing international popularity, Canadian distilleries continue to operate on a knife's edge.

In Canada, profit margins for distillers are very low. From an economic viewpoint, it makes little sense for a multinational firm to invest in its Canadian distilleries when, after all the taxes have been paid, the margin left for markup on expenses is about 18%. The same level of investment in Scotland, the United States, or emerging nations can bring double or triple that return. Only the extent of the international market for Canadian whisky, particularly in the US, can explain why, with such limited margins, these companies continue to support Canadian distilling.

Taxation has turned Canada's whisky into a cash cow for multinationals to exploit rather than develop through investment and innovation. It is time to turn this narrative around, because should it ever cease to be profitable to distil Canadian whisky, then the rum, vodka, and gin distilleries will also be replaced by tanker trucks arriving from abroad. Artisanal distilleries could never produce the volumes the legacy distilleries do, and Canada will have lost a major component of its cultural and agricultural heritage. The risk is real that decisions in foreign corporate boardrooms could wipe out a multi-billion-dollar industry and the farms that supply it, and with it, a unique element of Canadian distinctiveness that predates the "founding" of Canada in 1867.

At one time early in Canadian history, whisky was the single largest contributor to the Canadian treasury, the fabled goose that lays the golden eggs. Wouldn't it be ironic if, instead of killing this particular Canadian goose, as happened in the fable, our politicians simply took her golden eggs for granted until she flew away to lay them elsewhere?

QUALITY WORTH WAITING FOR

The consistent popularity of Canadian whisky relates to its quality. In 1890, it became law that all Canadian whisky be aged for at least two years. This was already the practice at several distilleries, but enforcing the age requirement brought a government seal of assured quality. Sales of Canadian whisky surged. This requirement speaks directly to quality, but it also created cash flow difficulties for many distillers. In 1890, when the requirement for two years of ageing became law, virtually all the small producers went out of business because ageing was, and continues to be, the most expensive part of making whisky. In 1974, the requirement was increased to a minimum of three years.

Straight bourbon, Scotch, Irish, and Canadian whisky are the most respected whiskies in the world. Each is different from the others, but they all share one commonality that sets them apart from other whiskies: the requirement that they be aged. A profusion of regulations in the US also allows American distillers to make dozens of different kinds of whisky that need not be aged. Essentially, in the US, if it contains at least 20% bourbon or rye, even neutral spirit can be called whisky. Technically, unaged grain spirit that has spent even a minute in a barrel or wooden box is also whisky there.

In 2009, talk began of a "rye renaissance" in the United States. When a few US-based independent bottlers decided to join this rye revival and began looking for rye whisky to bottle, they not only looked at home, but they also sampled some Canadian rye whiskies. To say the least, they were impressed. Enter the late Dave Pickerell, the renowned master bourbon distiller at Maker's Mark in Loretto, Kentucky. When he declared Canadian rye to be the best rye whisky in the world, that world suddenly took notice. The whisky web was abuzz with plaudits for WhistlePig Rye, a Canadian whisky that Pickerell had sourced for a start-up in Vermont. Others soon followed—Grand Grizzly in Mexico, Pendleton in Oregon, and, from California, Masterson's Rye—all with premium bottlings of Canadian rye whisky. The reaction from connoisseurs was practically gleeful. Producers such as Gibson's Finest, Crown Royal, and Canadian Club followed with premium bottlings of skilfully blended, powerfully flavoured whiskies.

If new things are happening with Canadian whisky, it makes sense that some of the lead should come from Canada's major market. And it does. The Sazerac Company of New Orleans and its master blender, Drew Mayville, formerly of Canadian Seagram's, have launched a series of new, richly flavoured Canadian whiskies, including a relaunch of the one-time number one bestseller, Seagram's

VO. Sazerac plans new offerings that reshape consumers' expectations of how good Canadian whisky can be. Early releases, including Caribou Crossing Single Barrel, Royal Canadian Small Batch, and Rich & Rare Reserve, have certainly delivered, and barrel samples from Sazerac-owned Collingwood and Old Montreal Distilleries reveal greater things to come.

New hope springs from the innovators and the individuals whose passion pushes them to take great risks. Innovation leaders today include small distillers, independent blenders, and larger firms as well. Innovation anticipates the market; it doesn't follow it. So bourbon's recent popularity may encourage bolder Canadian whiskies, but that does not mean they should taste more like bourbon. Similarly, finishing Canadian whisky in wine or other barrels merely follows the 1990s lead of Scotland's Dr. Bill Lumsden. Innovators do things differently to get positive results.

For instance, if a distillery makes its own wine from local grapes, then matures it in barrels that held whisky it also made, natural curiosity suggests a finish or added dash of it, as Forty Creek's Bill Ashburn has done with several releases, including his captivating Art of the Blend. This is the same Bill Ashburn who blended long-aged whisky, then redistilled and matured it to create the sui generis Master's Cut. When Stillhead's Brennan Colebank matures rye spirit in local BC blackberry wine barrels, he is capturing terroir. Or turn to the work of Andres Faustinelli of Bearface. He matures and finishes whisky or spirits he buys from others to reflect Canada's vast geography. Filling a barrel with wild-harvest matsutake mushrooms from the Monashee Mountains to make a blending wine, for example, gave Canada its first umami-laden whisky. And rather than knocking us over the head with it, he used his masterful blending skills to tease the flavours into subtle harmony. Similarly, James Lester and Jenna Diubaldo of Sons of Vancouver so skilfully wove powerful peat smoke into rye flavours, they created what no one else had done: a spectacular peated rye.

Just as innovation is found in Canada's littlest distilleries, the largest, Crown Royal, comes up with one sensation after another, year after year and in quantities large enough for all to enjoy. Their Whisky of the Year, Winter Wheat, was a colossal success, while back in their Montreal lab, they have sheer amazement in the works. Yet while innovators continue to work away inside some of the larger corporations, others that showed much promise may have lost their way. Think of staggeringly flavourful whiskies such as Wiser's Legacy, which seems to have evolved into a never-ending series of wine-soaked stunts and novelty wood infusions designed to generate publicity, then disappear or become contrived collectibles. On the other hand, the wonderful Lot No. 40 Dark Oak has the character and potential staying power to become a long-term bestseller. Let's hope Lot No. 40, with all its iterations, does not go the way of Legacy.

CANADIAN WHISKY: THE NEXT CENTURY

If Hiram Walker's whisky dominated the 19th century and Sam Bronfman's the 20th, already, with three-quarters of the current century yet to come, there are definite leaders. Based on sales alone, Crown Royal has a clear edge. Beyond sales, in the hands of Diageo, Crown Royal has become an innovations front-runner, releasing new connoisseur whiskies regularly. It has dedicated each of its four massive facilities to a specialty: St. Clair makes base whisky, Amherstburg does bottling and packaging, Valleyfield has become an innovations centre, and the fourth, Gimli, follows a one-of-a-kind fermenting and distilling regimen.

While the popularity of Forty Creek has slipped a bit in the US since it joined Campari, that is likely just a short-term transition hiccup. With its wild innovations, a solid connoisseur line, and a fanatic fan base, Forty Creek is clearly a whisky to watch. Another brand that leads the way in innovation and accessibility, and is well resourced, is Bearface, with its new and flavour-forward approach.

Sazerac, too, is a top contender, as innovations at Old Montreal and Collingwood, and the brilliance of blender Drew Mayville, demonstrate. Its stewardship of the Seagram legacy gives Sazerac a three-length starting lead in this horse race, though that just puts it nose to nose with Crown Royal. Of newer distilleries, one stand-out is Yukon Distillers. Their Two Brewers whiskies are world-class, but supplies are too limited to go global. The jury is out on Shelter Point, another top contender, since founder Patrick Evans sold a controlling interest while the brand was still finding its global sea legs. Alberta Distillers also has a powerful kick at the can. Already acknowledged widely as the world's greatest rye distillery, and named Distillery of the Decade at the 2020 Canadian Whisky Awards, ADL's growing emphasis on home brands, its revival of the Reifel link and romance, and its fabulous Reifel Rye are very encouraging. Beyond its much-awaited fifty-year-old, new developments and off-site blending talent also reveal tremendous potential for Hiram Walker's original whisky, Canadian Club.

A HISTORY DISTILLED AND A FUTURE BOTTLED

Whatever the future may hold, whisky has played a major role in creating Canada. From its early service as a source of comfort (and lucrative taxes) to the extent of employment it generates to its role as a gentle ambassador of Canadian quality, whisky has played its part with distinction and pride. It is a role that Canadian whisky is destined to keep playing long into the future.

Having read this book, you now know more of what makes whisky Canadian, and what makes Canadian whisky unique. You sample it, you savour it, you enjoy it. As you sit by the fire on a cold winter's night, glass in hand, remember all those generations of Canadians who spent their lives creating it. And place yourself in that ever-growing cadre of those who, like you, also find simple comfort in its simple pleasures.

GLOSSARY

ALC/VOL. Alcohol by volume (also written abv, or ABV). The percentage of alcohol in whisky or other spirit.

AMYLOLYTIC ENZYMES. Proteins that convert starch into sugar by breaking specific chemical bonds. Obtained from malted grain or fungi.

BASE WHISKY. Whisky made from spirit that has been distilled to 94% alc/vol, then matured in used barrels to emphasize flavours of maturation rather than materials.

BEER. The alcoholic product of fermenting grain mash with yeast.

BOND. A single batch of whisky, all of which was produced at the same time from the same materials.

CASK STRENGTH. The alc/vol of whisky in the barrel. This increases over time in dry climates and decreases in humid climates.

CHAR. The process of heating the inside of a cask until it burns, creating a layer of charcoal, which is also called char.

CHILL-FILTER. The process of cooling whisky, then filtering it to remove less soluble elements that sometimes make the whisky appear cloudy.

COLOURIMETER. An instrument used to measure the colour of whisky for comparison to a standard.

COLUMN STILL. A tall metal cylinder containing horizontal perforated plates, over which beer or high wines pass as they descend the column. Steam rising from below strips out alcohol and congeners and delivers them to a condenser.

COMMON WHISKY. The most basic and least expensive whisky. Historically in Canada, whisky made without rye grain.

COMPOUNDING. The practice of some US producers in the era before ageing whisky became common of making whisky by adding non-whisky flavouring agents to newly distilled spirit.

CONDENSER. A series of tubes that are cooled so that vapours passing through them will condense into a liquid state.

CONGENER. Any of a number of compounds that give whisky its flavours.

CONTINUOUS STILL. A column still to which distiller's beer or spirits can be added and distillate removed in uninterrupted streams.

CONVERSION. The transformation of starch into sugar.

COOPERAGE. Another term for barrels or casks. Also the place where they are made.

DIAMMONIUM PHOSPHATE. A chemical yeast nutrient used by some distillers to increase fermentation efficiency.

DISTILLATION. Separation of individual components of a solution by collecting vapours after heating the solution to a temperature where some components vaporize and others do not.

DOUBLER. Much like a small pot still. Vapours from the main still are bubbled through condensate from the still, enriching the vapours that then flow to the condenser.

ENDOSPERM. The portion of a seed that contains food, usually in the form of starch, for the new plant.

ENZYME. A naturally occurring protein that catalyzes specific chemical reactions.

ESTER. A sweet-smelling, often fruity congener in whisky.

FEINTS. Vapours containing undesirable congeners that are collected at the end of pot distillation or from a specific plate in a column still.

FERMENT. As a verb: to convert from sugar to alcohol and carbon dioxide through the metabolic activity of yeast. As a noun: the process of fermenting sugar into alcohol.

FERMENTER. The vessel in which fermentation occurs.

FLAVOURANT. *See* congener.

FLAVOURING WHISKY. Whisky made from spirit that has been distilled to 60% to 70% alc/vol and matured in new or used barrels to emphasize flavours derived from materials rather than from maturation.

FORESHOTS. The first distillate to come off a pot still or be extracted from a column still, usually containing undesirable congeners.

FUSEL OIL. Undesirable heavy alcohols, primarily amyl alcohol, removed during distillation.

GELATINIZE. To turn from a liquid to a gel. With starch, this involves changes in molecular structure.

GRAIN NEUTRAL SPIRIT (GNS). Flavourless alcohol produced by distilling and redistilling fermented grain sugars until all detectable congeners are removed.

GRIST. A coarse flour made by grinding grain.

HEADS. *See* foreshots.

HIGH WINES. New, twice-distilled spirit ready for rectification. Black Velvet uses lower alc/vol high wines in place of flavouring whisky.

HYDROPHOBIC CONGENERS. Congeners that are more soluble in alcohol than in water.

HYDROPHYLLIC CONGENERS. Congeners that are more soluble in water than in alcohol.

KETONES. A common component of foreshots, some ketones are sweet and caramel-like, but most produce undesirable flavours.

LIGNIN. This complex molecule, found in wood and bran, is a primary source of wood- and grain-derived flavours.

MALT. Grain, usually barley or occasionally rye, wheat, or corn that has been partially sprouted to activate the amylolytic enzymes, then dried.

MALTINGS. A facility where grain is malted.

MALTSTER. A business that produces malt.

MARRYING. The practice of holding recently blended whisky in barrels or vats to let the mixture equilibrate and, sometimes, to draw additional flavours from the barrel.

MASH. The process of mixing coarse-ground grain with water in tanks, or the mixture itself.

MASH BILL. The types and proportions of grains mashed to make a particular whisky.

MISCELLES. Microscopic spheres of alcohol that are suspended in water in mature whisky.

MOUTHFEEL. The way a whisky feels in the mouth. Usually characterized as creamy, mouth-coating, thin, or watery.

NOSE. As a verb: to smell whisky to identify aromas. As a noun: the aromas themselves.

PALATE. The flavour and feel of whisky in the mouth. The ability to differentiate subtle differences in flavour and mouthfeel.

PALETTE. What artists mix paint on, or the colours themselves. Similarly, blenders select from an assortment of distinct whiskies—their flavour palette.

PALLET. The wooden base on which barrels of whisky are placed for storage and transportation by forklift.

POT ALE. The leftover residue in a pot still after the alcohol has distilled off.

POT STILL. A large vessel, usually made of copper, in which beer is heated until the alcohol and desirable congeners evaporate and are separated from water and undesirable congeners.

POTABLE. Safe to drink or consume.

RACK HOUSE. A tall warehouse, usually made of wood, in which whisky is matured. Some bourbon makers call it a rick house.

RECTIFIER. Traditionally, someone who converted raw alcohol into whisky by filtering it and adding flavouring compounds. Today, the final column still used to produce or rectify new distillate.

RECTIFY. To make raw whisky more palatable by adding or removing certain flavours. Traditionally, whisky was filtered through charcoal, and flavourings and colour were added. Today, high wines are redistilled in a column still called a rectifier.

SACCHARIFYING ENZYME. An enzyme that converts starch to sugar.

SACRIFICIAL COPPER. Copper, often in the form of rods, tubes, or filings, placed in a still to neutralize or remove undesirable chemicals from the beer or vapour.

SINGLE MALT. Whiskies made from malted grain only, in a single distillery. *See* malt.

SLURRY. A liquid with solids suspended in it. Ground grain suspended in water.

SMALL WOOD. Canadian law requires that whisky be aged in small wood—casks of less than 700 litres capacity. In practice, distillers generally use casks with about 200 litres capacity.

SPENT GRAIN. The remaining grain and yeast residue after distillation. Usually quite rich in protein, it is used to feed animals.

STILL. A mechanical device used in whisky making to separate alcohol and congeners from water by heating them and taking advantage of differences in boiling temperature.

STILLAGE. *See* thin stillage.

TAILS. *See* feints.

TANNIN. An astringent chemical familiar in red wine, and also found in oak. In proper balance, tannins can give a refreshing mouthfeel to whisky.

THIN STILLAGE. The alcohol-depleted liquid left over after distillation in a column still.

TOASTING. The process of heating the inside of a barrel until it turns brown, but does not burn. Components of the wood melt and change chemical structure, contributing new flavours to whisky matured in the barrel.

VANILLINS. Various related chemicals found in oak that impart vanilla-like flavours to whisky.

VOLATILES. Congeners that evaporate easily.

WASH. The fermented liquid or slurry that is fed into the still. Also called beer.

WHEAT MIDDLINGS. A mixture of fine-ground particles of bran, wheat germ, and floury endosperm produced when milling white flour.

YEAST. A single-celled organism that metabolizes sugar into ethanol and carbon dioxide. Yeasts also produce many of the desirable congeners in whisky.

BIBLIOGRAPHY

Bronfman, Samuel. *From Little Acorns: The Story of Distillers Corporation-Seagrams Limited.* Montreal: Bronfman, 1970.

Broom, Dave. *The World Atlas of Whisky.* London, UK: Mitchell Beazley, 2010.

Brown, Lorraine. *The Story of Canadian Whisky: 200 Years of Tradition.* Markham, ON: Fitzhenry & Whiteside, 1994.

Chartier, François. *Taste Buds and Molecules: The Art and Science of Food with Wine.* Toronto: McClelland & Stewart, 2010.

Chauvin, Francis X. "Hiram Walker: His Life, His Work, and the Development of the Walker Institutions in Walkerville, Ontario" (working paper, Leddy Library, University of Windsor, Windsor, ON, 1927).

De Kergommeaux, Davin, and Blair Phillips. *The Definitive Guide to Canadian Distilleries.* Toronto: Appetite by Random House, 2020.

Dempsey, Hugh A. *Firewater: The Impact of the Whisky Trade on the Blackfoot Nation.* Calgary: Fifth House, 2002.

Dendy, William, and William Kilbourn. *Toronto Observed: Its Architecture, Patrons, and History.* Toronto: Oxford University Press, 1986.

Denison, Merrill. *The Barley and the Stream: The Molson Story.* Toronto: McClelland & Stewart, 1955.

Faith, Nicholas. *The Bronfmans: The Rise and Fall of the House of Seagram.* New York: St. Martin's Press, 2006.

Fiset, Richard. *Brasseries et distilleries à Québec (1620–1900): profil d'archéologe industrielle.* PhD thesis, Université Laval, 2001.

Gibson, Sally. *Toronto's Distillery District: History by the Lake.* Toronto: Distillery Historic District, 2008.

Gray, James H. *Booze: The Impact of Whisky on the Prairie West.* Toronto: Macmillan of Canada, 1972.

Hagelund, William A. *House of Suds: A History of Beer Brewing in Western Canada.* Surrey, BC: Hancock House, 2003.

Heron, Craig. *Booze: A Distilled History.* Toronto: Between the Lines, 2003.

Hunt, CW. *Booze Boats and Billions: Smuggling Liquid Gold!* Toronto: McClelland & Stewart, 1988.

Hunter, Douglas. *Molson: The Birth of a Business Empire.* Toronto: Penguin, 2001.

Jacques, KA, TP Lyons, and DR Kelsall. *The Alcohol Textbook,* 4th ed. Nottingham: Nottingham University Press, 2003.

Lea, Andrew GH, and John R. Piggott, eds. *Fermented Beverage Production,* 2nd ed. New York: Kluwer Academic/Plenum Publishers, 2003.

Leavitt, Thad WH. *History of Leeds and Grenville.* Belleville, ON: Recorder Press, 1879.

Livermore, Don. *Quantification of Oak Wood Extractives via Gas Chromatography—Mass Spectrometry and Subsequent Calibration of Near Infrared Reflectance to Predict the Canadian Whisky Ageing Process.* PhD thesis, Heriot-Watt University, 2010.

MacKinnon, Tanya Lynn. *The Historical Geography of the Distilling Industry in Ontario: 1850–1900.* Master's thesis, Wilfrid Laurier University, 2000.

MacLean, Charles. *Scotch Whisky: A Liquid History.* London, UK: Cassell, 2003.

Marrus, Michael R. *Samuel Bronfman: The Life and Times of Seagram's Mr. Sam.* Lebanon, NH: University Press of New England, 1991.

Miles, Fraser. *Slow Boat on Rum Row.* Madeira Park, BC: Harbour, 1992.

Molson, Karen. *The Molsons: Their Lives and Times, 1780–2000.* Willowdale, ON: Firefly, 2001.

Morris, John AH. *Morris's History of Prescott, 1800–2000.* Prescott, ON: St. Lawrence Printing, 2001.

Newell, Dianne, and Ralph Greenhill. *Survivals: Aspects of Industrial Archaeology in Ontario.* Erin, ON: Boston Mills Press, 1989.

Newman, Peter C. *King of the Castle—The Making of a Dynasty: Seagram's and the Bronfman Empire.* New York: Atheneum, 1979.

Okrent, Daniel. *Last Call: The Rise and Fall of Prohibition.* New York: Scribner, 2010.

Otto, Stephen A. *A Report on the Buildings at Gooderham & Worts' Distillery and an Assessment of their Heritage Significance.* Gooderham & Worts Heritage Plan Report No. 2, March 1988.

Piggott, JR, R Sharp, and REB Duncan, eds. *The Science and Technology of Whiskies.* Harlow, UK: Longman Scientific & Technical, 1989.

Poirier, Bernard. *Whisky with Dinner.* Burnstown, ON: General Store Publishing House, 1989.

Prince, Thérèse Lefebvre. *The Whiskey Man.* Yorkton, SK: City of Yorkton Municipal Heritage Advisory Sub-Commission, 2003.

Rannie, William F. *Canadian Whisky: The Product and the Industry.* Lincoln, ON: WF Rannie, 1976.

Robertson, Terence. *Bronfman.* Unpublished manuscript, 1969. Jack McClelland fonds, William Ready Division of Archives and Research Collections, McMaster University.

Rowe, David J., ed. *Chemistry and Technology of Flavours and Fragrances.* Oxford, UK: Blackwell, 2005.

Russell, Inge, ed. *Whisky: Technology, Production and Marketing.* London, UK: Academic Press, 2003.

Schneider, Stephen. *Iced: The Story of Organized Crime in Canada.* Mississauga, ON: Wiley, 2009.

Shepherd, Gordon M. *Neurogastronomy: How the Brain Creates Flavor and Why it Matters.* New York: Columbia University Press, 2012.

Shuttleworth, EB. *The Windmill and Its Times.* Toronto: William Gooderham, 1924.

Slone, Philip, ed. *Beverage Media Blue Book 1958–59.* New York: Beverage Media, 1958.

Stafford-Wilson, Arlene. *Lanark County Comfort.* Self-published, 2021.

Teatero, William. *Notes on the History of Wiser's Distillery Limited.* Undergraduate thesis, Queen's University, 1977.

Turin, Luca. *The Secret of Scent.* London, UK: Faber & Faber, 2006.

Vanderhill, Jason. *The BC Distillery.* Self-published, 2021.

Wilkie, Herman F., and Joseph A. Prochaska. *Fundamentals of Distillery Practice.* Louisville, KY: Joseph E. Seagram & Sons, 1943.

Woods, Shirley E., Jr. *The Molson Saga 1763–1983.* Toronto: Doubleday, 1983.

Wright, Steve. "Canadian Whisky—From Grain to Glass." *Ferment* magazine, n.d.

ACKNOWLEDGEMENTS

Continuing heartfelt thanks to my agent, Denise Bukowski, and her staff at the Bukowski Agency. Sincere appreciation to Appetite publisher Robert McCullough, and to Katherine Stopa for believing in this expanded third edition. Grateful thoughts also for my most helpful and cheerful editor, Whitney Millar, Andrew Roberts for his updated design, my past publicists, Josh Glover and Daniel French, and the continued marketing and publicity support for this book.

I am beholden to Janet de Kergommeaux for preparing the bibliography. Jan Westcott and CJ Helie, both of Spirits Canada, offered a wealth of information for earlier editions. Lunch conversations with retired Seagram's blender Art Dawe were illuminating and enjoyable. Thank you to the helpful folks at each of Canada's legacy distilleries and many of the new distilleries who made sure to answer all my questions.

While it's impossible to mention everyone who contributed to this third edition, Lawrence Graham and Frank Hudson of the Victoria Whisky Festival, Andrew Ferguson of Calgary's Kensington Wine Market, Randy Fitzpatrick and

Philip Dangerfield of Whisky Ottawa, and Frank and Jackie Scott of the New Brunswick Spirits Festival are high on the list.

Vancouver historian Jason Vanderhill, a wealth of knowledge and a patient guide, shared his old whiskies generously. Stephen Gye and Frank Hudson poured copious drams of Joanne Wolloschuk's BC Distillery rye. George C. Reifel shared anecdotes about the fabulous Reifel family and his childhood memories of Alberta Distillers. I also appreciate the ongoing support of Grant Stevely of Dubh Glas, Alex Hamer, and my writing partner at *Whisky Magazine*, Blair Phillips.

Whisky buddy Emmett Hossack, a much-appreciated source of reality checks and sales opportunities; Johanne McInnis, whisky friend and the queen of Canada's whisky fabric; and Mike "The Whisky Explorer" Brisebois, brand ambassador, promoter, and face of the new whisky generation.

My greatest thanks, though, are reserved for my family: Chris, Amanda, Tori, Danielle, Matt, Seneca, Ronan, Laurie, Murray, Kristen, Heather, René, Drew, Sarah, Olivia, Jordan, Tim, Eve, Jonathan, Marco, Karyn, Donna, Dad, and the guiding memory of my mother. And finally, my deep love and affection to my most understanding wife and best friend, Janet.

CREDITS

Author's collection: xv, 9, 23, 28, 43, 84, 98, 108, 115, 122, 145, 191, 216, 218, 221, 229, 254, 258, 271, 282, 292

Canadian Club Archives: 130, 132, 143

City of Waterloo Heritage Collection: 158

City of Waterloo Museum: 161

Dolph Shaw: 310 (Two Brewers Peated PX Sherry)

Duncan de Kergommeaux: 14

Glencairn Crystal: 71

Grimsby Museum, Ontario, Canada. GM 2011.3.2.1: 183

Jane Cameron: 266

Jason Vanderhill: 178 (Carrington; United Distillers Old Rye)

Kim Ratz, Grain Farmers of Ontario: 4

Library and Archives Canada: 89

Prescott Museum: 110

Reece Sims: 64

Reifel family: 172, 224

Richard Lee: 305 (Dubh Glas Wee Rock)

Tanya Cull: maps on inside covers

Sazerac Company: 214

University of Waterloo Library, The Seagram Museum Fonds: 48, 80, 86, 152, 186, 188

Whisky.Auction: 116

TASTING NOTES INDEX

NS means the alc/vol has not been stated

WHISKY	ALC/VOL	PAGE
158 SMWS Cask 152.1	64.5%	307
Adams Private Stock Aged 6 Years (1975)	40%	194
Ahoy!	44.4%	301
Alberta Premium	40%	230
Alberta Premium Cask Strength	63.5%	230
Antifogmatic Bliss	42%	303
Arbutus Canadian Rye	40%	302
BC Distillery Double Distilled	NS	178
Bearface Wilderness Series Matsutake Release	42.5%	17
Black Velvet Reserve Aged 8 Years	40%	236
Bush Pilot's Private Reserve 13 Years Old, Single Cask	43%	194
Caldera Hurricane 5	40%	302
Canadian Club 1858 Original	40%	150
Canadian Club 1950s	40%	150
Canadian Club 1960s	40%	150

WHISKY	ALC/VOL	PAGE
Canadian Club Chronicles Issue No. 5 Aged 45 Years	50%	150
Canadian Hunter	40%	57
Canadian Masterpiece	40%	194
Canadian Mist	40%	244
Canadian Rockies Aged 28 Years	46%	17
Captain's Table	40%	194
Caribou Crossing Single Barrel	40%	220
Carrington	40%	178
Century Reserve 21-Year-Old	40%	4
Cirka Premier Whisky Québécois	45%	303
CN Tower (1974)	40%	210
Collingwood	40%	244
Collingwood 21-Year-Old Rye	40%	244
Collingwood Double Barrelled	45%	244
Coopers Revival	42%	301
Crown Royal Aged 29 Years	46%	288
Crown Royal Black	45%	260
Crown Royal Fine De Luxe	40%	260
Crown Royal Noble Collection Winter Wheat	45%	260
Crown Royal Northern Harvest Rye	45%	260
Danfield's Limited Edition 21-Year-Old	40%	236
Dillon's Three Oaks Rye	43%	306
Downriver Small Batch	47%	310

WHISKY	ALC/VOL	PAGE
Dubh Glas Wee Rock	68.6%	305
Durham Home for a Rest	45.5%	304
Eau Claire Single Malt Batch 006 Aged 6 Years	48%	306
Fort Beausejour Peated Single Malt	46%	304
Forty Creek Barrel Select	40%	253
Forty Creek Confederation Oak Reserve	40%	253
Forty Creek Master's Cut	48.5%	253
Gibson Olympic Aged 16 Years (1960)	40%	288
Gibson's Finest Bold Aged 8 Years	46%	76
Gibson's Finest Rare Aged 12 Years	40%	17
Gibson's Finest Sterling	40%	288
Gibson's Finest Venerable Aged 18 Years	40%	36
Glynnevan Double Barrelled	43%	305
Gooderham & Worts Four Grain	44.4%	278
Gooderham's Canadian Centennial 15 Years Old (1956)	NS	105
Gooderham's Rich & Rare	40%	105
GrainHenge Elevator Row	58.2%	304
Harris Beach Rye 51	45%	305
Hiram Walker Special Old Rye	40%	280
Howitzer	40%	57
Hunter Rye	45%	57
JP Wiser's 10-Year-Old Triple Barrel	40%	280
JP Wiser's 18 Years Old	40%	278

WHISKY	ALC/VOL	PAGE
JP Wiser's Legacy	45%	278
Junction 56 Rye	40%	308
Laird of Fintry Tequila Barrel	42%	46
Last Straw Rye Cask 6, Whisky in the Six	60.5%	303
Liberator	42%	268
LMD Release 0001 Straight Rye 3 Wood	45%	46
Lohin McKinnon Single Malt	43%	306
Lot No. 40 Cask Strength 18 Years Old	56.1%	280
Lot No. 40 Dark Oak	48%	278
Mad Lab Single Malt Batch 2	40%	304
Masterson's 10-Year-Old Straight Barley Whiskey	50%	4
Masterson's 12-Year-Old Straight Wheat Whiskey	50%	4
McGuinness Old Canada	40%	210
Mister Sam	66.9%	170
Monashee Triticale	45%	306
Ninety 5-Year-Old	45%	268
Ninety Decades of Richness 20-Year-Old	45%	268
North of 7 Single Cask Rye	45%	4
Odd Society Wild Thing	46%	307
OFC 8 Years Old (1952)	43.4%	288
Patent 5, Single Barrel, Release 1	44%	309
Pendleton Directors Reserve Aged 20 Years	40%	17
Pendleton Original	40%	76

WHISKY	ALC/VOL	PAGE
Pendleton Rye 1910 Aged 12 Years	40%	76
Pike Creek 10-Year-Old	40%	280
Proof and Wood Good Day 21-Year-Old	52%	236
Raging Crow FN Rye	40%	307
Reifel Rye	42%	230
Resurrection Spirits 100% BC Rye	42%	308
Rich & Rare	40%	68
Rich & Rare Reserve	40%	57
Rieder Canadian Company	40%	253
Royal Canadian Small Batch	40%	24
Schenley Golden Wedding	40%	236
Seagram's 83	40%	170
Seagram's VO	40%	170
Seagram's VO Gold	40%	170
Shelter Point Artisanal Single Malt Aged 10 Years	57.8%	310
Signal Hill	40%	68
Signal Hill Founders Reserve	56.3%	24
Silk Tassel Aged 7 Years (1972)	40%	210
Sons of Vancouver Marshmallows over a Campfire	59.5%	305
Speaker Rota's Canadian Whisky/Rocking R 100% Rye	40%	36
St. Laurent Rye 3-Year-Old	43%	308
Stalk & Barrel	40%	309
Stampede Rye	40%	24

WHISKY	ALC/VOL	PAGE
Still Waters 12-Year-Old Single Malt	61%	6
Stillhead Rye Porty Spice	50%	307
Strath Ancient Grains Wine Cask Finished	57.4%	301
Taber Corn Berbon	45%	302
The Beast Wildfire Whisky Aged 6 Years	58.3%	309
The Scientist	53.2%	302
Trust Ancient Grains	44%	309
Tumbleweed 1888 Triticale	45%	6
Two Brewers Peated PX Sherry	58%	310
Two Brewers Release No. 37 Classic Single Cask	58%	301
United Distillers Old Rye	NS	178
Wayne Gretzky No. 99 Ice Cask	41.5%	24
Wayne Gretzky No. 99 Red Cask	40%	76
Western Grains	40%	310
White Owl	40%	268
Wild Life Wheat	45.8%	308
Willibald Greenhorn Colombian Rum Finish	59.1%	303
Windsor Canadian	40%	230
Wiser's De Luxe 10 Years Old (1974)	40%	129
Wiser's Oldest 18 Years Old (1949)	40%	129

INDEX

DAVIN DE KERGOMMEAUX is an independent expert who has been writing about whisky for more than a quarter of a century. He is the world's leading authority on Canadian whisky, and was named one of the most influential Canadians in Food and Drink by *The Globe and Mail*. He is a past contributing editor to *Whisky Magazine*, and has contributed to or co-authored eight other books about whisky, spirits, and cocktails, including most recently, *The Definitive Guide to Canadian Distilleries*. He writes full-time, and is regularly featured in many publications, including *Whisky Advocate*. De Kergommeaux is an IACP award winner and the founder and chairperson of the prestigious Canadian Whisky Awards.

canadianwhisky.org

@davindek

Author photograph: Nick Wons

appetite
by RANDOM HOUSE

www.penguinrandomhouse.com